He Loves Me,
He Loves Me Not

He Loves Me,
He Loves Me Not

A Memoir of Finding
Faith, Hope, and
Happily Ever After

TRISH RYAN

NEW YORK BOSTON NASHVILLE

Lyrics on page 116 are from "Here and Now" by Christopher Greco. Copyright ©
2001 by Christopher Greco. Used by permission. All rights reserved.

Lyrics on page 123 are from "Worthy to Be Praised" by Eunice Sim. Copyright ©
2001 by Eunice Sim. Used by permission. All rights reserved.

Lyrics on page 136 are from "You Have Entered In" by Jordan Seng. Copyright ©
2001 by Jordan Seng.

Scripture quotations are from The Holy Bible, New International Version®.
Copyright © 1973, 1978, 1984 by International Bible Society. Used by permission
of Zondervan Publishing House. All rights reserved.

FaithWords
Hachette Book Group USA
237 Park Avenue
New York, NY 10017

Visit our Web site at www.faithwords.com.

Printed in the United States of America

First Edition: April 2008
10 9 8 7 6 5 4 3 2 1

FaithWords is a division of Hachette Book Group USA, Inc.
The FaithWords name and logo are trademarks of Hachette Book Group USA, Inc.

Library of Congress Cataloging-in-Publication Data
Ryan, Trish.
    He loves me, he loves me not: a memoir of finding faith, hope, and
    happily ever after / Trish Ryan.—1st ed.
        p. cm.
    ISBN: 978-1-59995-713-5
    1. Single women—Religious life. 2. Christian women—Religious life.
    3. Mate selection—Religious aspects—Christianity. I. Title.

BV4596.S5R94 2008
248.8'432—dc22

                                                            2007028282

For Steve

Contents

PART II. During

PART III. Enduring

PART IV. Happily Ever After

A Polite, Heartfelt Disclaimer

There are three things you're likely to notice before you get too far into this book. First, I refer to God as He and sometimes I even capitalize (as Elizabeth Gilbert points out in her own spiritual memoir, it seems like a nice touch in the presence of the Divine.) The Bible makes it clear, however, that God encompasses all of masculinity and femininity. So if you decide to go through these pages and ink in an *S* in front of all the divinity-related pronouns, more power to you; I think God can handle it. Second, I have, on occasion, uttered four-letter words, a select few of which made it into this manuscript. Please understand: they are not there to show that I *can* say them, but rather to admit that I *did,* and that, on occasion, I *do.* I've sacrificed the chance to clean up my image in exchange for the ability to be honest. And, speaking of honesty—if you're someone who knows me, or used to know me, or (awkward moment) once dated me and are flipping through these pages in fascinated horror, wondering what I'll say—chances are I've changed your name. This book is a collection of my memories and thus may differ from yours. Some events and people have been combined, and (in an effort to avoid 346-page chapters) some time sequences shifted around. But as with the swearing, I haven't cleaned anything up; the words you find here are true, and my best effort at an honest account of how A led to B and then swerved around to C, D, and E.

He Loves Me,
He Loves Me Not

PART I

Before

Chapter One

The Road to Mr. Right

Imagine, if you will, the following:

I am thirty-two, single, and driving through Buffalo, where my large, loving family has gathered for an unexpected funeral. Yesterday morning, my boyfriend, Mark (whom I sometimes refer to as my "life partner" in a pathetic attempt to give our relationship a veneer of permanence), told me that he doesn't plan to get married—ever. I've had a nine-hour drive from Cambridge to western New York to think this over. Now I'm making my way down a nondescript highway trying to find my hotel, passing acres of strip malls, subdivisions, and driving ranges, listening to Sarah McLachlan wail on the radio and watching the minutes tick by. I think about my relatives—my parents and siblings, aunts, uncles, cousins—and their happy marriages, happy children, happy lives. I think about how much I want those things, and small tears roll down my cheeks.

Hanging out with these *families* decimates my carefully crafted story of how lucky I am to be unmarried, unencumbered, free to live a life of change and adventure. I feel like a character in one of those *Sex in the City* episodes that makes you think, "Wow—thank God I'm not *her*."

I'M her.

YOU SEE, THE pursuit of romantic happiness is (has always been) my secret obsession, the defining focus (and failure) of my first three decades of life. I believe in happy endings; I just can't seem to get there.

It's not like I haven't tried. I've spent years amassing a veritable smorgasbord of romantic advice, consulting everything from self-help articles to books on finding my soul mate. I've ruined far too many flowers in my lifetime, plucking off petals one by one, trying to figure out if some guy (or God, for that matter) cared about me. I'm "spiritual, but not religious" (as the form at my doctor's office puts it), drawn to suggestions with a supernatural element. I'm sure God is real, and suspect that the way I interact with Him (Her? It?) affects how things go in my life. At some visceral level, I believe that my search for God and my quest for love are intertwined; I just need to figure out how the whole thing works.

I've experimented: I feng shui'd my apartment one year, did miracle meditations the next. I've been to Mass, church, service, temple, sacred circle, Dance of the Inner Woman, and a ceremony to mark the movement of Jupiter into my second house. I've had my astrological chart done, my palm read, my energy evaluated, and my wristwatch scanned for psychic potential. I've kissed a frog, a toad, a snake, and at least three lizards, moving from amphibians to reptiles as if one of them might turn out to be "my type." I've even worked for the author of a best-selling book on spirituality and relationships, hoping to glean some wisdom from her expertise. All of these experiences were interesting, but none of them came through with the results they promised; none of them *worked*. And yet somehow, my dream of *happily ever after* lives on. It's an outlandish, resilient hope that counters my failures and cannot be silenced, asking, *But what if it's true? What might be possible then?*

I drive past a video store advertising a new release of *Cinderella*. "I want my Prince Charming," I whisper. "I want to get married, I want to build a real life." This is the first time in years I've spoken the truth out loud, even to myself. I pull to a stop at a red light and reach into my bag for a tissue.

That's when I hear the Voice. It comes out of nowhere and says, in the most matter-of-fact way possible, *I have more for you. I want you to want more for yourself.* It sounds (don't laugh) like James Earl Jones, calling from his wireless phone commercial to scold me for not living up to my potential. *I have a husband for you, and a family,* He says. *But you need to take Jesus seriously.*

I stare at the car in front of me and wonder what that means.

The truth is, Jesus baffles me. I can't figure out who he is or why he matters, or why Wal-Mart is filled with Max Lucado greeting cards embossed with a big cross and the words "He took the nails for you . . ." I can't think of an occasion where receiving that card would cheer me. All this talk about blood, sacrifice, sin, and death has nothing to do with my sense of a loving God—I don't understand why God, if He is *God*, needs this kind of drama. Over the years, even as I've charted the stars and moved my furniture to ensure the optimal flow of positive energy, I've never considered what it might mean if Jesus is who he says he is (the son of God) and did what he said he did (died, then rose from the dead to save me from my own bad choices).

A week after I return from Buffalo, my friend Maura gives me a little book entitled *If the Buddha Dated.* The very idea grosses me out—*who,* I wonder, *would date the Buddha?* Skimming through the pages, I don't think much of the big B's dating advice—I'm just not that transcendent. If a guy tells me he's going to call, for example, I expect him to call; you can talk to me all day long about nonattachment and emancipation from my desires; in the end, *I still want him to call.* It makes me tired, all this pretend not-wanting, and cranky. I throw the book away. But as I begin to consider Jesus (a more attractive guy, in my opinion), I can't help but wonder, *what if Jesus dated?* At the very least, I think, Jesus would call.

A few days later, I'm home in bed with a cold. My dog, Kylie, is curled up at my feet, and I'm working my way through a towering pile of magazines stacked on my bedside table, reading story after story about women wrestling with life—searching for ways to be happy, or fulfilled, or at the very least enlightened. My heart aches with recognition; each of these women is searching, as I am, for the right higher power, some personal connection to the Divine.

I read about a spiritual seeker just back from a yoga retreat on the West Coast. She's evolved, and now she can sit still for over an hour in the midst of a swarm of bugs.

I read an interview with a powerhouse feminist playwright who describes how nothing "happened" in her life until she stopped living in her head and started living in her vagina.

I read about the despair of four single women in New York, and a psychologist's suggestion that they look in the mirror, give themselves a hug, and say, "You *are* beautiful. You *are* valuable. You *are* loved."

And I sense Jesus looking over my shoulder, asking incredulously: *This is my competition?*

Chapter Two

Humpty Dumpty Sat on That Wall

From the time I was five years old, there were two things I knew for sure: that God loved me (and not just me, but all of us) and that someday He would send a handsome prince to find and marry me. I was pretty sure my prince and I would have a dog, and perhaps a nice castle by the water.

I'm not sure where I got this idea. I had a rather idyllic childhood, it's true: I was raised by two parents whose loving marriage was filled with affection, fun, and vague allusions to a secret passionate life we kids weren't part of. My brothers, Chris and Eric, were just enough older to seem like super-heroes to me, and my sister, Meg, was just enough younger to be my willing accomplice in all manner of imaginary fun. (This often meant spending hours dressing up one of our Barbies in elaborate formal attire, as if Ken might arrive at any minute to whisk her away to the opera. We had no Ken doll, so Barbie had lots of time to get ready.) It's not that the earthquakes of life never rumbled through our home. But when they did, some inexplicable sense of *family* held us together, so that when the rumbling was done we were all still there, safe and more or less sound. I liked this feeling. So at some point, I guess, I decided that the key to continuing this wonderful life was to find my own happy marriage, and that God was probably the one in charge of making sure this happened. No one told me this. I just *knew*, the way little girls with big imaginations sometimes do.

My concept of God—who He was, what He thought about—was pretty much self-generated at that point, as our local Catholic Church didn't offer much in the way of inspiring imagery. To me, Sunday Mass was just a giant blur of dull, beige words blending in with the beige carpet, beige paneling, beige altar posts, and beige pews; on every sensory level, it was like sitting in a giant bowl of oatmeal.

My mother's diligent efforts on behalf of our young souls ensured that Meg and I made it to church each week. But the truth was, despite years of immersion, I never really got it. I picked up the routine as quickly as any other kid: stand, cross, beg for mercy, bow, sit, stand, kneel . . . shake hands with everyone around you, watch Mom take Communion, put on our coats, go home; I just couldn't figure out why we were there, standing, kneeling, begging, and crossing ourselves. Perhaps I just wasn't liturgical—I never connected the dots between all those gestures, never saw the sacred mystery or understood why we called Mass a "celebration." Try as I might, I couldn't see how the forty-five minutes we spent shivering in that sanctuary,

listening to Father McNamara mumble while we stared at a
life-size reproduction of Jesus' maimed body, had anything to
do with, well . . . anything. I couldn't find the take-home point.

There was one Sunday morning, though, as I sat in the icy
classroom with my Sunday school class, all of us rubbing our
little hands together trying to stay warm, when I had what you
might call a spiritual breakthrough. Our teacher, Mrs. Falcone,
in a rare off-script moment, burst into a bubbling description
of her prayer life, explaining how her days of dreary housework
were lightened and brightened by her conversations with God:
"When I get up in the morning, I start talking to God . . . I do
my ironing, and I'm talking to God . . ." She sang this in a half
rhyme, like a Catholic rendition of "Whistle While You Work,"
walking around our table with a bouncy step, making her chats
with God sound like the best fun ever.

I chatted at God with some frequency after this, and from
time to time He'd answer. Nothing big—it certainly never
struck me as anything special—just small conversations about
whether He thought I should try the triple-toss turn around
at the end of my baton-twirling routine, or if He remembered
that I thought Scott Stewart, a boy in my class, was cute. (Yes
on both counts.)

For a time I thought I might be Jewish, spurred by the arrival of a kid named David Goldman in my English class. One
day when we were supposed to be copying vocabulary words, he
turned to me and said defiantly, "You know what? I'm a Jew. I
don't believe in Jesus." *Like me*, I thought. No one had explained
Jesus to me—who he was or why he mattered—in a way I could

understand, so I proceeded on the assumption that he wasn't all that important. If God was immortal, my reasoning went, He didn't need a son to take over the family business. After reading Judy Blume's *Are You There God? It's Me, Margaret* (and discovering I wasn't the only little girl who believed God had a hand in making my love life work), I thought that like Margaret, we all got to choose whether or not we wanted the Jesus part of the story. (I was stripped of my Jewishness fifteen years later by my law school boyfriend's mother. Within seconds of meeting me, Mrs. Lowenstein stormed off to the kitchen, hissing to her husband, "She looks like a map of *Ireland* . . ." Apparently, Jon hadn't mentioned that his new girlfriend was named after St. Patrick.)

Prayer worked for Margaret, so I prayed every night before bed, as she did. The impetus for my prayers was not so much to grow closer to God, but rather to obtain His help: Margaret prayed every night and she got her first bra; I hoped the same formula might work for me. I prayed, for years, varying versions of the same words, strung together by endless series of ellipses so as to not inflate or diminish any one request in relation to the others:

> Dear God please bless Mom and Dad and Meg and
> Chris and Eric and our dog Ginger and Bill and Paul
> and Bill's other friend whose name I can't remember and
> Susie and Barbie and Timmy and Aunt Janet . . . (deep
> breath) . . . God, thank you for my cute new belt and
> pink T-shirt, and that I was picked to be the featured

twirler for Homecoming . . . please, please, please, don't let me drop my batons on the football field, and don't let me look fat in the parade. Please don't let people make fun of me . . . And please, God, let Mom buy me a bra . . .

I don't remember much else of the content of my prayers in those days, only the format. I remember viscerally, however, my certainty that omitting anyone from my blessing list somehow left them outside of God's protection, rendering them vulnerable to bad things. It was a horrible sort of power I possessed, the lives of everyone I knew balanced on the breadth of my young memory. I sensed, even then, that there was spiritual power in the world, and that I needed to make careful choices to negotiate the maze of life in front of me. I just wasn't sure how.

WHEN MY TEEN years hit, my spiritual searching was quickly replaced by a new object of curiosity and worship: boys. While friends experimented with drinks and drugs and daring each other to jump from high places to ease the dullness and panic of our impending adulthood, I turned to boys to ease whatever ailed me at the moment.

I don't remember much about the beginning of dating my first boyfriend, Dan, only the kissing. We were in eighth grade, and we made out constantly, everywhere: in the hallway between classes, behind the curtain on the stage in the gym, on the dock overlooking the river, in the hammock in his parents' backyard. We lived in constant fear of getting caught, of hearing grown-up footsteps closing in on somewhere we'd snuck off to kiss. It was my first experience with requited love, and my first experience of the flip side of romance, jealousy. Dan's former girlfriend (his love from the year before) was a beautiful girl with long hair who left school early every day to pursue her career in ballet. That's why they broke up, as I recall, because she didn't have time to date anyone. Even at thirteen this seemed foolish to me, choosing your career over a man. I worried that she'd see the error of her ways, quit ballet, and want him back.

Dan was a fabulous introduction to coupledom: he held my hand at football games and wrote me romantic notes during study hall. He carved the word "LOVE" into a block of wood and gave it to me on Valentine's Day. For my birthday he sent me tulips because I'd mentioned once that they were my favorite. With each of these gestures, he shaped my understanding of what true love could look and feel like, neither one of us realizing how impossibly high he was setting the bar for every man I'd date thereafter.

Dan was also the first boy to break my heart.

If I'd been a little older, or a little wiser, or a little more something, I might have learned from this experience to wait before stitching my life to someone else and getting all entangled. But I was hooked, blinded by the awareness of how much better I felt as one-half of a whole than standing alone. I liked the kissing, and the cuddling, and knowing someone would call at night to encourage me when algebra seemed insurmountable, so I focused on re-creating that circumstance as quickly as possible, adding my budding romantic life to my prayers.

High school was a blur of melding for me, of wide-eyed

hopefulness crashing into every cute boy who wandered by like a pinball searching for tilt. I picked myself up off the ground over and over again when it didn't work out. It was fun, though—the wondering, the waiting, the flirting, the hoping. And I was good at this game of attraction, almost entrepreneurial, in a way. If they gave out varsity letters for getting into new relationships, I'd have been a shoo-in for the all-star team.

When the time came to pick a college, I surged off on a quest for new lands (read: new men) to discover. But to my utter astonishment, after a tour of New England campuses, I fell in love with Wheaton College—an all-women's school just south of Boston.

I wasn't the only one who was surprised. Indeed, it's a fair indication of how devoted I was to the pursuit of romantic happiness that when I announced that I'd decided to apply to Wheaton, nobody believed me.

"You . . . at Wheaton?" my friend Matthew said, trying unsuccessfully to hide his laughter. "You're kidding, right?"

"Oh—you must mean Billy Graham's alma matter in Illinois?" my guidance counselor said, trying to clear up what was obviously a misunderstanding. Apparently, it was easier to believe that I'd been born again on my first college excursion than voluntarily chosen a school with no men.

WHEATON COLLEGE WAS in transition when I arrived in the fall of 1987, a roiling hotbed of fury and feminist angst unleashed by the recent (and somewhat ironic, in my case) decision to abandon 150 years of exclusive women's education and admit men. Walking to the dining hall on my first day there, I stared wide-eyed at the stately elms and maples lining the center of campus: they were strung with dozens of colorful bras, like an eco-friendly Victoria's Secret commercial. I learned that this assortment of feminine underpinnings had been flung into the branches by angry seniors, a protest against the encroaching testosterone. I couldn't help but wonder if the female power message wasn't lost on the seventeen- and eighteen-year-old boys who visited campus that first year—if they didn't think they'd landed on the ultimate *Fantasy Island*, where lingerie literally grew on trees.

Given my varsity-dating accomplishments in high school, I was oddly ambivalent about the sudden shift to coeducation. To me, college was the beginning of *real life*, and dating here held greater significance. This was where my prince would arrive, where we'd sow the seeds of our *happily ever after*. I didn't need lots of guys anymore; I just needed one—The One. Greater Boston was loaded with colleges filled with men, I reasoned—it couldn't be all that hard to find one.

I met Chip at 2:00 a.m. one morning, a month into my freshman year. Walking to the bathroom in my floral flannel pajamas and fuzzy blue slippers, I was surprised to see a tall blond guy walking down our hall with two friends. *He looks like Freddy from Scooby Doo*, I thought sleepily. The crest on his navy blue windbreaker indicated he was from the local military academy, which sent a shiver down my spine. Men were not allowed in our all women's dorm unescorted under any circumstances, but military guys were banned altogether from our campus—the result of a scuffle in which one of them had thrown some girl's boyfriend into the pond. We'd been warned that these guys were only after *one* thing (a thing it was presumed that Wheaton girls were not interested in providing), and that we should avoid them at all costs.

But Chip was cute, and funny, and he smiled as he leaned against the wall to talk to me as my big pink glasses slid down my nose. We went our separate ways after a few minutes, but a mutual friend set us up on a date, and after that we were inseparable. The rest of Wheaton was welcome to protest against the men; I was happier with my boyfriend.

A FEW DAYS later I met my soon-to-be best friend, Kristen, an elegant, preppy blonde who sat in front of me in European History. I was a bit awed by her. She strolled into class each week and casually shrugged off her leather jacket, telling a friend about spending the weekend at her boyfriend's beach house, or how he'd taken her to see Bruce Springsteen in concert; she seemed impossibly sophisticated. We were paired together for a project on the ascension of monarchical dynasties and bonded almost instantly over two things: a shared disinterest in the entirety of nineteenth-century Europe (Kristen eventually developed an affinity for the antiques of the period, but that was a decade, several boyfriends, and a considerable fortune later), and our mutual conviction that the quest for the perfect man was the defining characteristic of our lives. As academically curious and accomplished as we appeared on the outside, inside, we were throwbacks to the founding days of Wheaton, when it was a fine institution where women were groomed to become wives.

"I'll never feel secure until my boyfriend proposes," she told me. I knew just how she felt.

•

LIKE SO MANY schools at this time, Wheaton's message about male-female relationships was rather awkward, as the faculty and administration waded into the morass of collegiate gender dynamics. Those first two years were littered with hours of thoughtful workshops on strategies to help men and women communicate with one another in our newly coed living environments; as if men and women hadn't been communicating with one another in coed living environments since Adam first met Eve. It was the beginning of the political correctness movement, and Kristen and I, along with an expanding group of friends, learned to alternate our pronouns, identify oppression in everything from great literature to restaurant menu pictures (one memorable guest speaker convinced us all that the plate of clams advertised by a local seafood chain was nothing short of pornographic), and ignore cultural differences. We absorbed the ethos and strove to treat people of all shapes, sizes, colors, and dating preferences with open-mindedness and acceptance.

Oddly, though, this barrage of acculturation training ignored our most obvious social challenge, offering no help at all in negotiating the labyrinthine world of heterosexual romantic relationships. As our minds steeped in almost three decades of feminist *womyn's* progress, our leaders were loath to acknowledge that, as nice as it was to befriend international students and even a lesbian or two to broaden our horizons, the relationship that would most influence our lives, should we decide to enter it, was marriage. We majored in the typical array of liberal arts subjects: political science (me), English (Kristen), and history (our friends Francesca and Tracy), which provided occasional opportunities to discuss marriages that struggled and/or ended badly (the Kennedys, Sylvia Plath and Ted Hughes, the whole Henry VIII debacle). But we rarely discussed unions that succeeded. We never talked in our classes or workshops about what characteristics made for a good husband, or whether we had any responsibility to be good wives. We admired accomplished alums like Leslie Stahl and Christine Todd Whitman, but never asked, "What are their marriages like? Are they happy with their sex lives? Do they ever see their kids?"

In our off hours, though, we asked. We spent hours contemplating past boyfriends, current boyfriends, prospective boyfriends, and where one might find new members of the male species on the upcoming weekend. Like scientists, we analyzed the behavior of the men in our lives, determined to assign some motive or meaning to every word or gesture. And we consoled one another when things didn't work out.

Kristen's perfect boyfriend broke up with her, and she barricaded herself in her room, refusing to come out. Francesca, Tracy, and I sat outside her door for hours, cutting pictures from the J.Crew catalog and shoving them under her door to remind her how many other cute, preppy guys there were in the world. She finally emerged, her sniffling giving way to giggles. A few weeks later she ran smack into a guy who looked just like one of our paper-doll cutouts. He swept her off her feet, then spent the next year telling her she was fat.

This is where some real advice on male-female communication patterns might have been helpful—some tips on sorting out the good guys from the bad, perhaps, or coaching on how and when to send a jerk packing. But there wasn't anyone to teach us that; it just wasn't on the agenda. The purpose of a liberal arts education, it was understood, was to prepare us for *our future*—our careers, our unique contributions to the planet, our pride-infusing legacy for subsequent generations. Husbands and children were nice accessories, the theory went, people we'd come home to after a day out living our lives. How we acquired them was entirely up to us.

Indeed, the only school-sanctioned dating advice I received in my four years of college (other than the ubiquitous workshops on preventing date rape) came via a psychology course called Friendship and Love. On the first day of class, twenty-three of us sat in a circle, staring with rapt attention at our professor, a white-bearded man in his late fifties. Passing around a detailed syllabus, he told us that he was a Buddhist, that he and his wife had an open marriage, and that the goal of this class was to help each of us recognize that "faithfulness" is a momentary concept, not be confused with—or degraded by—long-term commitment.

"I could have a successful relationship with any one of you," Professor Big Love said, running his gaze slowly around our circle. He didn't say if any of his students had taken him up on this offer. "As we learn to redefine our vision of relationships in terms of meaning, rather than duration," he continued authoritatively, "we will transcend our obsession with ownership and learn to enjoy real love." Our reading list consisted of titles such as *Brief Encounters: How to Make the Most of Relationships That May Not Last Forever.* I wrote my journal entries about my wonderful new boyfriend, Chip; Professor Big Love awarded my efforts with a long string of Bs, and encouraged me to broaden my horizons. The official school belief seemed to be that we could do/be/

accomplish anything we wanted, and we didn't need a husband to make it happen.

Or, for that matter, God. Along with our future husbands, God was rarely mentioned on campus. Aside from a semester-long class on comparative religion (which dismissed Jesus and his trinity in a curt, fifteen-minute overview the day before the final), I rarely thought about God at Wheaton; I was too busy expanding my mind and living up to my potential. God was like a benevolent grandfather, a vague-yet-beloved relative I'd visit dutifully—albeit infrequently—when I remembered.

Indeed, the closest thing I had to a spiritual experience in college was the night Kristen drove us to a local Catholic shrine devoted to the Virgin Mary. We weren't there for worship, but rather for the famed Technicolor light show they put on each year at Christmastime.

"Omigosh!" Kristen exclaimed as we turned into the main entrance. "Do you see that?"

"JESUS IS THE REASON FOR THE SEASON!" Francesca recited, reading the six-foot neon letters hovering over us from the roof of the main building. This set us into a fit of hysterical giggles, and we spent the next two hours wandering through acres of fluorescent, blinking reindeer and Santa Clauses, reminding each other of this catchy truth and sipping beer from our soda bottles. Jesus was no more real to us (or at least to me) than Santa's little elves. But for months after that, whenever we needed a moment of levity to lighten the load, Kristen would look at us earnestly and say, "Remember: JESUS IS THE REASON FOR THE SEASON!" and all our worries would be momentarily subsumed in an uncontrollable fit of laughter. It never occurred to me that God might provide anything beyond this sort of momentary stress relief. Honestly, it never occurred to me that I'd need Him to.

CHIP PROPOSED TO me at the beginning of my junior year. I wore my new diamond with pride, happily checking off one more item from my to-do list for assembling the perfect life. We planned our wedding, and I was enveloped in dreams of lace and tulle, the perfect party for a prince and princess on their way to becoming king and queen of the world.

"I NEED TO tell you something," Chip said one night on the phone a few weeks later. He was crying. I'd never heard that before.

"What is it?" I said softly, wondering who had died.

"The party last night," he stammered. "There was this girl. I drank too much . . ." The story tumbled out in one awful sentence after another: he had hooked up with that girl, on the couch in his parents' living room. Chip had cheated on me. "I was showing her our engagement picture," he cried. "I don't know what happened."

I was stunned. Waves of nausea knocked me over onto my bed, and I curled up in the fetal position, mumbling incoherently into the telephone, "How could you?" We had a whole *life* planned: I'd applied to law schools in distant cities to be near where he'd be working, after which we'd move back to New England to be close to our families. We had it all laid out. And now, in one stupid, drunken night, he'd ruined everything.

My family tried to comfort me. "It's an awful part of life," my dad admitted, "but people you love will let you down. You can't hold it against them forever."

"We love you," my mom reminded me. "Whatever you decide to do is okay with us."

The next few months were agonizing as Chip and I assessed the wreckage of our relationship. He begged for forgiveness; I tried to forgive. I'd always sworn that if any man ever cheated on me, I'd dump him immediately and never look back—but as I'd made those bold pronouncements, I never considered what I might have to lose. And when the time came, I didn't know how to choose between righteous indignation and swallowing my pride. Always more resilient than independent, I chose option number two. And I closed down, not telling anyone—even Kristen—what had happened.

Chip treated me reverently after that, like a fragile piece of art. This was worse, almost, than if he'd just turned cold and told me to get over it. Suddenly, he had no backbone: as much as his cheating bruised me, it broke him, almost beyond recognition. The phrase "a shell of a man" came to mind as he showered me with all manner of supplication and apology.

When all was said and done (and cried and yelled and anguished over), I couldn't go through with the wedding. I couldn't face the prospect of spending the rest of my life missing how things used to be. Two months before my graduation, I called the whole thing off, even though my fluffy white dress was not returnable and it's hard to find a use for two hundred pre-embossed cocktail napkins celebrating a couple that has just broken up.

"What do you mean, Chip cheated on you?" Kristen asked me, stunned, when I finally told her. "That doesn't make any sense." Exactly. Chip was my balancing force, my safe place, the one we all counted on to take care of me, no matter what. Everyone agreed: He was *that guy*, the one who could never do anything like this. And yet here I was, my life sprawled out in front of me like the shattered pieces of Humpty Dumpty, with no viable plan for reassembly.

"God," I cried in bed, my pillow drenched with tears. "How could you let this happen? Help me . . ."

Chapter Three

Build a Bridge and Get Over It

Three weeks later, I met Josh and assumed my prayer had been answered. It fit my fairy-tale worldview perfectly: I was in trouble, so God sent a handsome man to rescue me. And while it's true that there are few things as amazing as how quickly new love can piece a hurting girl back together, it's also true what they say about assumptions.

WE WERE THE only two people in the dorm hallway on a Sunday afternoon, walking in opposite directions. We smiled as we passed each other. He was beautiful—a Nordic giant with an easy smile and a relaxed confidence. He looked like the man I'd dreamed of as a little girl, the square-jawed Ken that Meg and I had imagined as we dressed and re-dressed our Barbies. Almost involuntarily, I turned around to check him out and found him looking back at me. A warm feeling oozed through my body, soothing all the jagged edges of my freshly torn heart. *I'll see him again,* I thought, even though I had no idea who he was or where he came from.

A few days later, Kristen and I were sitting on a bench outside the dining hall after dinner. Out of nowhere, he walked by. "Don't I know you?" he asked, turning around. I pretended that he did, because it felt like the truth. I gave him my phone number. It seemed natural. Destined, even.

"Who was *that?*" Kristen asked when Josh headed inside.

"I'm not sure," I told her. "It's no big deal," I lied.

The next night he called, and we talked for an hour. We went out that weekend.

"He's gorgeous!" Kristen admitted after meeting him for the first time. "But I keep catching myself wanting to call him Chip . . ."

The first time Josh kissed me good night, I was certain my world was firmly back in place.

I was still burning from the shock of Chip's betrayal, and the stark realization that my own instincts were not enough to keep a man—or at least keep him faithful. I cast about for strategies to hold Josh's interest, somehow forgetting that I had caught his interest without this sort of plan. Much of our two-year relationship can be summed up by the afternoon we spent meeting his family in Vermont.

It was a hot day in May, and his brother suggested we all go down to the "swimming hole" to cool off. I pulled on my new bikini and resolved to impress Josh as a brave, outdoorsy type of girl who could still keep her French manicure pristine.

I wasn't either of those things—brave, or outdoorsy. But I was determined to be what I thought he wanted.

Twenty minutes later, I was dangling by my perfect nails from a rock face thirty feet above a ribbon of river. I was terrified of heights, but even more scared of looking like an idiot in front of Josh's entire family. How could he love me if I wimped out? So I jumped.

Afterward, as we floated in the chilly water, I stared into Josh's deep blue eyes, drinking in his admiration. *How could he not love me?* I thought. I didn't consider the false picture I was painting, how I was encouraging Josh to fall for a high-flying, adventure-seeking, throw-caution-to-the wind version of me that existed only in onetime snapshots. I thought one jump would give me lifetime bravery credit, like a merit badge in Girl Scouts, and then we could move on to the next project, something involving cuddling or romantic dinners. Dating Josh marked an evolution for me: it was my first experience with lying about who I was and what I wanted, of guessing what a guy wanted and then pretending to be exactly that.

During this time, Josh promised me the moon. He loved to dream and plan, loved to seek adventure. I graduated and went off to law school; he skied in Colorado, dove for pearls in Majorca, smoked pot for the first time on a layover in Singapore. ("Are you kidding me?" I asked. "Of all the places in the world to get stoned, you picked a place where it's a capital offense?") And then he came back and adored me, sweeping me into his arms over and over again like a hero back from war, casting dreams for our future together late into the night.

"We could move here, you know," he said one evening in

Oregon as we sipped wine and watched the sun set from our private hotel deck overlooking the Pacific. "You can take the bar exam anywhere in the country, right?" he asked as if mapping out our future. We'd looked at diamonds earlier that day—a two-carat pear-shaped stone had been his favorite.

"I could," I said, realizing for the first time how broad my options were.

"Imagine the life we could have here," he said, his eyes sparkling with fun and promise. On our way out the next morning, I tore the legal section out of the yellow pages, wanting a point of reference for when the time came to look for a job.

I wouldn't admit it to anyone, but something inside me still held fast to my childhood notion that everything in my life would be better once I was married to the right man; Josh, I thought, was that man. And while I knew from reading articles in *Glamour* and *Cosmo* (not to mention my own experience with Chip) that I wasn't supposed to look to a man to save me, I also knew this: I couldn't save myself. I *wasn't* cool, together, and independent like I pretended to be; I *did* feel like half a life waiting to be made whole, and despite everything I'd been told to the contrary, I did believe that a man—this man—could complete me. I devoted myself to Josh as though he was my personal messiah.

THE NEXT SUMMER, I was clerking for a criminal court judge, and I got a call announcing that I'd made *Law Review*—the brass ring for every law student with dreams of success and greatness. Once again, it seemed like everything was coming together. Upon hearing my good news, the judge graciously offered me the phone in his chambers to call my parents. I called Josh instead.

He didn't say much as I raved about what this appointment meant for us in terms of job opportunities and earning potential. After a long pause, he responded. "Yeah—um, that's great. Well—um—hmm. Yeah. There's something else I've been meaning to tell you. I guess this might not be a great time, but . . ."

Ten minutes later the judge found me sobbing into his phone, tears and snot running down my face, littering his immaculate desk with piles of wadded-up tissue.

WHEN JOSH BROKE up with me, it was like someone hit the "pause" button on my brain. All but the most involuntary forward momentum of my life stopped, and I lost the will to keep going.

"I guess this is how it is for me," I told Kristen that night on the phone. "I sew up one end of my life, and the other end just comes unraveled."

I moved in a sort of semifunctional hibernation, going through the motions of finishing my clerkship, attending classes the next semester, pretending to take notes. I had a mountain of student loans (a mortgage on my brain, as one friend called it) that kept me from quitting. So I soldiered on, dragging my body from class to class, not caring a whit about corporate reorganization strategy or the intricacies of federal taxation. I'd look at the pile of photocopied caselaw stacked next to my desk and think, *Who cares?* I couldn't see the point to being a lawyer—to being anything, for that matter—if no one loved you, if no one chose you to build a life with him.

Night after night, I gulped down shots from the bottles in my roommate's liquor cabinet, hoping they would help me sleep, or maybe even get me addicted. It's a fair depiction of how far I'd fallen from my perch on the "I've got it all together" pedestal that I actually envied people who qualified for twelve-step programs: alcoholics, drug addicts, sexual compulsives; from where I stood, they had it made. Preconstructed groups of friends—people obligated to love them if they just showed up—stood waiting to welcome them, exorcize their demons, and invite them to gatherings to smoke and drink coffee. I longed to stumble into that sort of ready-made network. But people like me who couldn't seem to stomach more than two drinks at a time had no such group. I poured out my heartache in my journal, scribbling worriedly: *I'm afraid I'll remember my twenties as the decade I just floundered about.*

Wandering through a bookstore one day, I came upon Elizabeth Wurtzel's bestseller, *Prozac Nation: Young and Depressed in America.* As I pulled fourteen dollars from my wallet, I told myself that reading her story would help me recognize signs of depression in people I cared about, to empathize with their plight and love them through it. It was a nice rationalization, but the truth was I wanted a point of reference from which to evaluate my own instability, to see if things were as bad as I suspected they might be. A quick scan of some middle pages was reassuring; I wasn't slicing myself with a razor (something I hadn't before thought to celebrate). But I was intimately familiar with the feeling she described in the beginning of the book, of waking up in the morning, terrified she might *live*.

Looking around, I could tell I wasn't the only girl losing ground in the relationship wars. On the surface, my friends and I were the accomplished single women magazines raved about: we had advanced degrees, cute haircuts, nice cars. Poised and together on the outside, but baffled and heartbroken underneath, we were the women people always asked (earnestly and with the best of intention), "Why aren't you married yet?" expecting a cogent answer.

We found different ways of dealing with our stress: Alicia said rosaries to repent for impure thoughts; Janna joined the Junior League—"Wealthy women have wealthy husbands who have wealthy friends," she explained. "I'm accessing a higher quality talent pool."—Kate pined her nights away wallowing in an unrequited crush; Liza hooked up with every guy she fancied—as well as a few she didn't—wanting to capitalize on her opportunities. "Carpe diem!" she'd cry, ordering another round of tequila shots. Holly clothed herself in pious virginal innocence, while Laura learned to bake gourmet cupcakes. Annie dated two best friends who were both named Brad, hedging her bets that one of them would come through with a ring. Heather spent a year in shocked denial when her boyfriend burst out of the closet on the night he was expected to propose.

Kristen called me from her new apartment in Manhattan one night. "Help me! I have a date tonight with a guy who looks like Benjamin Franklin!"

"How did that happen?" I asked, trying not to laugh.

"I didn't want to be rude," she explained, sounding despondent.

"Well," I said, "have you tried imagining what Ben Franklin might look like with a fashion update? You know, like a nice suit from Brooks Brothers?"

"That's what he was wearing the other night," she said. "I still felt like I was talking to the head on a hundred-dollar bill."

We were all doing the best we could, but no one seemed to know the secret password that would get us through to our next stage in life.

THE NEXT FEW years are a bit of a blur.

I graduated from law school, passed the bar exam, and went to work for a firm that defended grocery store chains against the claims of people who'd fallen on wayward foodstuffs. My caseload included an eight-year-old boy who said he'd slipped on the floor of the men's room (requiring a site visit to photograph urinals and antiskid mats while trying to keep the bullet holes out of the picture), and a woman alleging that her sex life was ruined by soft tissue injuries sustained when she slipped on a grape. It was ridiculous work, and I was miserable. So miserable, in fact, that my father begged me to make up something—anything—good to say in my weekly calls home to my mom. For months, we talked about the weather.

Kristen married Ben Franklin. They bought a Volvo, a cocker spaniel, and an apartment on the Upper East Side. I felt like Little Orphan Annie, curled up alone in my studio apartment with a half-dead plant.

I read a horrifying magazine article, a profile of four single women in their late thirties, each of whom claimed to have "made peace" with her apparent destiny as a single woman. I panicked. *Where,* I thought frantically, *did they get the idea that if we aren't married by a certain age, it's time to give up and make alternative plans?* Was this written down someplace? Was there an official deadline? *And if there isn't,* I thought angrily, *why would anyone, at this point or any other, take up the task of making peace with such a plight?* I hated these women, with their efforts to "draw meaning" from their spinster fate. I hated how they gave up, battened down the hatches, and settled in for lonely, barren lives, recouping what pieces they could through single parenthood or adopting stray cats. I did not want to be one of those women.

Still reeling from Chip and Josh and how far off track my life had gotten, I started dating randomly: a series of men who took me to nondescript restaurants and waxed poetic about their amazing good fortune, how they couldn't believe someone like *me* was going out with someone like *them.* (This would be obnoxious for me to say if it weren't so true, if I weren't dating so far outside the realm of viable romantic partners that my family and friends watched in rapt horror, wondering if maybe they should intervene. Suddenly, it was as if I would consider only men who had dropped out of high school, filed for bankruptcy, or been convicted of drunk driving. Bonus points for guys who still lived at home yet hated their mothers). No longer sure that a real prince would have me, I essentially dropped my asking price and declared a blue light special. I couldn't get to *happily ever after,* it seemed, so I settled for *I guess this will do for now.* As one candid friend put it, I seemed to have broken my chooser.

Chapter Four

Becoming a Fascinating Woman

One night in the middle of this mess, I turned on the television. Larry King was interviewing a pretty redhead; she was wearing an elegant suit and talking about spirituality.

"The answer to our relationship problems is simple," she told Larry with a knowing smile. "All it takes is a shift in perception. We need to approach life from a perspective of love, rather than a perspective of fear." It seemed so simple—change my mind, change my life; as if my destiny was up to me. I was captivated.

Her name was not Jayme Brass, although that's what I'll call her. She was on *Larry King Live* to promote her new book about love. She explained how her book was based on a spiritual program called *A Course in Miracles.* The premise of the *Course,* she explained, was that only love is real, everything else is imagined, and *we* are what stands between us and the magnificent lives we wish for. She described how the teachings of the *Course* had set her free from her fears and neuroses, allowing her to succeed in life and love. "We have no right to think of ourselves as lowly worms, foraging for enough to get by," she said. "That's not what we were created for. We were created by a higher power, for the good of the universe. We should be asking ourselves 'Who are you *not* to be everything you were created to be? Who are you not to be brilliant, gorgeous, talented, fabulous?'"

Exactly! I thought. *Who am I not to be brilliant, gorgeous, talented, fabulous?* It was the wake-up call I'd been waiting for.

Jayme appeared the epitome of her own sage advice: smart, beautiful, self-assured, funny—she was the type of woman I wanted to be. That night, I became her disciple.

I skipped class the next morning and went to the bookstore, where I bought Jayme's book, along with three of her audio-taped lectures. I read her story cover to cover, highlighting passages and feeling like a whole new world of understanding and possibility was opening up in front of me. *Oh—of course!* I kept thinking. It all was so obvious: only the love was real.

Following Jayme's lead, I bought my own copy of *A Course in Miracles*. It was daunting: thousands of whisper-thin pages and tiny print, all bound together in a heavy, navy blue volume. These were, the book explained, the newest teachings of Jesus himself, channeled through an atheist professor at Columbia University to correct errors in the Bible. *Why not?* I thought. Despite my years of Catholic Sunday school, I'd never read the Bible, or thought much about Jesus; I had no basis for evaluating whether or not this sounded like something he might do. I was just glad I hadn't wasted time on the first edition when there was an updated, 2.0 version to read instead.

The next morning, I poured myself a mug of coffee and started in on the first of the *Course's* 365 meditations, ready to purify my thought forms and shift my perspective from fear to love:

"I have given everything I see all the meaning it has to me," I read out loud. *What the heck does that mean?* I wondered. Following the instructions, I repeated this phrase over and over again, looking at all the objects in my bedroom that I had, apparently, given all the meaning they had to me.

Over the next few weeks, I continued this daily training, often having no idea what I was saying. I hoped that eventually these bizarre declarations would add up to some enlightenment and I'd catch on. The lessons each followed a similar pattern, describing how the negative things in the world—sickness, poverty, disappointment, pain—were illusions. Our job as students, it said, was to learn to see past these falsehoods, to the healing, abundance, perfect circumstances, and joy that were really there. *What about people with cancer?* I wondered. *Or women whose husbands hurt them?* O. J. Simpson had just been filmed fleeing the police in that white Bronco; I couldn't imagine how Nicole Brown's family would be helped by the news that her suffering and death weren't real. I pushed these thoughts out of my mind, though; apparently I was still too unspiritual to understand.

Jayme's advice was easier to apply. "Relationships are divine assignments," she said, sharing about a man who'd once left her for another woman. "They can be devastating, but remember: even the bad ones teach us something the universe knows we need to learn." I devoured her stories of relationship misfires, comforted that even she had been stood up, dumped, told she was too crazy/too demanding/too weird. "We overcome our disappointments when we recognize that *we* are the problem," she claimed. Jesus could help us, she explained, because he was our divine big brother—a powerful example of all we could be once we reached our own divinity. This was the first reasonable explanation of Jesus I'd ever heard.

With each day that went by, I saw myself less as a lawyer gunning for partnership, and more as a spiritual pilgrim searching for a higher road to happiness than billable hours and sharp suits could buy. I didn't talk to anyone about my newfound woo-woo perspective of universal abundance and light; there didn't seem to be that sort of conversational opening in our partner-associate meetings or at happy hour on Friday nights. I knew I wasn't your typical candidate for psychic transformation. But as I looked to Jayme's example of what a higher, spiritual life might look like, her words of hope were like an IV drip of reassurance, connecting me to alternative truths and hope the partners in my firm didn't seem to have. To me, Jayme was living proof that I could feel this bad now, and yet someday look that good.

ONE NIGHT AT the gym, a tall, dark, handsome man hopped on the treadmill next to mine and started talking.

"I know you," he said, his eyes sparkling. "You were on that rock-climbing trip to the indoor walls last month."

I've never been one of those chatty runners, so this was a bit disconcerting. "Mmhmmm," I replied winningly, struggling to conserve my breath. "Thatwasme." I typically had about fifty-seven seconds of conversation in me before I'd start to audibly gasp for air.

"I'm Tim," he said, extending a long arm to shake my hand.

"ImTrish," I replied, praying my palm wasn't clammy.

Over the next twenty minutes, Tim and I somehow kept up a witty train of banter, and I forgot all about my tiny, oxygen-starved lungs as he smiled at me and flirted. Tim was an engineer; he lived around the corner. He invited me to a party that weekend and I, suddenly breathless again, accepted. *Here it is,* I thought, *my first chance to apply my miracle-minded perspective to a real guy.*

Three nights later, at the swank martini party, sparks flew as we shared potent drinks and flirted. At the end of the night Tim walked me home in the rain, pulling me in for a kiss that made the streetlights above us spin. The next day, he called—right when he'd said he would. We talked for almost an hour: he told me how he admired Ayn Rand and that *The Fountainhead* was his favorite book. I told him about my spiritual work, and my commitment to focusing on love rather than fear. Remembering Jayme's chapter on "Being a Fascinating Woman," I assured him that I wasn't one of *those girls*—you know, the dull ones who only want to get married. Tim was silent as I said this. I suspect he'd never had a woman start a romantic relationship by assuring him that she didn't expect anything to come of it.

"I believe in the *experience* of our relationship," I explained, "not the title." I'd learned from Jayme and the *Course* that evolved people don't worry about the *form* of a relationship—dating, exclusivity, marriage. "The form of most relationships," she'd explained, "is like an ornate frame encrusted with diamonds and rubies." That heavy frame was bad, according to the *Course*—the diamonds were our tears and the rubies were our blood. Insisting on a particular frame (such as marriage) diminished the content of the picture (the relationship). "The alternative," Jayme said, "is for the form to be light and unobtrusive, something you can barely see or feel that holds everything together lightly so you can focus on the content." Secretly, I assumed that once Tim got to know me, the *form* would take care of itself.

SEVERAL MONTHS LATER, as we sipped wine at our favorite Italian restaurant and celebrated how wonderful it was to be *us*, Tim rhapsodized about how amazed he was to find me, how lucky he felt to be with someone who shared his values, who agreed on what was important in life. "Especially," he concluded, "since I can't see myself getting married for at least another four years."

A piece of pasta lodged in my throat and I coughed until my ribs hurt, my eyes filling with tears. I'd been dreaming of the engagement ring I hoped might be under the Christmas tree that winter. "Why?" I asked, lower lip trembling.

"I don't know," he said casually. He seemed oblivious to my shock. "I'm still figuring out what I want to do with my life. Maybe I'll travel, maybe I'll move . . . maybe I'll go to law school."

Law school? Tim had never—not once, even in passing—mentioned this before. He never asked me about my cases, or if I thought *Law Review* had been worth the time and effort. We made it through entire episodes of *Law & Order* without discussing litigation strategy or wondering how a real judge would rule.

"So, you might want to go to law school," I repeated slowly, feeling my stomach churn. "What would that mean for us— what would we do?"

"We'd do what we've been doing," he responded, looking confused by my reaction. "What's wrong with that?"

"You mean date perpetually?" I asked. By this point I was struggling—and failing—to hide my alarm. "You want to spend the next four years dragging our stuff back and forth between our two apartments, rather than building any sort of a life together?"

"Well," he replied, hesitant for the first time all evening. "I mean, it doesn't have to be like that. We could each have a drawer in the other's apartments . . . and even room in the closet."

I didn't know what to say. I was devastated, but—in light of my new training—desperately trying not to be. I excused myself to the ladies' room to pull myself together.

"I have given everything I see all the meaning it has for me," I reminded myself sternly in the mirror. I repeated mantras from the *Course:* "Instead of disappointment, I can choose to see love. Instead of rejection, I can choose to see love. This situation is perfect!" I insisted, hoping to convince myself, "it's a divine opportunity for me to learn!" I dabbed my eyes with cool water and took a deep breath, then headed back to our table. I'd reined in my emotions, but nothing inside me had changed. I was still disappointed, rejected, wondering how to handle the bull that had just wandered uninvited into my fantasy china shop.

Thinking of Jayme's words, I prayed for the universe to unite us with our highest good.

A few nights later, I called Tim to check in about our plans for the weekend.

"Hello?" he answered.

"Hi," I said softly, hoping to bridge the gap that had grown between us. "It's me . . ."

"Laurie?"

Tim, apparently, was building bridges in other directions.

AFTER TIM AND I broke up, I kicked myself for all the things I'd done wrong. Turning to the *Course*, I focused on our universal oneness, and spent hours trying to *overcome my fear-based ego responses that would have me judge my brother*. Yet try as I might, I couldn't see Tim through the judgment-free eyes Jayme promised. And despite my new spiritual awareness that everything other than love was an illusion, my hurt felt awfully real.

I became a regular at new age bookstores, amassing a vast library on alternative spirituality and metaphysics, trying to speed up my enlightenment and attract the life I wanted. I read volumes about the power of my intention, the importance of reciting affirmations of what I wanted to draw into my life, and the universal principles of abundance that were mine to tap into so long as I kept my thinking positive. On the surface, I was still just another single girl in a little black dress on Saturday night—the only difference being that when a guy wandered over to buy me a drink, I talked about God and metaphysics rather than tennis and my 401(k) plan. But on the inside, I felt like something must be happening, like all this effort had to be getting me closer to the top of this spiritual mountain I was climbing. But I couldn't understand why the results weren't better.

I cycled through another round of bad first dates (each of whom I'll call Bob just to keep things simple). Bob #1 was a handsome emergency room doctor. We went mini golfing and he inquired several times about the regularity of my bowel movements. I met Bob #2 at the dog park; he took me out to dinner and told me how he was studying to be a psychoanalyst. "If you'll excuse me," he said politely between courses, "I need to go to the men's room." Halfway across the room, he turned and came back to our table, an accusing look in his eye. "I'm not sure what I'm supposed to do here," he said angrily. "I'm attracted to you, and I have to pee, so now I have to go and touch myself. What the hell do you expect of me?" This was followed by several evenings with Bob #3, a long-haired painter with low self-esteem who drove slowly by my apartment building for weeks after we broke up. I struggled to see these guys—the Bobs—through the eyes of love, rather than fear. But each time I fizzled out at the last moment, realizing the horrible, frustrating, unspiritual truth that yes, I *did* want to get married, and no, I didn't want a husband with weird obsessions about bodily functions—his or mine—or an inclination to stalk me.

"The problem isn't that you keep meeting the wrong men," I heard Jayme tell someone in one of her lectures. "It's that you keep giving them your number!" *Touché,* I thought. But I had no idea how to prescreen these guys who kept wandering into my life. I believed Jayme's unspoken point, though: that if this wasn't working, the problem must be me. I redoubled my efforts to live a life of "true" love, free from the boundaries of "form." Not because this was what I wanted, mind you, but because I thought it was my only option; I thought it was *the truth*.

Chapter Five

Stars, No Stripes

O ne weekend I attended a seminar on some vague topic like "The Essence of Spiritual Living," where a fellow seeker named Jed asked my astrological sign. I was pretty sure he wasn't trying to pick me up; this was just the kind of small talk one made at these types of gatherings.

"I'm a Capricorn," I told him, "but I don't believe in that stuff—Capricorns are supposed to be studious, boring, and conservative, and that's not me at all."

"What's your rising sign?" he persisted. "That's what tells me who you are." He explained the impact of my rising sign—the sign on the horizon at the moment of my birth—on the rest of my astrological picture. Determined by consulting various charts, my rising sign described the *type* of Capricorn I would be, how I would manifest my "Capricorn personality."

Noting that my rising sign was Leo, Jed looked at me and

said, "You're that Capricorn goat, which means you can climb to heights other people could never reach. It takes you a long time, though, because every ten minutes you turn around and yell, 'Hey everybody! Look at me!'"

It was the most accurate—albeit embarrassing—description of my inner workings I'd ever heard. It explained why I'd worked for months as a child perfecting my baton-twirling technique so that I could march in the *front* of our town parade; how I'd won multiple public speaking awards but couldn't get through a solo chemistry experiment; and why I'd lost interest in law school as soon as I realized that most people don't like lawyers nearly as much in real life as they like them on TV. Without an audience—cheering me on, giving me pointers, acknowledging that who I was and what I did had value (even if only because I did something inherently silly better than anyone else they knew)—I lacked the will to apply myself, or even care what the outcome or benefit might be.

Inspired by this spot-on assessment, I went back to the bookstore (the "spirituality" aisle was practically my church, at this point) and bought an ephemeris—a book charting the movement of the planets through the past, present, and future—and immersed myself in signs and forecasts. I found an astrological interpretation guide that explained the personalities of everyone I knew, and a book of rituals for seeking the beneficial energy of each planet. It felt like I'd found my key to unlock the mysteries of the universe. The planets were orderly, explainable, predictable. *This* was a spirituality one could plan around.

"When's your birthday?" I asked my colleague Evan one morning at work. "Where were you born? What time?"

"April 17, 1968," he replied skeptically. "Washington DC. Six-fifty-two p.m. Why? Who wants to know?"

"Ah—you're an Aries," I exclaimed knowingly, "with Scorpio rising—that explains why you're so stubborn!" Evan went on with his work, pretending to ignore me and my odd metaphysical outburst. I was about to tease him, to ask if his girlfriend of the month knew what she was getting into. Suddenly, though, I stopped. *He's more sensitive about that than I thought.* I wasn't sure where this awareness came from.

That night, when I asked my friend Jenny about her birthday, the same thing happened: *She's just playing along,* I realized. *She's afraid of conflict and doesn't want to upset me.* This made no sense at all; Jenny was perhaps the most confident person I knew. If she thought this zodiac stuff was silly, why wouldn't she just tell me?

Over the next few weeks, I discovered something astounding: my new understanding of astrology, remedial though it was, opened up a whole realm of personal, private information about people, things I never would have known on my own. People's birthdays told me how they thought, what bothered them, what motivated them to do certain things. It was as if I had access to secret files on them, an internal database providing whatever information I wanted. If the *Course* was my spiritual foundation, astrology became my Palm Pilot—the structure by which I organized my days and friends and choices.

"You might not want to go camping this weekend," I warned my sister one day. "Mercury is in retrograde—that's when accidents happen."

"Sure I'll come to New York," I told Kristen a few weeks later. "This weekend has awesome planetary alignment—who knows who we might meet?"

I discovered that I got along great with Cancer women like my new roommate Celia (so easygoing!), yet found the men a tad wimpy for my taste.

Naturally, I charted the astrological parameters of my ideal man. I lingered over his chart with such careful attention that I wouldn't have been at all surprised if he materialized, fully formed, right off the page. He would be an earth sign—Capricorn, Taurus, Virgo—grounded and secure, unthreatened by the exuberant personality of my attention-loving Capricorn-Leo self. I vowed to never, under any circumstances, date another Sagittarius (they struggle so with monogamy), or a water sign that might try to quench my fire. Soon, it seemed like the most normal thing in the world for me to turn down a dinner invitation from a handsome man because he was born in early December. *Why bother?* I thought. *It will only lead to heartache.*

A FEW WEEKS later, I bought a fishbowl at a garage sale and set it up in the living room. Celia came home, saw it, and gasped in horror: "Water!" she exclaimed. "It's activating our childbearing corner!" I had no idea what she meant, but as two single women with nary a date on our calendars, activating our childbearing corner seemed like something to avoid.

After relocating the bowl to a bookshelf across the room, Celia spent the next two hours teaching me the finer points of feng shui, an ancient Chinese system of arranging one's belongings to ensure good fortune.

"The goal of feng shui," she said, "is to maximize the flow of auspicious chi energy to the important areas of our lives—work, family, health, wealth—while minimizing pernicious chi that cuts off success and happiness." I was struck by the notion of an unseen battle between good and evil forces waging all around us, and I loved the idea that the key to victory was good interior design.

I rearranged my furniture with a vengeance, determined to cut off the pernicious edges and corners keeping me from the life of my dreams. I scoured Celia's guidebooks, focusing on their prescriptions for love. I used a compass to locate my romance corner (this was tricky at first, as there were two opposing schools of feng shui, with two different opinions as to which corner applied), ultimately deciding that the key to my romantic success was a thin sliver of wall between my window and closet. I blanketed that little sliver with all the items of love it could hold: nine rose quartz crystals to activate the earth energy, pink flowers to bring romance to bloom, lit candles to ensure great passion, a carving of lovebirds to symbolize life-long partnership. My room now looked a bit like a Chinese restaurant, but as I surveyed my handiwork, I could almost *feel* my synchronicity with the benevolent flow of the universe. Certain I had my spiritual bases covered, I commanded the universe to bring me a man.

Surprisingly (or not), it worked. Both Celia and I attracted far more men than we had before; indeed we each had numerous potential suitors seeking to avail themselves of our charms. But what we didn't account for, in our enthusiastic embrace of these spiritual practices, was the lack of quality control.

I responded to the advances of a minister named Drew, a rugged blond with a razor-sharp sense of humor. On the surface, he was everything I wanted—fun, athletic, spiritually inclined. He was immersed in the juxtaposition of politics and religion, two of my passions, and—most important—he had a great last name that went well with either Trish or Patricia. Before we'd even had our first date, I told my friends about how well feng shui'ing worked, sketching out furniture arrangements for their apartments on happy hour cocktail napkins.

"Do you like Ethiopian food?" Drew asked as we strolled toward the restaurant on our first date. "You must. I know you will. Don't worry, it's spectacular. You'll love it."

It was a gorgeous summer evening, and as we walked along our conversation turned to the common first date topic of the awkward nature of dating and love.

"I've wrestled with dating lately," he shared. "It seems so much more complicated than it used to be." I laughed, ready to agree how much higher the stakes seemed now that we'd crossed into our late twenties and were searching for marriage partners.

As we reached the restaurant, he continued, "Ever since I started fantasizing about men, it seems like everything is different." Then he requested a table for two outside, as if we were normal people on a normal date rather than two strangers in the midst of an unexpected disclosure of bisexual inclinations.

Drew ordered for both of us, and then segued into a tale of his recent trip to Mexico as a relief worker. I forced his male-fantasy revelation to the back of my mind, and went along with his story of struggle in the Mexican harvest fields, trying to convince myself that I must have misheard; he couldn't possibly have said what I thought he had said.

The food arrived: a massive platter of unidentified meat and brown sauce on top of spongy bread. Drew scooped the thick mixture into his mouth with his hands and returned to the topic of his budding bisexuality. He raved about his counselor on the relief trip: how he'd dreamed of cuddling with him, how exciting it was when they got to share the same tent.

"This shouldn't have any impact on us," he paused to assure me. "I'm mostly into women. And for the most part, I'm monogamous."

I stuffed pile after pile of the meat mixture into my mouth, praying for one of the passing cars to make a sudden swerve and crash into the restaurant to end this conversation. I flashed back to what had been, until that night, my ringer story for "worst date ever"—dinner with a Philadelphia writer who told me in graphic detail about his brother's job at a salmon farm, which required him to fondle fish until they ejaculated. Sitting there with a plateful of unidentifiable food while Drew worked his way out of the closet, I wondered why I hadn't given the Philly guy more of a chance.

Trying to bring us back to some form of common ground, I asked Drew about God. It seemed like fair game, given his occupation, and I lobbed him an easy question about the role of miraculous intervention in the lives of the Mexicans he was so worried about.

"God?" he repeated. "Oh, I don't believe in God."

As it turned out, the most embarrassing part of my date with Drew was not his assumption that I'd be comfortable with his budding bisexuality, or even what happened to my gastro-intestinal system as that spongy bread expanded inside me until I thought I might explode. Rather, it was the fact that when he asked if we could get together again the following week, I said, "Sure."

A few weeks later, Drew broke up with me. He decided that it couldn't work out between us because he didn't think I was passionate enough about the most important things in his life: politics and spirituality. I was a lawyer, with a growing assortment of esoteric spiritual practices, being dumped by a bisexual atheist because I wasn't sufficiently interested in politics or spiritual matters. In my quest for a husband with a good last name, I'd dropped my standards to an all-time low—and ended up flattened by a man I neither liked nor respected.

Celia fared almost as badly. She met a beautiful boy who played the trombone. *A musician,* she thought, *how romantic!* We soon discovered, however, that Celia's "Jazz Man" was a third-chair volunteer in his community marching band. He had smoked so much pot in college that he had no recollection of four entire years of his life, and his big dream, at the age of twenty-six, was to repeat college in its entirety so that he could further his trombone studies and join the swim team.

"WHEN ARE YOU pretty girls going to get married?" one of the elderly ladies in our building asked Celia and me (week after week after week).

"As soon as the right guys come along, Mrs. Karamakis," we'd reply dutifully. "As soon as they get here, we'll let you know."

"Don't wait forever," she warned ominously. "You won't always be young and pretty!"

Heeding this warning, Celia and I arranged our furniture and plied our spiritual wares, desperate for the day when we'd have a better answer for her. Strangely, we were not dissuaded by our obvious lack of progress. Knowing these spiritual principles—the *Course*, feng shui, astrology—made us feel special, like we were privy to secret sources of information other people passed by. It also gave us something to *do* while we waited for our dream men to arrive, a way to feel like we were in control, that we weren't just waiting around hoping something might happen.

"We just need to change our energy," Celia encouraged me. "We need to cleanse our auras and fill our space with more positivity."

"You're right," I agreed. "We attract people and experiences into our lives for a reason," I recited, parroting one of Jayme's lectures. "It's a basic metaphysical principle. We just have to affirm that the next guys we meet will be better."

It never occurred to us that these "glitches"—Drew, Celia's trombone man—were any bigger than our crossing the paths of the wrong men (and our subsequent decisions to date them); we never considered that our spiritual foundation might be unstable. Celia dated an older man from work who'd stop by our apartment at midnight to say hello. I dated a younger man from work who'd come over whenever I told him to. Somehow, though, it still didn't seem like this intentional attraction thing was working. But our reaction to these misfires was to reassure one another that things had to get better soon. Then we'd "smudge" the negative energy out of our apartment by swirling a burning hunk of sage throughout our apartment, repeating a Native American incantation to ward off evil spirits. It smelled terrible, and it didn't seem to work.

What would Jayme do differently? I wondered.

Chapter Six

Some Who Wander Are Really Lost

L ater that summer, after the fishbowl and the atheist minister and the lovebirds guarding the energy of my romance corner, I learned from Jayme's Web site that she would be leading a spiritual pilgrimage to Greece that August. *This is it!* I thought. *My chance to see her in action!* The trip sounded amazing: touring Athena's temple and Minoan ruins, exploring sacred sites under Jayme's tutelage, gleaning their power through her insight and wisdom. Unfortunately, the price tag was equally amazing. I signed off and hopped in the shower, exchanging my dreams of world travel for the mundane reality of the day ahead.

As I washed my hair, a voice in my head said, *Write to her—ask if she needs an assistant.*

That's ridiculous, I thought. *Who writes to celebrities and asks for a free trip to Europe?*

An hour later, as if propelled by some unseen force, I was walking to the mailbox with an audacious letter addressed to Jayme, introducing myself as a lawyer who admired her work and offering to accompany her to Greece as a personal assistant. I even claimed to make great coffee—*If she'll take me to Greece,* I thought, *I'll learn!*

Two weeks later, Celia brought the phone to me, cradling it in both hands like a holy relic. "It's *Jayme Brass* . . . for you . . ."

It was, indeed, Jayme Brass. She did not need an assistant for her upcoming trip, but she wanted someone to help with her eight-year-old daughter while they travelled—would I be interested in that instead?

"Of course!" I blurted. "I mean, I'd be honored."

"Wonderful," Jayme replied. "I'll be in Washington next month giving a lecture on Capitol Hill—perhaps we could meet for lunch?"

SITTING AT LUNCH a few weeks later, stirring sugar into my iced tea as Jayme perused the menu, I tried not to stare. She seemed so *real.* I braced myself for a hard-hitting interview to determine my fitness for the position, and asked if I could answer any questions or offer her a list of people to vouch for my character.

"Don't worry," she said. "I'm sure you and Sara will get along famously." I was unnerved by her nonchalance.

"You'll be fine," she insisted. "Now tell me about yourself— what are your dreams?" I was stunned. *Jayme wanted to know about me? Not as a babysitter, but as a person?* "What do you plan to do with your life, your education, your intelligence?" she prompted.

Surprised by her directness, I stuttered my replies. I knew what I hoped to do with my life, my education, my intelligence—I wanted to be like *her*. Having no idea how to say this, however, I choked out a condensed version of my grad school application essay, something about "wanting to be at the intersection of spirituality and political justice."

I was astonished to be lunching with Jayme Brass; that *she* was interested in *me* was too much to fathom. She was different from what I'd expected. She wasn't like the Dalai Lama, wearing robes declaring her spiritual preeminence; she didn't punctuate every sentence with relevant spiritual quotes, or regale me with tales of her pious hours of prayer and meditation. And when she corrected the way her young daughter used her utensils, there was no deep spiritual underpinning to the correction.

After hugging her and Sara good-bye, I spent the rest of the afternoon in a daze. I had Jayme Brass's home phone number in my cell phone, and a ticket to accompany her and her daughter to Greece in my pocket. Suddenly, my life was a whole lot more interesting; I couldn't wait to see where this new road would lead.

Two months later, on our first full day in Delphi, we pilgrims—all ninety of us—gathered in the midst of a stream of water thought to be a source of prophetic power. Jayme stood high atop a rock like an ancient priestess, and began teaching us about the mysteries and sacred essence of this place. As she spoke, we trailed fingers in the shallow waters and dangled our toes in its clear current. I removed the gold cross I was wearing and dipped it into the water, hoping, I guess, that this gesture might imbue the charm with some power, prophetic or other-wise, that would give direction to my life. I looked up to see a plump young woman from our group stripped down to her un-derwear (full coverage briefs and a pointy support bra), sitting right in the middle of the shallow current, struggling to im-merse herself in those six inches of water. It was an odd sight, but as a spiritually correct new age follower, I tried to look beyond her doughy nakedness, willing myself to be impressed by her open quest for insight. Inside, though, I cringed. *Is that what it takes to make this work?* I worried. This fear stayed with me for the rest of the trip, taunting me that the breakthrough I hoped for was just beyond my reach. *I guess I'm still unenlightened,* I thought sadly.

When our spiritual adventure drew to a close nine days later, I struggled to hide my disappointment. Despite my close prox-imity to Jayme, and the hours of meditation, contemplation, and endless circular discussions of spiritual principles, I still had no idea how to make this stuff work. I still didn't under-stand how Jayme managed her real life, how she applied the spiritual power she exuded in her talks and writing.

On the long flight home, Jayme and I talked for hours about politics and spirituality, and she asked me to be the new director of her nonprofit organization. Thrilled, I jumped at the chance. Rather than going home to my mun-dane life, I'd have a new job, and another chance to observe Jayme firsthand—an apprenticeship, of sorts. I could learn from her, and see how she applied the *Course's* principles to her everyday life.

•

FROM THE MOMENT we stepped off the plane, I was enfolded into Jayme's whirlwind lifestyle, living out of a suitcase in her guest room and participating in everything she did. She treated her massive bed as a command center, and soon I was sprawled out on her silk comforter surrounded by phones, books, papers, and laptops. CNN streamed from an enormous television in the corner of the room, and I stared in awe as her coterie of people wandered in and out and around us—bringing food, cleaning the bathroom, assessing logistics for Jayme's upcoming engagements. We'd spend the morning recruiting a board of directors that read like a who's who list of *New York Times* spiritual best-selling authors, then sit down for an afternoon snack and talk about astrology and men.

The next two months were like a surreal fantasy: I attended Washington meetings on Jayme's behalf, networked with publicists, lobbyists, and wealthy spiritual seekers who desired her attention in exchange for their support, and waded through the never-ending list of people who wanted to hitch their wagon to Jayme's train. In a way, it was a dream come true, my opportunity to travel and tell the world about spiritual things at the side of my mentor; witnessing firsthand how she navigated the ups and downs of her very public spiritual life. But my close proximity to her private life revealed something that I'd never imagined.

Despite her bestseller status, it appeared Jayme had no more idea of how to make a relationship work than I did. She told me stories of the men she'd dated over the years, men impressed with her success and drawn to her charisma. They came, and then they left. It seemed she had no hope that there was a special—single—man for her, and so she availed herself of those who wandered by. She used the *Course's* principles of formless love to justify these dalliances, never recognizing how empty—and alone—these choices left her. Despite her convictions about the generous provision of the universe, Jayme was, I realized, even more likely to settle for whoever came along than I was.

Her stories shook me. Here was a beautiful, successful woman—the epitome of what I hoped to be—and she was alone. I was stunned to see that Jayme's advice, the words that sounded so beautiful and true in her books, didn't seem to be working in her life, just as they hadn't worked in mine. I looked into my future and was unnerved by what I saw: another two decades of relationship disappointment, eroding my hopes and leaving me willing to compromise everything for scraps of attention from men who took my love but gave nothing but baubles and fading memories in return. It was as if God was putting a giant, flashing sign in front of my nose: *This Is Where You're Headed! Turn Around! Turn Around!*

After three months, unable to reconcile the spiritual promises I'd read with the emptiness of what I'd witnessed, I resigned. And suddenly, for the first time in almost a decade, I had nothing to lean on, no spiritual mooring to keep me from drifting out to sea. Like Dorothy in *The Wizard of Oz*, I'd made my way to the Emerald City, only to pull back the curtain and find that my wizard had no magic. It seemed clear that I'd been wrong as a child: God couldn't be counted on to provide the life I dreamed of. So I returned to my other object of devotion and worship: men. Walking down the street one day, I announced to the universe: "I am so tired of having *boyfriend* problems! I am ready to have *husband problems!*"

And somewhere out there, some malevolent force rubbed his palms together in glee and said, *I'm so glad you asked . . .*

Chapter Seven

What About That?

R ight on cue, the universe acknowledged my request: I met a man who embodied each and every item on my wish list (tall, good looking, athletic, ready to get married, willing to marry me). *It works!* I thought delightedly, waltzing into my newly manifested love. But the problem with giving the universe a wish list, I'd soon discover, isn't what you ask for—it's what you forget to mention.

WE MET AT a mutual friend's boat launch party. I didn't care for him much at first—he was cocky, the slightest bit too anxious to show off his status as an eligible bachelor. As he drove away that evening, something in me said, *That guy is bad news. Watch out for him.* I didn't pay much attention to that voice, though; it never occurred to me that I'd see him again.

A few weeks later he called and asked me out. I was horrified by his audacity—I'd dated one of his friends (albeit briefly); weren't there rules against such things? "Just meet me for a cup of coffee," he said. "No obligation."

"Fine," I agreed, not wanting to offend him. We made plans to meet at a coffee shop that Sunday afternoon.

He's better looking than I remember, I thought, seeing him walk toward me. We sat down, started talking, and the warning words I'd issued myself faded slowly into the background as I relaxed into our conversation. He told me about the two daughters he was raising, the business he had built, and how much he relied on God to hold it all together. He was eleven years older than me, but as the minutes ticked by, this revelation shape-shifted from a red flag into a green light, as a romantic picture of wisdom and security flooded my mind. *What might life be like with a man who is truly grown up?* I wondered. *A man who wants to be married again because he understands how much better life is when you approach it as a team?* When he asked me if I'd consider a real date with him, I relented. What if this unlikely man might indeed be my Prince Charming? I vowed not to blow it this time, not to judge him unfairly or be overly critical. I promised myself that no matter what happened, I'd keep an open mind.

He gave me a gold bracelet on our first official date, slipping the long velvet box into my hands as I slid into his front seat. "You have beautiful hands," he said. "They should be shown off. Have you ever thought of getting a manicure?"

That's offensive, I thought, before pushing the negativity aside. I turned my wrist back and forth, watching the late-evening sun shimmer off of the golden links.

"I want to take care of you," he told me later that night. "Let me buy you a spa package—you deserve it."

He wants to take care of me! I thought. "Yes," I agreed blissfully, "I would love to get my nails done."

"What's up with that color?" he demanded harshly when I walked out of the salon waving my new French manicure. "Did you choose that or did they force it on you?" I stared at him in shock, putting my hands behind me in shame.

"I thought it was pretty," I confessed. "You know—kind of elegant."

"You're better than that," he said. "Next time, I'll go in with you."

He just wants to take care of me, I told myself glumly. *Don't make such a big deal out of it.*

For our next date, he brought flowers, a toy for my dog, and a necklace. We dined by the river and spent the evening watching the stars from the docks. It was perfect. Well, almost. Every once in a while something awkward popped up: his ongoing litigation with his ex-wives (there was not one, I learned, but two), a critical comment about something I wore, hints that he wasn't particularly skilled at controlling his anger. *He needs a lot of attention,* I thought. *Don't judge!* I countered quickly, reminding myself not to be so picky.

Our dates rolled by like a fairy tale, albeit one in need of a little editing. For the most part, this relationship was everything I'd dreamed of: he was devoted to me, he made grand pronouncements of love and adoration. And while these factors were sometimes tinged by the occasional dig or social gaffe, these were easy to overlook, quickly forgotten in the shower of extravagant gifts and ever-growing plans for our future. He wanted to get married as soon as possible. It was the first such offer I'd had in almost a decade; as far as I was concerned, we couldn't walk down the aisle fast enough.

SIX MONTHS LATER, he took me to New York City to buy an engagement ring. He picked out a breathtaking solitaire diamond set between two smaller pear-shaped stones. My mind swam, barely able to grasp the idea that I would get to wear this ring, every day, for the rest of my life. I felt like Cinderella.

"It looks so beautiful on you, baby," he enthused.

He paused, then went on. "You know what? It would probably be best if we used your credit card to pay for this, so we can keep my debts low for when we buy our new house." We'd been looking at property for a new home the weekend before; my dream of finally settling down into a real life was becoming a reality.

"That sounds smart," I responded, never taking my eyes off of my sparkling left hand as I opened my wallet and handed him the card.

WE DECIDED NOT to have a big wedding. My new fiancé did not get along with his family, and had few friends of his own. Part of me wanted to wear a white dress and walk down the aisle, but I happily sacrificed this dream for the chance to finally be married—to get the completer set for my engagement ring and no longer be the "still single" cousin at family gatherings. We eloped on a Wednesday afternoon in the mauve-and-teal living room of a justice of the peace, after which I went home and he went back to work. Overnight I morphed from single girl in the city to suburban housewife, complete with two step-daughters, a new four-bedroom house, and two luxury cars in the driveway. On paper, it all looked so, soooo good. Like a dream, in fact. Like my destiny.

But as I dug into my dream life, it was hard to ignore that my tall, good-looking husband had an emerging anger management problem. What had appeared to be a slight tendency to overreact during our months of dating now expanded into regular full-blown episodes. I won't belabor the point except to say that ups and downs of our new marriage proved a bit more difficult—"volatile" would be the proper word—than the usual tiffs and challenges associated with the first year of wedded bliss.

He found fault with unexpected things—I put the soda away on the wrong side of the refrigerator, I was out too long walking the dog. "Why don't you dye your hair darker?" he asked me sharply one day at lunch. "You'd look better with dark hair." I didn't have any friends in our new community—he didn't think we had time for that. He took me on a romantic trip that fall—a belated honeymoon, he called it. The first night, after our dinner waiter smiled at me and took my order first, my new husband flew into a rage, a furious storm that lasted for seven hours. "You knew what you were doing," he accused me again and again. "You *made* him smile at you."

I lived under constant accusation, carefully monitored by my new husband who was certain that my days were spent seducing every gas station attendant, coffee barista, or airline worker who crossed my path. At the slightest provocation, he would blow, screaming at me in restaurants, at the gym, outside his daughter's school. "You're lucky I married you," he'd sneer, "because no one else would have someone like you for a wife." His eyes burned in fury as I shrunk back into the corner, bewildered.

The next morning, he'd always apologize, showering me with loving overtures as I choked down the low-fat cereal he bought me to maintain my weight.

"You know how much I love you, baby," he'd croon, eyes now soft and liquidy. "You forgive me, right? I just get a little carried away sometimes." Later there'd be another velvet box—a ruby ring, a silver necklace, small gold earrings. They came from the pawnshop next door to his business, I knew by now; he had "an arrangement" with the pawnbroker. All my precious jewelry was tainted with painful histories of other people's disappointment, picked up for a pittance by my husband to distract me from his inability to control his anger.

Did he hit you? people ask, when they hear about my first marriage. Even when they don't ask, they wonder. The answer is *He didn't have to.* Smart men know better than to hit you, because hitting is the line we draw between husbands with poor stress management skills and husbands who belong in jail. My first husband balanced precariously on this line, leaning his whole body across, but always righting himself an instant before he fell. It was the only control he ever required of himself when it came to me. Hitting was off limits, because that's what awful men do. And for him to be an awful husband would have required him to forfeit his utter conviction that I was an awful wife.

WE'D BEEN MARRIED just under a year the first time he came home with a girl's phone number in his pants pocket. A few days later I found the business card of a woman I'd never heard of lying on the kitchen counter near his phone. Two ex-girlfriends called the house to speak to him. "Don't be ridiculous," he said when I questioned him about why he was still in contact with these women. "It doesn't mean anything," he insisted. "They're just people I know."

Before long I was numb to it all, walking on eggshells, accepting admiring compliments about my beautiful ring, agreeing that, yes indeed, I was fortunate to have such a wonderful husband. "He's so handsome," a colleague chided me one day. "You'd better appreciate how good you've got it—there are a lot of us out here who would give anything to have what you have." I nodded dutifully and resolved to focus on my excellent circumstances. I had a husband, a house, a beautiful diamond. What was wrong with me that I wasn't satisfied? *Every marriage has tough times,* I told myself sternly. *Try harder.*

I was determined to succeed as a wife, to hang in there until I figured out how to make this marriage work. *The first year of marriage is hard,* I told myself, *everyone goes through this.* I didn't dare tell my sister or my parents or even Kristen how bad things were. I hinted at times, making jokes about the traditionally rocky first year of marriage. But I was too embarrassed to admit that I still couldn't get a relationship to work.

Not sure what else to try, I pulled out my old feng shui

books and focused on harmonizing the energy of our home. I pushed and pulled the furniture, painted the walls in soothing earth tones, and bought a giant fish tank for our living room filled with seven fancy goldfish that would, according to the expert authors, quench the angry fires causing us to fight and bring us prosperity. My stepdaughters named the fish, and we marveled at the speedy snails that glided along the glass walls of the tank to keep it free from algae. We even had a special dinner that night to celebrate our new turn of fortune.

Two days later, the tank morphed into a scene of grim carnage: one of the snails ate all the others, leaving a trail of empty shells along the bottom of the tank. Smiley, the yellow fish, was stuck haplessly to the filter, gasping for air as the current flew by, while BoBo, the black fish, floated upside down, his eyes wide as he bobbed across the top of the tank. The other fish swam frantically in the bottom corner, biting at each other and searching for a place to hide. I spent the next week flushing our hopes down the toilet one at a time, wondering what to try next. *I guess fish and snails aren't built to handle this kind of pressure,* I thought.

IN A LAST-DITCH effort to save ourselves, we tried Christian counseling. We'd been through two marriage counselors already—one of whom told me privately, "I can't imagine how you stay with him." We hoped that paying one of God's people to deconstruct and rebuild us might yield better results.

We met with an impossibly meek and earnest woman named Tabitha, who asked us to begin by describing our *feelings* about the marriage. Desperate for tangible help and scared of what my marriage was becoming, I jumped in and admitted, "He punched a hole in the wall last week. I'm not sure a full analysis of our feelings is the best place for us to start."

Turning to my husband, Tabitha asked, in all sincerity, "What do you think *Jesus* would want you to do about that now?"

"Jesus," I interjected, too frantic to notice the storm I was stirring up, "would not have punched the wall in the first place!"

By the end of our hour with Tabitha, my husband was so in touch with his feelings that he screamed at me, without stopping, for the next five hours. He screamed on the drive home, weaving in and out of thirty-five-mile-an-hour traffic at fifty-two miles an hour; he screamed at me in the kitchen, the bathroom, the bedroom, then followed me all throughout the house like a possessed madman. It was like standing in front of a firing squad, watching bullets whiz by and wondering when it might ever be over, almost longing to be hit. Finally, sometime after midnight, I locked myself in the guest room. He pounded on the door for another thirty-five minutes, taunting me with threats of what he'd do to me if I ever tried to leave him.

That was the end of Tabitha.

WHEN WE'D BEEN married about a year, my mother came to visit. After two days with us, she took me aside, looked into my eyes, and spoke the truth I'd never dared consider: "This is not your fault," she said, "and this is *not* normal." She begged me to leave, and reassured me that the things she saw were not the traditional struggles of a newly married couple. My mom, perhaps the most dedicated wife and mother I know, handed me a fistful of cash and told me to *run*.

Leaving was harder than I thought it would be. Before I left I had, like most people, read horrific accounts of abused women who stayed with their husbands too long, stories of women like Hedda Nussbaum and Nicole (formerly Simpson) Brown, and wondered, along with everybody else, why—how even—they stayed. In a life so awful, with specific evidence that something was very, very wrong, how could any woman let things reach that point? Why did they wait until the decision was taken out of their hands, until the emergency room doctor noticed that they'd broken fifteen bones in the last eight weeks, until they were found on the elegant rug in the living room, blood seeping out of a slash wound? *How*, I wondered along with everybody else, *does this happen?*

Here's how, I discovered: there is a cost to leaving. A huge price to pay to fall out of the societal acceptance and comfort that comes from having a husband and a home—even if you get screamed at for hours every night behind the walls of that home, and even if the kids hide in their bedrooms with the music cranked up to drown out the noise, and the dog spends most "family time" cowering under the bed. Even with all that, it's still easier to stay married than to start over. That's the truth. We point to well-intentioned social programs like battered women's shelters and "dress-for-success" nonprofit organizations that help women get out from under abuse and wonder, *Why didn't she seek help?* But even as we're wondering—seated at our kitchen tables waiting for kids to get off the bus and husbands to call to let us know they're on their way home from work—few of us wonder how we'd cope; what we'd choose, given those options. Even at the worst points in my marriage, when I was seated at my own kitchen table wondering about *those* poor abused women, I never considered that I was one of them. And despite the frantic offers from the people who loved me most, I figured that at a certain point their enthusiasm and/or expendable resources would wane, and I'd be left on my own to make something of myself. I wasn't sure I had it in me, or that the results would be worth it. *Better the devil you know*, as they say. So despite the fierce devotion of my family and friends, it took a miracle to pry me out from under my own kitchen island.

ONE BRIGHT SPOT through this harrowing time was my job. I worked as a sales representative for a home-building company in a new housing development (you know, the kind that makes you feel like you could be in any suburb in America, the same house repeated over and over again outside cities like Syracuse, Toledo, Kansas City, Houston). The development was about forty-five minutes outside the city, in acres of felled trees and about twelve tons of mud. I met with prospective buyers in my pretty model home, wowed them with blueprints and architectural renderings, and painted elaborate mental pictures of the delightful new life they could have here in "Trishville." Then I'd pull out my calculator and attempt all manner of financial gymnastics to qualify them for the monthly payment they'd owe on this new life.

Trishville, as it was, was not what most people envision when they dream of what a half-million dollars can buy. Our architectural renderings barely disguised the naked truth that we were selling long, skinny houses, six feet (that's seventy-two inches) apart from one another. Fire code meant no windows on the sides of the houses, and tight lot lines meant next to no backyard. And yet the houses were not the problem. They were perfect, for example, for people who valued privacy over yard work. The problem was the neighborhood. Trishville was located in the middle of the NIMBY ("Not in my backyard!") trifecta, bordering a sewer treatment plant, an Amtrak station, and a federal maximum-security prison.

Because of these "community challenges," the company had modest projections for sales in Trishville. I was expected to sell perhaps two or three houses a month; four got me a nice bonus and an "Attagirl!" from management. I did well enough at this that I enjoyed my job, and the generous paycheck my dream building earned. Selling the dream of the perfect life somehow took the edge off the fact that my own "perfect" life was falling apart.

One quiet day, sitting in my model, I wondered, *How can I keep this job if I leave my marriage?* It wasn't safe for me there in the model home, alone on an isolated piece of land. My husband's propensity toward violence was escalating with every fight we had, and he had a gun. *If I leave,* I realized, *I have to leave everything.*

But there was money on the line—a lot of it. I had no money of my own—my husband controlled our joint bank account, keeping the checkbook with him at all times. I'd squirreled away a few $10 bills after my mother's visit, trying to build up a bit of a stash, but he found them; I'd made up a story about saving to buy him a birthday present to quell his rage.

I challenged God: "If you want me to leave this job, God, I need you to make it clear. Give me a sign." Then I heard myself blurt, "If you want me to leave, let me sell eight houses this month!"

Well, I thought, *that pretty much answers that.* I heard the Amtrak warning horn blow as the train rumbled through, and got back to work, convinced I was in for the long haul.

I sold one house that first week, another the second. Week three—nothing. But when I arrived at my model early on the fourth Saturday morning, three couples were pacing outside the door. All three had been in to see the model on my day off, and all three were ready, checkbooks in hand, to sign contracts. And as that last week wound down, people came from far and wide, all ready, willing, and anxious to secure their strip of land in this aesthetically challenged neighborhood. (One man even bought *two* houses, sure his brother wouldn't want to miss out on such a great opportunity.) By the end of that month, I had eight new contracts sitting on my desk, signed and ready to go. Three weeks later, I resigned, not sure what I (or God) was doing. I had my sign, but no idea what to do next.

FINALLY, ONE BAD morning (not the worst, but certainly one of the more memorable) my husband picked up the giant water bottle where we stored loose change. "If you ever leave me," he vowed in a matter-of-fact tone that sent chills down my spine, "this will be the closest thing to alimony you ever see." He hurled the bottle to the floor, then stormed out the door and went to work. I got on my knees and started rolling all those nickels, dimes, and quarters. I heard a song coming from the radio, a woman singing angrily to her abusive husband: "How can I forget the times you said no one would want me? How am I supposed to think about all the shit you've done to me?" and something inside me broke.

Kristen called. "I don't know if I can do this any longer," I gasped, crying so hard I couldn't hold the phone steady.

The next morning, an envelope arrived from FedEx. Inside I found the key to Kristen's summer house in Connecticut and a check for $1,000. That was the day I decided to run away.

Chapter Eight

Exile

When the decision point came, I didn't really understand what I was choosing. I naively thought that leaving a marriage—especially a volatile one, where I had a solid excuse for my departure—would return me to my former single status, like hitting "restart" on a video game.

Wow, was I wrong.

I didn't realize it until I landed in Kristen's kitchen and she reached into her junk drawer for a pen. *My God,* I thought, *I don't even have a junk drawer . . .*

Before I left, I had no way to calculate the gazillion little things I'd no longer have, things I had taken for granted a mere twenty-four hours before. As ugly as my married life was, it was *a life*—I planned dinners (and could afford groceries), went to work (because I had a job), did laundry (because I had a washer and dryer, and—for that matter—*clothes*). My mind spun, amazed by the silly things I'd grabbed on my way out—I'd packed my Kate Spade purse but no coat, elegant strappy sandals but no winter boots. It was like I'd thought I was going to a cocktail party.

Then there were the practical matters: I had my dog, but no way to put food in her hand-painted bowl. I had a credit card and a gas key, both of which my enraged husband closed out once he realized I was gone, erasing any means of support or sustenance I might count on to survive without him. I no longer had a cell phone or computer, not to mention the bulk purchases of tampons and toothpaste and toilet paper that had made me feel so prepared for life, so *adult*, as I'd lined my linen closet. Now, I didn't even have a junk drawer. All I had were a few people who loved me enough to help while I figured this all out.

I spent the next three months in motion. I lived at Kristen's, but bounced between my parents' house on the coast, my sister's house in the woods, and my brother's house on the side of a mountain, trying to remain unfindable. I changed my last name to an imaginary word I made up using a numerology chart; left my luxury car in a supermarket parking lot and told the loan company to take it away; pawned my engagement ring and hid the cash in an ever-changing series of hiding places among my scant possessions. For all intents and purposes, I disappeared.

My husband turned up from time to time—a strange car pulling into my parents' driveway, an endless series of phone calls to my sister and brothers and college friends. I considered taking out a restraining order after one harrowing run-in, only to realize that if you want the police to tell someone they can't come within one hundred or two hundred or fifteen thousand yards of where you are, they have to tell that someone where it is they're not supposed to be. This rather blows the point of hiding. I guess I would have known if he was near by watching my dog, who would have done what she always did in his presence: leaked a panicked pile of poop on the rug and thrown her trembling body underneath the nearest bed. Thankfully, it never came to that. Instead, I moved around, crashing at friends' apartments in New York and Baltimore and Cambridge, all the while creating a new, semisecret life.

WHEN PEOPLE ASK me what I did during those long days squirreled away in the Connecticut countryside, I tell them the truth: I cried, and I ate pasta. That's almost all I remember. I must have brushed my teeth, taken walks, played with my dog. But I don't recall much besides the singular thrill of eating fettuccini with pesto sauce, every night, for three months straight. It had been almost two years since I'd been allowed to choose food without supervision; as I plunged back into the world of endless possibilities, it turned out that all I wanted was platefuls of carbohydrates coated in pine nuts and basil.

And when I wasn't making dinner, I cried. I'd start out with other intentions—reading a book, watching TV. But I'd always end up in a heap on one of the house's many plush surfaces, sobbing until I passed out. I felt like a composite character from *The Wizard of Oz*, needing a new heart, a new brain, a shot of courage; I was a human Build-A-Bear waiting to be stuffed. Crying, I discovered, is great for your complexion, as well as quite a workout; under the right conditions it's almost aerobic. There were many nights I'd see my bright-eyed reflection in the hall mirror and think, *Anguish: the beauty routine I've been waiting for.*

At that time, I didn't realize how prominently the theme of *exile* figures in the Bible. In my dull childhood Sunday school, I never caught on to this narrative thread in God's story, how heroes were always taken far away from everything they built their lives upon so they would learn to depend on God. In contrast, I thought I was being taken far away from everything so I would learn to depend on *me*: to focus on my inner truth, become self-aware and self-sufficient, get healing for my issues like all the self-help literature told me I should. That's what I thought I was supposed to be doing in Connecticut, even though I had no idea what that might look like. The cathartic crying/getting in touch with my emotions/reaching into my dark places/facing my inner demons part I had down, but it all left me feeling like a murky swamp that needed to be dredged; like my kidneys should be hooked up to my brain to filter out all the muck floating around in there. I salvaged what I could remember of the old me—pieces of dreams and tiny shards of hope I found floating in the flotsam and jetsam of my clogged up head. But try as I might, I couldn't find anything in there to take me from where I was (miserable, desperate, disappointed) to where I wanted to be.

One day I decided to meditate—it seemed like a "filter out the garbage" thing to do. I set myself up on a comfy pillow in Kristen's living room, determined to empty my mind. "Omm-mmmm," I chanted (like I'd seen monks do on the Discovery Channel), closing my eyes and trying to open myself to the light of the universe. I took deep breaths in and tried to follow them out. It didn't feel like much was happening. After a few minutes, though, things got more interesting, but not at all in the way I'd anticipated. As I breathed in, a violent shiver surged through my body, and I was overwhelmed by the distinct sensation that someone was standing over me with a sledgehammer, about to crush my skull. I cringed in anticipation, sliding back off of my pillow and scooting around the corner into the dining room. Panting heavily, I didn't dare look. *What the hell was that?* I thought angrily. *The Dalai Lama never mentioned a guy with a hammer . . .* I stood up and glanced back into the living room, which naturally, was empty. The sun shone in through the windows, my pillow lay abandoned on the floor.

A few days later I tried a guided meditation, sure that the soothing voice of a renowned spiritual expert drifting out from my CD player would keep any monsters at bay. I lay back on the floor as my guide described the gentle stream of mystical light and energy coursing through my body—starting in my toes, continuing up the backs of my calves, filling my thighs and hips and abdomen. At first, I felt the warmth of the gentle stream, but then it made me a little jumpy. My heart started beating faster, and by the time the gentle stream started toward my chest, I had the visceral sense that poison was seeping through my veins, like I was being executed by lethal injection. My whole body jerked, and I slammed my hand against the CD player, ejecting the disc and sending it skittering across the carpet. Breathing heavily, I considered something for the first time: that perhaps not all of the spiritual forces vying for space in my brain and body were good, that not every higher power had my best interests at heart. It occurred to me that at a practical level, *empty your mind* is actually a terrible suggestion. I felt like the kid on the camping trip who gets hungry and starts munching on random berries—sure, they might tide me over for a little while, but the odds were equally good that they'd kill me.

ONE MORNING I pulled on a giant fleece jacket that had belonged to my father, poured myself a cup of coffee, and went out to Kristen's backyard. I sat by the pool in the brisk fall air, wondering, in the most matter-of-fact way possible, what would become of me. *How did I get here? How did this happen?* The cold wind blew over me, and slowly, the truth came:

I was not brave, I was scared. I had not, historically, made decisions as the strong woman I thought myself to be, but rather as an annoying, spoiled child who stomped away when life didn't follow her plan. In my hysterical pursuit of marriage, I'd lost sight of reality: that when I married this man, I'd have to live with him, that along with his beautiful diamond ring came his demands, his expectations, and his maniacal insistence that my life operate on his terms. Surrendering to my desperation, I had abandoned years of training in faith, spirituality—even the simple knowledge that not every loud frog is really a prince. Yet even as I realized all of this, I wasn't sure what to do differently, or even what to do next. So I made some bold decisions: "I will never get married again." I declared, letting the words echo out across the yard. The idea of being bound to someone I couldn't get away from—a situation I had once pursued with my entire existence—now terrified me. "I will never let a man have that kind of control over me," I continued. "I will never entrust my life to someone else, and I will never bring children into this world that might tie me to a man and make it impossible to get away. I won't do that, not ever." I took a long sip from my now lukewarm mug of coffee and looked at the fallen leaves blowing by. Everything around me felt cold and hopeless and dead.

THE NEXT DAY I went to Wal-Mart. I wanted to find some music to lighten my desperate outlook, preferably something that wasn't filled with sappy lyrics about how the right man's true love saves the day. As I wandered past a small section called "Christian Inspiration," a white CD cover with four happy, smiling people on it caught my eye. *In a Different Light* it was called. On a whim, I grabbed it. On the surface, at least, this chic group of two men and two women looked happy—like they had life figured out. Avalon was the band's name. *Like the Arthurian Legend,* I thought. Their shiny world felt so far from where I was, like such an impossible dream, that I bought their CD to see if a tiny bit of what they had might rub off on me.

I listened to that CD over and over and over again, surprised by how good it made me feel. I skipped the weird songs about Jesus and his wonderful death on the Cross, but the others— upbeat tunes about trusting God, how His love could strengthen my heart—began to resuscitate my flattened spirit. I played one song repeatedly. It was written as if God himself was singing, promising, that if His people prayed, if they reached out to Him with broken hearts, He would heal them.

Please let it be true, I prayed.

I COULDN'T LIVE in Connecticut forever, even though I kind of wanted to. It wasn't a bad place to convalesce—a five-bedroom estate with a Jacuzzi tub, 257 cable channels, and a pool, not to mention a gardener and a maid. I took weekend trips to the ocean. I spent quality time with my dog. Really, it could have been worse.

The thing was, though, none of it was mine. Kristen and her family came on the weekends to reinhabit their lives, and I'd realize—mortified—that I'd eaten her husband's favorite crackers or drank the last beer. I lived in constant fear of breaking, spilling, denting—I was like one of those uber-conscientious campers, trying to erase all traces of my existence, determined to leave this pristine, antique-filled habitat unsullied by my presence. That Kristen would let me live in her weekend house was a gorgeous act of generosity; that her husband—whose opinion of me hovered somewhere between contempt and utter disdain—allowed me in the house at all was, in fact, a miracle. (I suspect it is recorded in heaven as his one kind gesture toward a registered Democrat.)

And yet I could tell that everyone was watching me, wondering what would happen next. No one asked, or even hinted. But it was clear that I couldn't go on like this, that I couldn't spend the rest of my life planning my day around a bath, a long walk, and the latest episode of *A Love Story* on TLC.

"Why is Trish crying?" Kristen's five-year-old daughter asked one afternoon.

"She's sad." Kristen replied. "Sometimes grown-up life makes you really sad."

Chapter Nine

My Get-a-Life Coach

M aybe you need professional help?" Celia suggested one day over the phone, after I'd described the grim sum total of my circumstances: the hiding, the fictitious last name, the man with the sledgehammer haunting my attempts at meditation. We both agreed that my life was getting a bit too much like a James Bond movie. She sent me an article from the *New York Times* describing a new source of help for people who were not, as the author gently put it, where they wanted to be in life. Rather than spending all our money on psychoanalysis and updated editions of *What Color Is Your Parachute?* under-performers like me could hire a new breed of personal adviser, what the article called a "life coach," to sort us out and help us find our way. Not quite a therapist, not quite a guru, a life coach was a trained professional whose specialty was helping people reach their personal and professional goals.

I found a listing for one of these life coaches in the yellow pages. I took it as a sign. (It's remarkable how omnipresent signs are when you're determined to see them . . .) The woman's name was Mary-rama Jacobson, and she invited me to her office for a free introductory session. Undaunted by her name—I'd certainly come across more unique ones in my travels—I decided to meet her and see what she had to offer.

When I walked into Mary-rama's office that first day, I found myself in a cornucopia of spiritual tchotchkes: angels looking down from bookcases, crystals dancing in the summer sun, and a giant welcome mat at the foot of the stairs announcing "You are HERE" with a giant X to mark the spot. Harp music plunked cheerfully in the background. Mary-rama greeted me with a warm handshake and an offer of distilled water. She reminded me of Jane Hathaway from *The Beverly Hillbillies*—efficient, precise, and more than a tad off center. We sat down at her desk, where she ate the last of her eleven almonds (she was experimenting with the precise regulation of her protein intake). Her eyes glowed as she explained the genesis of her unique name: how the universe revealed her *true identity* one day as she was driving down the road.

"*Spirit* insisted," she said as if that explained everything. "My birth name was Mary Ellen; changing it was a vital step in the declaration of my inner truth. Expanding the reach of my name out into the universe connects me to my larger presence," she exclaimed with glee. My new age training in nonjudgmental acceptance kicked in at this point, and I nodded in what I knew was a positive, spirit-affirming manner. The first thing I learned

from Mary-rama was that the key to selling people on a preposterous idea is to present it with absolute confidence.

"My mission is to help clients obtain RESULTS," she explained. (I'd soon learned that the word "RESULTS" was
always, *always* capitalized in Mary-rama's world.) She spoke
deliberately, using hand gestures to emphasize each point of
her coaching paradigm. "As we explore your inner self, you'll
become more self-aware, self-contained, and self-expressive! We
can reframe our difficult experiences into delightful opportunities, therefore expanding our experience of well-being!"

I stared at her quizzically, not sure how to respond.

"For example," she soldiered on undaunted, "last weekend I
ate a brownie."

"You ate a brownie . . ." I repeated. Was this her idea of a
difficult experience or a delightful opportunity?

"I ate a brownie," she confirmed. "I wanted to feel the experience of sugar, so I wrote myself an action step, and then
followed through on that step and acted with intention to purchase a brownie. Then," she continued, eyes sparkling with pleasure, "I affirmed myself for completing these tasks, therefore
acknowledging my commitment to full-cycle living. After eating the brownie, I charted my self-experience of this endeavor,
monitoring my enjoyment of the brownie on my Well-Being
Chart where I chronicle my satisfaction with my life decisions."
She handed me a sheet of graph paper with rows and cells col-
ored in with different shades of highlighter, marking her enjoyment of everything from the last movie she saw to her breakfast
cereal. "As you can see, when you make the right choices, your
experience of life will increasingly synchronize with your de-

sired RESULTS—last week, I achieved eighty-three percent satisfaction with my self-experiences!"

Is she kidding? I thought skeptically. But then again, who was I to mock? By any standard, my efforts thus far lacked RESULTS. But could it really be as simple as reframing my lemons as lemonade and keeping a chart of how much I liked dessert? Could I stand to spend more time analyzing my "self"? I struggled to see past her mannerisms and focus on her message.

"Life is like a game of tennis," she continued, flipping to yet another worksheet. "The goal of my work as a coach is to help you figure out what you're doing when you're *not* hitting the ball."

"When I'm not hitting the ball?" I parroted back to her. What on earth did that mean?

"It's what happens between the hits that determines how often we get the RESULTS we want," she explained patiently, clearly delighted with this insight. I wasn't sure what to do with this information, but it seemed like something I should write down and think about later. *Between the hits?!?* I scribbled in my notebook.

Then Mary-rama told me to get up. "Stand at the edge of that throw rug over there. Great. Now, if you would, walk back toward me, starting with the third step." I started to walk, and then paused, not sure what she was talking about. I looked at her, baffled.

"Go ahead . . ." she encouraged, "take that third step!"

"But I can't . . ." I admitted.

"Exactly!" she crowed, rising from her chair and enveloping me in a hug. "You *can't* start with the third step! This is the most important thing you can learn. Until you discover steps one and two, you can't take the third even if you want to!" She beamed at me, thrilled by our breakthrough. "We," she assured me, "are going to find your first step!"

Her methodology was silly, but I had to admit she had a point. I had no idea what my first step should be (or how to position myself between the hits for that matter), so I set the time and date for my next appointment. Mary-rama promised that she'd help me establish my life purpose, then set up my "ladder for winning" to take me toward my goals.

Two weeks later, we had our Life Purpose Determination meeting. We played a word game where she asked me a series of questions about my favorite memories.

"Tell me about a time you succeeded at something," she said, scribbling furiously on her pad as I responded.

"Now tell me about a time you felt loved." We went on to discuss a time I'd connected with someone I cared about, a time I'd been completely happy, and a time I felt like I was exactly in the right place. She wrote down my answers and then pulled out every fourth word (or some such formula), then left me alone for a half an hour with a pile of verbs and adverbs and adjectives from which to craft my purpose. I looked at the sheet of sample purpose statements from Mary-rama's previous clients:

To successfully engage my dynamic creative being!
To manifest my childlike wonder in a fully conscious context!
To help others attain optimal life-enhancing practices!

I couldn't imagine how any of these statements could help pay the bills. Never one to blow off a potentially life-changing project, though, I dutifully considered my words. Fifteen minutes later, it was decided: my life purpose was *to encourage others that more is possible in life!* It sounded good, like something that might be helpful. But still, I couldn't see how to connect this jaunty statement to, as Mary-Rama would put it, RESULTS.

Chapter Ten

That's Me in the Corner

Before leaving my marriage, I had RSVP'd to an alumni event at Wheaton. As I'd signed up for the dinners and booked my hotel room, I'd entertained visions of my grand return: driving my luxury car, showing off my gorgeous ring. No one there would know the truth about my marriage; I'd looked forward to a weekend of pretending that things were how they were supposed to be. But now, as the date grew closer, the ring was gone, the marriage was gone, my whole facade was shattered.

As I considered whether or not to go, one thought kept popping up, like a beach ball I couldn't keep underwater: *What if someone there can help me? What if someone there is the key to my new life?* If that was true, it would be worth it—worth the embarrassment of showing up at the low point of my life rather than as a conquering heroine; worth the embarrassment of admitting that I needed everything imaginable to start over: a place to live, a job, friends; worth the embarrassment of admitting how far I'd fallen from our collective ideal of what happens to graduates after being magically launched from college. Bolstering my courage, I decided to give it a try.

As befits my long history of dramatic romantic rescues, I met a man my first day back on campus. Mark was also a Wheaton graduate, from a class a few years behind mine. A friend of his knew a friend of mine, and so we spent the day immersed in the same activities, making small talk and drinking lots of beer. At one point he asked, "How come you never say anything about yourself? Are you in hiding or something?" I choked on a chicken wing and admitted that yes, I *was* in hiding, which was why he didn't recognize my name or remember much of anything about me.

Mark was interesting to talk to, and not bad to look at. He had caramel eyes and broad shoulders, and his mellow temperament put me at ease in a way I'd forgotten was possible. "I'm applying to grad school," he told me. "I want to get a degree in disaster relief management." *How perfect,* I thought. By all accounts, I was a disaster.

"Mark is *such* a great guy," one of our fellow alums told me later. "You can count on anything he tells you."

Two months later, I drove from Connecticut to Cambridge for our first date. Mark took me to a French restaurant and fed me platefuls of hors d'oeuvres and compliments by candlelight.

"I'm never getting married again," I warned him, later, trying to be forthcoming.

"That's perfect," he responded happily. "I don't believe in

marriage." He took my hand and smiled at me. As reluctant as I
was to admit it, it felt a bit like a miracle.

A MONTH OR SO later, when one of his roommates moved
out, Mark offered me a space in the dilapidated Cambridge
apartment he shared with three other guys. Despite my recent
vow that I'd never again live with a man, I began the process
of relearning who I was by surrounding myself with hairy,
testosterone-laden creatures.

It was January, and each morning as the sun streamed through
my eastern window, I'd pull on yards of wool to protect me
from the winter cold, leash up Kylie, and head out through the
piles and drifts of snow to the coffee shop around the corner. As I walked through this neighborhood—my neighborhood!—it seemed as though anything was possible. Everything
felt cozy and welcoming and alive, like the whole atmosphere
buzzed with some frequency that enhanced my ability to think,
to create, to *be*. (With Harvard's science labs close by, this buzzing may have been more real than I imagined.) For those first
few months in Cambridge, I had an undeniable certainty that
something was happening; that perhaps—just maybe—my life might
be getting better.

The cultural climate in Cambridge was perfect for someone
like me, someone fresh off of a disaster with no real grip on
her life—few places in America are more devoted to acceptance
of alternative lifestyles. Residents describe our city as "the
People's Republic of Cambridge" in a tone utterly devoid of
irony; attitudes are monitored by a rabidly devoted citizen mili-
tia determined to protect unorthodox life choices from even the

slightest raise of an eyebrow. (Indeed, the only thing Cambridge enforces more seriously than open-mindedness, I've discovered, is parking laws. If you ever get a ticket in Cambridge, *pay it*; they will hunt you to the ends of the earth until you do.) Our tree-lined street was a bustling enclave of bourgeois political correctness. On one end was a single entrepreneur who got out of the dot.com boom before it went bust; the other was anchored by a pair of college professors who jointly published books on topics like "the philosophical evolution of the park bench in twentieth-century urban design." Across the street was a bisexual woman who ruled over her cowering whisper of a husband and their two young children (who had been conceived through some undisclosed—although almost certainly sexless, everyone agreed—miracle of science). To their left lived glamorous up-scale hippies (rumor was that the husband had had a minor folk music hit in the early 1970s). They were all lovely to chat with; we were all exceedingly polite.

Spiritually, Cambridge's citizenry was even more diverse, a surreal mix of Catholic/Hindu/Buddhist immigrants living in and among a hodgepodge of atheist academics, self-proclaimed psychics, Wiccans, and experts in past-life analysis. With this level of diversity, I quickly discovered that one could say almost anything at a dinner party in response to the question "What do you do?" and be met with wide-eyed interest and a series of appreciative questions. (Unless, of course, you said something ridiculous, like "I lobby against increased funding for the new arts initiative" or "I'm thinking of moving to Texas to enroll in Bible college." But no one ever said anything like that.) Mark had an active social circle he brought me into, and I had no viable answer to that inevitable question. I was living under a made-up name, in a town where I knew no one. I decided to try on a few different personas, to see if anything would stick.

"I'm a golf pro," I told a linguistics professor one night as we sipped single malt scotch.

"I'm a yoga instructor," I told a portrait artist a week or so later at open mike night. (I quickly dropped this from my repertoire—everyone in Cambridge is a yoga instructor, I discovered, and I hadn't paid enough attention during the three classes I'd taken to hold up my end of the conversation.)

"I'm a motivational speaker," I told a girl at a wine-tasting party.

"I could use some motivation," she said dryly, "given that four years of therapy hasn't gotten me any closer to a functional life." She described some of her ups and downs, a sad tale of dashed hopes. But in spite of this, she seemed quite lovely—the type of girl anyone would want to work with or befriend. I told her so. And somehow, by the end of our little chat, she was up and running again, filled with a sense of possibility. *Where did that come from?* I marveled. *I didn't know I could do that.* Then I got myself another glass of cabernet and forgot all about it.

THE ACCOMMODATIONS IN Cambridge were a little different than those I'd enjoyed at Kristen's summer mansion, and not just because we didn't have a pool. The upside was that I had a room, and it was mine. *A place of my own*, as Virginia Woolf would say. The apartment was part of a two-family house owned by a series of landlords who were, shall we say, *unorthodox* in their approach to maintenance. There was a giant bucket under the kitchen sink for the plumbing leak that never got fixed, and several gaping holes in the ceiling where Cambridge firefighters chopped into the wall in search of an electrical fire started by the landlord's redecorating efforts. The dining room featured a seven-foot patch of exposed drywall from where they took over one of our bedrooms, and the spring after I moved in we were overrun with giant flies. (Whenever the topic of this apartment comes up, my friend Amy always says, "Tell them about the flies!")

For no reason we could ascertain, giant cluster flies hatched by the thousands and swarmed through our house that spring, giving us a real-life experience of what it might have felt like to live in the time of the biblical plagues. They swarmed through our rooms like old-time fighter pilots from a World War II movie, bouncing off our chins and foreheads, getting tangled in my long hair. We all learned the dangers of inhaling too deeply.

My roommates and I smushed flies with our shoes, smacked them with rolled-up newspapers, and sucked them up by the dozens with a shop-vac. We left the halogen lamps on, willing the flies to be drawn to the nine-billion-watt light. Even Kylie did her part, catching flies in midair while leaping from her perch on the edge of the couch. By the time the siege ended, we were surrounded by insect carnage—in our light fixtures, our dishes, our clothing; it was months before I could use my printer without a random wing or leg coming through on each page. Our landlords didn't understand why we didn't think a small break on that month's rent was enough to reimburse us for our trouble. The words, "implied warranty of habitability" were tossed around, but in the long run nothing ever came of it. That was kind of how it was with that apartment: we all knew we could do better, but each of us had our own reasons for leaving well enough alone, despite the water under the sink and the flies.

DURING THIS TRANSITION, I spent a lot of time talking to God (even though I was quite mad at Him and reminded Him on a regular basis that we were not speaking). I still had problems to deal with, and He was the only one I could think of who might have solutions. First on my list was my marriage. I knew that I needed to formalize the legal aspects of disentangling myself from my former husband, but had no idea how to do this without letting him know where I was. I'd grown so accustomed to hovering below the radar that it seemed both foolish and precarious to pop up again to ask for a divorce; I felt like the target in one of those whack-a-mole carnival games, knowing full well my ex would do everything in his power to smash me with a giant mallet if given the chance. Trying to prepare myself for the inevitable battle for my freedom, I asked God how I could fight for my share of our assets while maintaining my hard-won anonymity.

You can't. The Voice came from somewhere in my head, but it wasn't me that thought it.

"What do you mean, I can't?" I replied. *Could this be God?* I thought, confused. *Would He say something like that?* "That's not fair," I complained.

This is a decision point, He said. *The choices you make now will de-*

termine whether or not you become that woman—*you know: bitter, angry,
terrified; defined by your never-ending, contentious divorce.*

I did not want to be that woman.

If you walk away from the money, He promised, *I will take care of
you. You will always be okay. But if you fight,* He warned, *if you focus on
how you've been wronged and you deserve better, it will never be over, you'll
never win, you'll never be free.*

Somehow, in the middle of a sea of good advice about protecting myself and getting my share, I knew the Voice was right.
I didn't want the money; I wanted to be free. So I sent my former husband an e-mail saying he could have all our joint assets
(my father called it my ransom money) and deleted my online
research on winning contentious divorce proceedings. I didn't
stand up for myself, as everyone told me I should. Per God's
suggestion, I stood down instead.

Three months later, the papers came and I signed them. My
ex got the house, the car, the business, all our assets; I got my
freedom. To mark the occasion, I dug my wedding band from
the depths of my underwear drawer and walked down to the
corner. I held the ring over the sewer grate and announced, "I'm
done with you, forever. No one will ever control me like that
again." The ring bounced off the grate as I dropped it, rolling
in a circle out into the street. I kicked at it in a wave of frustration until the ring finally disappeared into the depths of the city
sewer. I wondered if it could still haunt me from there.

WHILE MY FINANCIAL status faltered, my romantic life
showed signs of flourishing. Mark was wonderful—handsome,
fun, gainfully self-employed. His mellow disposition was like a

balm, soothing the frayed edges of my nerves. He never yelled, never argued, never even worried about much.

My presence gave him a chance to practice his disaster-relief skills: he understood that violent movies made me jumpy and made decisions when I couldn't answer basic questions like "What would you like for dinner?" We were all misfits in this house—none of us would have been there if our lives had worked out the way we'd planned—but somehow our collective determination to laugh at our disappointments created the perfect atmosphere for me to heal, and to relearn what it was like to interact with men who didn't yell at me.

Like every new couple, Mark and I thought our relationship was unique, special, *destined*, even. We agreed that we didn't need the conventional romantic structures (marriage, children) to define us; we were above that. *As long as I can leave*, I thought, *he'll treat me well.* We agreed that it was better to *choose* each other, every day, than be shackled in the legalistic noose of marriage. We thought we were forging our own way, and that our rebellious independence from societal demands would immunize us against the ghosts of fear and regret from our pasts. We truly believed that our determination alone would allow us to sail on unhindered, the wind of romance always at our back.

It worked at first, in the way new relationships do. Mark was attentive and adoring, and he was a Taurus—my ideal partner, astrologically speaking. We moved to Montreal for the summer because he had friends there and the exchange rate was good, and because, well, *we could.* There was nothing holding us back—no kids, mortgages, jobs. We bragged about the joys of living free from the stifling confines of tradition.

I spent the next three months choking on those words.

Montreal is a city that prides itself on an elegant sort of sexual openness. ("We're not like you stuffy Americans," one man told me. "We're not afraid of what can happen when we give in to our true nature.") And summer is the time when that openness flourishes after months of icy winter cold and thick wool sweaters finally break. I tried to fit in, to keep up—to raise my game, so to speak. I traded my Cambridge fleece and flip-flop combinations for cute skirts and Pucci-print halter tops. I went out for chocolate martinis at midnight and double-cheek-kissed everyone I met. I engaged in flirty banter at elegant dinner parties and intrigued people with my confident spiritual theories. "Mark and I believe in magnetic and dynamic power," I explained, "that's what makes our relationship so unique . . ." I played the pretty, witty, fun girl to the hilt, working harder than I've ever worked in my life to appear effortless and carefree. Somehow, though, I was always just shy of pulling it off.

As I struggled to find my balance, scantily clad women of every description threw themselves at Mark like so many starving hyenas on a carcass, puffing up his ego and ripping us to shreds. Because of our unshackled status, there was little I could say. We had no formal commitment, no long-term plan, and I had no standing to challenge his minor (to his credit there were no major) indiscretions. Once again, I'd assumed that my devotion alone was enough to ensure a man's faithfulness. I bet the house on our "I choose you" daily opt-in commitment, never dreaming that his response might be, "For the next few minutes at least, I choose *her* . . ." I missed the irony that even though I'd abandoned the *Course*, I'd somehow enrolled myself in exactly the sort of "formless" relationship it advocated.

Despite my determined open-mindedness, the dynamic between Mark and me peaked, then started a slow downhill decline as the summer wore on. We were fine, and then we weren't. I'm not sure where it started, but suddenly, we were awash in all the symptoms of a relationship about to die: he frequented porn sites, there was nothing I could say. He planned a three-week trip to Brazil without me, there was nothing I could say. For my birthday, he gave me an extra-large T-shirt he picked up in the São Paulo airport, with the lyrics to "The Girl from Ipanema" written out in Portuguese. There was nothing I could say. The signs of his declining interest closed in on me, and what had started out so wonderfully unfurled into a long series of hurts and disappointments. I was haunted by the unshakable feeling that no matter how close we were physically, psychically he was still in a world all his own, a world marked "No girls allowed." I thought making love would bridge this divide, but it widened it, somehow, leaving me dangling precariously over an abyss of questions, wondering if he'd bother to catch me, pretty sure he wouldn't.

We moved back to Cambridge at the end of the summer and I sank into a puddle of despair. I couldn't play by these rules we'd established. There was no *quality* to this lifestyle, only fear. *How do people live like this?* I wondered. *More important, why do they bother?* I drove Mark's car down long highways, thinking about how easy it would be to drive right off the edge, or into the side of a bridge. This was the bed I'd made, though—I'd settled for twenty-four-hour chunks of devotion, an at-will tenancy of our relationship, relying on the best my magnetic power could conjure up.

Trying to shore up my career prospects while my romantic life wavered, I decided to parlay my former connection with Jayme Brass into a speaking career. *After all*, I thought, *Jayme was a lounge singer when she started. If she can do it, why can't I?* Cambridge was filled with alternative churches, yoga studios, and new age centers that offered outside programming, and after chatting with a few of them and describing my brief apprenticeship with Jayme, I soon had a full schedule of engagements. My audiences were varied: one week I'd have sixteen women at a Unity Church who wanted the universe to fix their broken relationships, the next week I'd face five guys who had inexplicably signed up for a seminar on "Finding Your Feminine Magnetic Power," at a yoga studio.

"Um, guys," I told them. "I hate to break it to you, but you don't *have* feminine magnetic power. What else would you like to talk about today?"

"Of course I have feminine magnetic power," one man argued, clutching his coffee with fingers bedecked in silver rings set with turquoise and amethyst. "I've been working to actualize my feminine side for almost nine months now, and I'm ready to give birth to my power!"

"That can't possibly be what you want," I countered. "You're a man—you don't give birth; that's not the way it works. Besides, I saw you flirting with the girl working out front before the class started, so I don't believe that feminine power is what you want to pull out of yourself. How about we access some of your masculine power, so you can ask her out and let her provide the feminine side?" Mr. Semiprecious Jewelry stared at me bug-eyed, then stomped out of the class in a huff. Looking at my four remaining students, I began to fantasize about out-fitting them all in denim and plaid flannel and dropping them over the border into New Hampshire for a month so they could learn to chop wood and change the oil in a Ford F-150.

The next week was better, as I spoke to a group of eager professional women about finding a spiritual path to guide our lives. I mixed in a hodgepodge of material: a few of Jayme's words, basic principles of astrology and metaphysics, sentences that just *seemed* right about how the universe responds to our call. I even quoted *Jonathan Livingston Seagull*: "If you love some-one, set them free." I was convincing myself as much as any of my students, trying to believe—despite all I'd seen and experi-enced—that it might somehow be true.

And against all my better judgment, I found myself wonder-ing out loud where Mark and I were headed, whether we were building a future together or just living day to day. He told me that he absolutely meant it when he said he'd never get married, and that he wasn't sure what our future together would be. "I love you," he said in a grim tone, "but I don't ever want to be tied down."

That was the week I drove to Buffalo and finally admitted that despite Mark's reluctance, I wanted to be married again. That's when (as you may recall) I heard James Earl Jones declare that he had more for me, but the time had come for me to *take Jesus seriously.*

PART II

During

Chapter Eleven

You Can't Get There from Here

When I heard the Voice, I figured it must be God—who else would ask me to do such a thing? But when I thought about *taking Jesus seriously*, all I could think of were all the weird people who had hurled that name at me over the years, like the group of earnest teens I'd been stalked by one day as I walked through Harvard Square: "If you get hit by a bus and die today," they'd asked me solemnly, "do you know for sure you'll go to heaven?" They handed me a small square pamphlet featuring a stick figure character falling into the pit of hell, then darted away, looking over their shoulders furtively to ascertain if I'd been saved yet, or if a bus had come to mow me down. *One good bus incident would do a lot to further their cause,* I'd thought at the time.

I'd had other run-ins with Jesus' people over the years: a hysterical woman standing in a scripture-covered sandwich board in the Philadelphia subway station, shouting through her bull-horn that I was going to hell; a law school friend's little sister, determined not to kiss her fiancé until their wedding day; a preacher in Virginia who delivered a rousing sermon on why our pets won't be in heaven. The strangest thing about these fervent believers, I thought later, was how none of them asked me, in their attempts to sell their faith, what was going on in my life—what was missing or what I was searching for. None of them told me how Jesus could make my life better, because they didn't ask what needed fixing. They guessed—assuming I worried about things like life after death, purity before marriage, the soul of my pet. They were wrong. I worried about my apparent failure in *this* life, whether I'd ever be married again, and whether my dog was the only family of my own I'd ever have. Amazingly, none of them suggested that Jesus could help me with any of this, that Jesus could help me here and now.

But here God was, suggesting exactly that: that if I'd take Jesus seriously, He could help me—here, and now. And in that moment, it seemed (oddly) like a spectacular idea—good, right, and entirely possible. So despite the odd message of some of His earthly sales reps, I agreed to God's proposal.

I had no idea what taking Jesus seriously might entail, although I had a few guesses: I suspected that a fluffy bouffant hairdo loomed in my future, and I'd probably have to give up my lifelong dream of dancing in a Janet Jackson video. I'd have to cancel my subscription to the *New Yorker*, purchase all nineteen volumes of the Left Behind series, and attach an aluminum fish to my car. (I didn't have a car, but I thought that sticking the fish to my purse or the back pocket of my jeans might suffice. *Would that be inappropriate?* I wondered briefly.) I might even be overtaken by an irresistible compulsion to vote for Pat Robertson in the next presidential election. And my live-in, doesn't-want-to-get-married boyfriend Mark? Well, he'd probably have to go.

But what if it works? I thought, curiosity overcoming my dismay. The bottom line was, I needed something. And if this voice could come through where every other promise had failed, it would be worth it, even the big hair.

"I'll do anything you ask, God," I said a few moments later. "I'll take Jesus seriously. Just please, *please* make my life better."

You realize, don't you, God replied, *this means no more sex until you get married?* I am the only person I know whose salvation story begins with a direct request to stop fornicating.

OVER THE NEXT few weeks, I was surprisingly calm as I calculated the cost of accepting this offer. Strangely, it seemed like the most natural thing in the world to tell Mark how God had told me that I needed to change the course of my life, and while I could refuse, it was worth it to say yes—even if my yes to God meant no to Mark, effective immediately. Secretly, I was certain that faced with the prospect of losing me, Mark would beg me to marry him. This was God's way of prompting me to stop the free milk supply, I reasoned, so that Mark would buy the cow. So I wasn't surprised when Mark acquiesced to my announcement that our relationship would no longer be sexual. I was flummoxed, however, by his utter refusal to consider marriage.

"You knew this about me when we started dating," he reminded me, obviously frustrated. "You're the one who prompted our seven thousand 'why we should never marry' conversations. Why are you changing everything now?"

"Because I changed my mind. I *do* want to get married," I said, hating how pathetic it sounded. "I think it's important—you know, legally."

"Legally?" Mark asked. "You mean like joint checking accounts and stuff? Is that what this is about?"

"No. Yes. Sort of. I don't know. There are benefits to being married," I insisted. "Like, if I'm ever in a coma, you know I don't want them doing weird things to me to keep me alive. But if you're not my husband, they won't listen to you!" This wasn't quite how I'd expected this conversation to go.

"You want to marry me so I can pull the plug if you get run over by a bus?" he asked, incredulous. "They have *forms* for that kind of thing; it's not a reason to get married."

He was right. This was crazy; my arguments were preposterous. And yet. Something inside me was awake now, insisting that marriage mattered, even if I couldn't explain why. On the surface, I knew Mark was right—there were no tangible, provable benefits of marriage; we could keep on as we were, merging finances and signing documents about how we'd like things handled in the event of a catastrophe. But that wasn't enough; I wanted more. And since that day in Buffalo, it seemed like that more would come through Jesus, if I could just figure out what that meant.

ONE MORNING AFTER that conversation, I turned on the television, looking for one of those decorating shows where people hijack rooms in their neighbor's houses and paint them shades like eggplant and cerulean that make the rest of the house look dingy and plain. Surfing through the channels, I paused at the sight of a woman in a bright pink dress, standing behind a lectern in the middle of a huge stage.

"Now let me tell you this," she said. "If your circumstances today are hopeless, if you don't know what to do with your life or how things can ever get any better, *Jesus* is the answer you've been looking for."

Mark wandered in and I flipped to CNN, pretending to be immersed in the market predictions for the day. But when he left, I flipped back, enthralled by the idea that this woman might know something about taking Jesus seriously.

Looking out at the audience, she asked, "Do you have everything the Bible says you can have?" It had never occurred to me that the Bible said I could have anything; I thought it was more a list of what I couldn't have. The truth was, for all my spiritual searching, I'd never really looked at the Bible. I'd been told it was a patriarchal, misogynistic book, written by early church leaders to repress women. Accordingly, I'd never bothered to read it for myself. (*Contempt prior to investigation*, I believe that's called.) But suddenly, I couldn't stop watching this woman who talked about the book like it was the key to life itself. Her name was Joyce Meyer. She was, I learned later, a big deal in Christian circles, traveling around the world with her husband and family, talking to crowds of thousands. "You need to decide that whatever the very best is that God has to give to anybody, you're going to have it!" she declared. "Press into Jesus—that's where the miracles are!" Joyce Meyer was the first person I ever heard use the Bible like a self-help book. Her version of self-help was different, though. There were standards to following Jesus, negative things we'd have to walk away from ("I had to give up my belief that I had the right to be bitter, or the right to nag my husband," she shared.) in order to get God's very best. Her show was like a half-hour infomercial for Jesus, touting his features and benefits and making outlandish claims about how he'd helped other satisfied Bible customers. All that was missing was a 1-800 number to call to have my six-month supply of Jesus shipped straight to my front door.

I liked what she said in her broadcast, or at least I thought I did; I wasn't altogether sure what to make of it. At first, her message seemed pretty straightforward, as she told us, "I get along so much better with my husband since I loosened up and decided to enjoy my marriage." But then she attributed this shift to incomprehensible sources, such as "Jesus' finished work on the Cross," and being "set free from the sins of bitterness and unforgiveness." Despite my various run-ins with Christians over the years, I still had no idea what to make of statements like this, or why Christians focused so determinedly on Jesus' murder when really, the only "good news" I could find in the story was that three days later the guy came back to life. I wasn't sure bitterness and unforgiveness were *sins*, per se, although they were frowned upon in spiritual circles. "Transcend," we were told. "Embrace your oneness with your brother." But Joyce wasn't talking about transcendence. Whatever it was Jesus did for her on that Cross, it changed her, somehow. It made her into a more easygoing, happier person. That seemed like a miracle. *She's kind of like Jayme,* I noticed. *Except that her life is better.*

Could this be true? I wondered. It wasn't so much that I doubted her, but rather that I couldn't fathom how, in twelve years of spiritual searching, I had never heard anyone else suggest the Bible as a viable guide for daily life. If what Joyce said was real, wouldn't someone else have picked up on it by now?

I dug out a copy of the Bible I'd received once from a friend who'd heard I was "spiritual" and flipped through its whisper-thin pages, looking for evidence that Joyce was changing things or taking them out of context to come up with this preposterous idea that Jesus could do the things she claimed: make marriages work, stave off depression, give people the power to overcome past failure and change their lives, just to name a few. I was stunned by Joyce's compelling stories of how Jesus helped her recover from terrible things from her past (including, I noted, a bad first marriage). They encouraged me that I might not have made up this whole "God promised me a husband" thing. If Joyce was telling the truth, God had saved her from a disastrous heap of a life and then given her a wonderful husband, children, and a purpose for living.

That's what got me. When I looked at Joyce, and the other "Christians" I saw on television (in my mind, "Christians" were always lumped together with quotation marks, convinced as I was of their collective disingenuousness), it was hard to deny that they—much more than the spirituality/self-help crowd I'd frequented—had the type of relationships I wanted. Most of them were married—and enthusiastically committed to staying that way. They didn't have "open" wedding vows laden with language about "journeying together until we're called our separate ways," but rather talked about lifelong covenants. They didn't assume marriage was a place where God partners you with someone unlikely in order to shave off your sharp edges, but rather a place where God chooses your partner for you, then knits you together and makes you one. According to the Bible, they said, I was created to be part of something bigger than myself, for true love with an awesome man and a marriage that lasted for life. Commitment was assumed, and measures taken to help the men and women making these vows live up to them. Joyce Meyer was walking proof that God could make good on such a promise.

I wanted what those "Christians" had, but I didn't want to tell anybody; I didn't want to be forced into something I didn't believe in. I wanted to edge up on Jesus, to see what he might have to say.

Edging up on Jesus was kind of like what happens when you're thinking about buying a new car: suddenly, that car is everywhere. You see it in every color, on every highway, in every commercial break. When I considered the possibility that I might be in the market for a new spiritual leader, Jesus popped up everywhere, introducing himself from a safe distance that allowed me to weigh my options, rather than prodding me into an impulse buy.

I secretly purchased more Christian CDs and listened to them alone in my room. I liked the lyrics about how much is possible in life and how much God loves me. They didn't make me feel hopeless and pathetic the way the songs on the radio did. But I skipped the songs about Jesus' blood or his "wonderful" death on the Cross. I didn't want to be covered in anybody's blood, and I didn't feel like God required it of me. I sang along happily with the others, blissfully unaware that most of the words came straight from the Bible. (Hearing the Bible quoted at a later point, I thought it was plagiarizing Christian recording artist Stephen Curtis Chapman.)

As I explored—watching Joyce, listening to my new CDs, circling Jesus to see what he was about—I uncovered incredible information no one else ever mentioned. No one told me that the Bible had *way* more to say about life and love and romance and happiness than just "keep your clothes on until after the wedding." No one told me about Jesus' offer of redemption for all my mistakes, or his promise to turn the ashes of my life into something beautiful, or how he could give me wisdom and confidence to make better choices. Amazed, I circled closer and closer to this Jesus, drawn by his teaching, his healing, his hope. Then one day, I felt like he said, *Trish, I have the keys to the relationship and the life you dream of. What is impossible for you is possible for me . . . and I don't need you to move the furniture or chart the stars.* I wasn't sure what he meant, or how I was supposed to respond.

Some days, at the end of her show, Joyce offered those of us watching at home the chance to accept Jesus' gift of salvation. She prayed a prayer, inviting us to pray along—confessing that she was a sinner, and that she believed Jesus' death on the Cross set her free. She claimed the healing power of his blood, and asked him to rule her life. This was where she lost me. Her words about sin and blood didn't apply to me, or to anyone else I knew; we were all doing the best we could, trying to be good people, picking ourselves up and starting over every time we fell. The last thing we needed was some negative perspective about how we were all hopeless sinners. I could accept, in a metaphysical sort of way, that the answer to my problems might be

Jesus, but it didn't make sense that such help required the blood from a two thousand-year-old murder. That sounded more like a spell than a prayer, so I opted out.

Over the next few weeks I didn't *do* much with what Joyce said, but I thought about it a lot. Even that small step seemed to make a difference, like Jesus was loosening the hard-packed soil around my brain, pulling out the weedy half-truths that had grown there for so long. Gradually, in a hundred different subtle ways, I changed. I felt better—calmer, more hopeful. Even Mark commented on how much nicer I was after I had my "time with Joyce." Which helped, given our questionable relationship status, suspended between my insistence that the next time I had sex would be with my husband, and Mark's firm conviction that he didn't want that job.

Through all of this—listening to Christian music, watching Christian television—it somehow never occurred to me that God might want me to *become* a Christian. Despite their enviable perspective on marriage, "Christians" still struck me as a somewhat peculiar and oppressed people, with bad outfits, dull sex lives, and a strange preoccupation with Jesus' brutal death. There seemed to be a few normal ones—the singers in Avalon, Joyce. Still, I was pretty sure that becoming a Christian just wasn't something that happened here in the Northeast.

And yet I wondered about them—"the Christians." What did they do all day? What were their lives like? I went to the bookstore and pored over Christian books the way anthropologists study aboriginal tribes, searching for clues about this strange people group and how its members functioned. I knew some basics: they read the Bible every day and didn't have much sex. They didn't smoke, or drink, or (if the movie *Footloose* was to be believed) dance. It sounded like a rocking good time. But in the midst of all this not doing, I wondered, what, exactly, did they *do?* I wanted to understand why they were so afraid of everything—alcohol, astrology, secular music, Hillary Clinton. I wasn't sure how they built lives around all the things they *weren't* doing—if they got up each day and didn't drink, didn't check their horoscope, didn't listen to the latest Jay-Z song or admire the new swimsuit line from Tommy Hilfiger, what did they do? *Pray?*

Chapter Twelve

Welcome to Wine Country

O ver brunch one morning, my friend Julie, a recent graduate of Harvard Divinity School and a spiritual-explorer type like me, told me about a church she'd heard about called the Vineyard.

"They're Christian," she said, her blue eyes wide with awe. "You know, *really* Christian—no sex, confess your sins—the whole bit. But they have hundreds of people there every week meeting in a school gym. I don't know how they do it."

Propelled by a surge of curiosity, I decided to find out. I quivered at the prospect of seeing live Christians right here in Cambridge; it was like learning that the circus had come to town. Julie and I had often talked about starting our own church (*All of the God, none of the guilt* would be our slogan). We were curious—and concerned—that this upstart church might capture all the spiritually inclined Cantabrigians. "I hear they

bribe people with bagels," she said. "That's not playing fair."
I decided to stop by the next Sunday to see if carbohydrates
alone could connect me to Jesus.

I ARRIVED AT the Vineyard fifteen minutes before the second service, eager to discover how God's message of guilt and
judgment was playing in our liberal city. I was surprised to see
so many normal-looking people streaming into the elementary
school. There were college students in cargo pants and T-shirts,
jeans-clad married couples wrestling kids into strollers, people
of every demographic, all gathering on Sunday morning to sit
in a gym and learn about the Bible. I was baffled. I knew this
sort of thing happened in Texas, but Cambridge?

I made my way through the throng, noting the piles of bagels and carafes of steaming coffee filling long tables in the
lobby. People of every shape, size, and description hugged one
another, laughed, and tossed around stories about what they'd
done the night before. It took me a full five minutes of bobbing
and weaving to make my way through the crowd, but I finally
made it to the gym doorway, where a smiling girl in jeans and a
sweater handed me a program.

"Thanks," I mumbled, averting my eyes. I was afraid that if I
made direct contact with anyone, they'd identify me as a nonbe-
liever—for all I knew, Christians had spiritual X-ray vision and
could sense these things—and force me to give my life to Jesus
right there on the spot.

I edged into the gym, pausing at the door to take it in. I saw
hundreds of pink padded chairs facing a stage set up under the
basketball net, with a full rock band—two keyboardists, a cute

guy on bass, and even a funky guy hammering away on some bongo drums—warming up a song that sounded like a tune by Dave Matthews. My feet throbbed in my high heels as I stood there, the percussion vibrating through my packed toes. I'd tried to dress like a churchgoing Christian that morning, in a long-ish skirt and loose sweater; I wanted to blend in. In retrospect, though, I might as well have worn a blinking sign around my neck, announcing Never Been Here Before! I'm New!

I took a seat near the foul line and glanced through the program. There was a long list of pastors, instructions on where to bring your kids. A blue index card with room for my name and address, with boxes I could check off if this was my first visit or I wanted more information about Jesus. A few minutes later the service began, and the band started playing for real. People poured into the gym, clapping their hands or and throwing their arms in the air. It was like being at a rock concert at eleven-thirty in the morning. The lyrics flashed on huge screens on either side of the stage as the lead singer sang: "Here, O Lord, is the place where I belong. Now is the time for me to find my place in your design. Here, O Lord, is an opening of your grace. Now is the time to step inside and follow—I follow you—into the place of greater power, into a time of abundant praise, into the place where all you've placed in me reveals your face—here and now."

As I opened my mouth to sing along, my throat closed and my eyes welled up with tears. Mortified, I stared at a rope ladder dangling from the ceiling, ignoring the lyrics and their applicability to my life: how despite all my efforts to fake it, I was still searching for my place in the grand design of things, a break that would put me where I was meant to be. Suddenly, I felt like they knew everything about me, these people—like God clued them in before my arrival: *This one is a tough nut to crack—let me show you her soft spot.* I distracted myself from the tears by staring at the drummer—an indie-looking guy in a goatee and cargo pants. He was rather hot, by spiritual standards (new age men are not noted for their rugged masculinity). Then I noticed his wedding band. *Damn.*

Stop it! I scolded myself. *You're a spiritual seeker. You're here to find the truth, not find a man. Okay, that's a lie,* I admitted. *But at least stop gawking.*

Looking around, I saw that the gym was filled to capacity, with people sitting on bleachers and on the floor. The music was good—catchy, upbeat. Certainly preferable to what I'd heard at other spiritual gatherings. (New age "music" can be anything, I'd learned in the course of my travels—a woman plucking a harp; an angry man yelling poetry while pounding on a drum; hippie folk singers stuck in a Woodstock time warp, celebrating the early work of Judy Collins. The common denominator is that it's mostly bad. Exceptionally bad, as if musical excellence somehow diminishes the spiritual value of the effort. Enthusiasm is the sole requirement in new age circles, and if your effort is heartfelt, well, you're guaranteed a healthy esteem pump from any number of similarly untalented seekers celebrating your effort.) Not so here at the Vineyard, I acknowledged, somewhat relieved. These guys were *good.* As the band finished the song, a giant man in a polo shirt and khakis took the stage, welcoming us and inviting us to join him in prayer. Again, my guard went up. *I'll stay until he says something obnoxious about hating women, or how*

Democrats will be scourged in the tribulation, I told myself. *As soon as he starts that Jerry Falwell stuff, I'm out of here.*

IF YOU'D ASKED me during my early years at the Vineyard to describe that first visit, I would have told you that it was Mother's Day, that they gave chocolates to all the moms, and that a very tall pastor named Dave gave a helpful sermon about money.

As it turns out, though, that's not what happened. Recently, I listened to the download of that first sermon and found myself in a different scenario. Yes, it was Mother's Day, and, yes, there were chocolates. But when Pastor Dave took the stage, it was to introduce a man named Ron, an earnest traveling missionary whose "testimony" ended with the story of how a homeless man slit his throat one day and left him for dead by the side of the road. The take-home point, I guess, was that he didn't die; he lived to offer more rides to homeless strangers in the name of Jesus.

I'll admit that the first time I heard it, Ron's story didn't stir up in me a sense of God's amazing grace. But it does now. Not so much because of Ron's survival, although I agree that this was a good thing. What strikes me now is how God blotted this story from my mind. I wasn't looking for a church where I could risk my life for the Lord, so this could have been one more sermon about Jesus that had nothing to do with me, one more church I wandered into, then wandered back out of, never to return. But God kept me blind, deaf, and dumb that first week—not to mention distracted by the prospect of handsome men—and then brought me back to this gigantic group of casually dressed church goers so I could sort this Jesus thing out once and for all.

THE NEXT WEEK I came back to more music, and more shiny, happy people, clapping and celebrating Jesus. "God, thank you for being here with us this morning," Pastor Dave prayed after the opening song. "We trust that you have something for us today. Speak to us, Lord. In Jesus' name we pray." I didn't understand why Christians had such a compulsion to tag *In Jesus' name* onto the end of every thought and prayer. It bugged me. *A lot of things about Christians bug me*, I thought, sitting in my pink chair at the top of the key. I squirmed in my seat, agitated. *I bet they have terrible sex lives*, I reassured myself, looking at the couples sitting around me. Yet I had to admit that these couples—holding hands, leaning into one another to whisper secret observations, sharing smiles and nods—didn't look starved for conjugal affection. In fact, they might have been the happiest collection of married people I'd ever seen. One couple in particular caught my eye—the guitarist from the band came down off the stage to join his wife for the sermon, wrapping his arm around her shoulders and squeezing her from time to time. They looked like they were on their honeymoon. Later, when their three-year-old son ran in to join them, I felt like I was on the set for a Disney commercial: "Cue the cute kid!" I ached for a life like that. I wanted to run up to them and ask, "How did you get here? What did you do?" and, more important, "Where do I go to sign up?" I couldn't imagine having a boyfriend or husband come to church with me. Sure, one or two dates had accompanied me on my various spiritual exploits, but only because they were trying to impress me, never because they were looking to satisfy any spiritual hunger of their own. I had never dated anyone who was curious about God. This guitar player with his arm around his pretty wife seemed curious, though. It was as if he liked being here, that this was something they did as a family, part of the fabric of their week. I couldn't imagine what that might feel like.

An elegant girl with auburn hair turned to me after the music ended. "Hi—I'm Gwen," she said with a smile.

"I'm Trish," I responded, trying to hide my surprise at her chic outfit—were Christian women allowed to shop at Ann Taylor? *Perhaps she's new, too,* I thought. "Have you been coming here long?" I asked.

"For a little while," she said, in what I'd later learn was a classic Gwen understatement. She was practically a founding member of the church, as it turned out, and had been there since the days where the "congregation" was twenty people sitting in a circle singing along while one guy played the guitar. She introduced me to her mother, an equally elegant woman with a lilting British accent. Their sophistication blew my preconceived notion about Christian tackiness to pieces, and I snuck glances at them throughout the service, trying to pick up cues on how to fit in.

Afraid Gwen might think I was stalking her with all my sidelong looks, I tried to focus on the sermon. It was about money. I tensed up, waiting to hear some declaration about how I should write the church a huge check before expecting anything from God. Instead, Dave suggested that our financial health depended more on God's blessing than on our earning power. He quoted several passages from a book in the Bible called Proverbs, warning us not to trust in money to keep us safe or make our lives work. Money disappears, Dave pointed out, which makes it an unreliable foundation for our lives. I had once read something on a wall plaque about how if we build our house on sand it will be blown away when a storm comes, but a house built on rock will survive (I didn't learn until later that these were Jesus' words). Money was sand, it seemed, but I still didn't know where or what the rock was.

"Honor the Lord with your wealth, with the first fruits of all your crops," Dave read from the Bible verse printed on our programs. "Then your barns will be filled to overflowing and your vats will brim over with new wine." He suggested that passages like this teach us how to leverage our lives to get the most return, how to position ourselves so that God will shower us with blessings. He told a story from his first year as a pastor, when he and his wife were newly married and thinking of starting a family. Supported by this fledgling spiritual enterprise, they were just scraping by. They gave God the "first fruits" of the little money they had but didn't see how this would be possible if they added kids to the equation. "So I asked God what to do," he said. "And I felt like God asked, *Dave, will you continue to be faithful with your money in the ways that I have taught you?* I said yes, and I sensed God promise, *If you stick to what you've always done, I will provide for you.*

"Of course," Dave continued, "we got pregnant right away. And then we had a major financial windfall. We trusted God, we put it all on the line, and God provided." The extent of that provision was obvious when I saw his wife—a pretty blonde in the front row with not one but *three* children, all of whom looked happy and well cared for.

Surprisingly, Dave closed his sermon on money without asking us for any. Instead, he prayed for us, asking God to bless us with a feeling of being abundantly provided and cared for. I was still living in the chopped-up, fly-infested house near Harvard, surviving on the remaining pennies from hawking my diamond ring. *Could this stuff teach me how to "leverage my life" for more?* I wondered. I'd never read Proverbs, but it sounded like the quintessential self-help book. No stories, no parables, just a straightforward collection of suggestions from God: *Do this, and your life will go well. Do that, and your life will be a disaster.* I pulled my Bible out of my bag and flipped through while one of the other pastors read announcements.

"Trust in the Lord with all your heart, and lean not on your own understanding" was the first thing I saw. That seemed like good advice. I wasn't sure I had any understanding of my own at this point; all I had were questions. I flipped to the end of the section: "He who finds a wife finds a good thing and obtains favor from the Lord." This was certainly a novel perspective on marriage. It suggested that men who marry get something good, not the burden of a ball and chain the way our culture tends to depict it. I noticed the use of the verb "find," as if men should be looking for wives—not hanging back until they were captured by some determined female. I tried to picture what it would be like to be pursued in that way, to be seen by a man as the good thing he wanted, the connection to receiving increased favor from God. I filed that away to think about later and sat up a little straighter. Maybe I could be the "good thing" God designed for one of the single men I saw around me?

After leading us in a closing prayer, Dave called the band back up on the stage. They sang lyrics that made my eyes well up again, even though I had no idea why: "Will I not lift my hands? Will I not sing? Can I not rejoice in the land you have given me? Will I not choose to praise? Will I not believe? Can I not dance on the day that you set me free? For you are worthy to be lifted above the highest honor, you are worthy to be praised beyond what words can say. Jesus, I leave all that I'm worth, and come into this place. For you are worthy and I'll sing of your glory, you are worthy to be praised."

Gwen and her mother sang with arms stretched heavenward, while all around us people were singing and crying and waving their hands in the air. It was clear something was going on, something I wasn't part of. "Jesus, I leave all that I'm worth, and come into this place," they sang. Was that something I was willing to sign on for? I was overwhelmed but intrigued—by the music, the message, the people, the tears that filled my eyes for no discernible reason every time the keyboardist hit a note. *I want more of this*, I realized—more of what Dave could tell me about this book, more of what the Bible said was possible, more songs about taking my place in God's design. Suddenly, next Sunday seemed too far away.

After the service, Gwen invited me to a barbecue she was having the following weekend. I accepted enthusiastically, knowing I wouldn't go. How could I face a whole yard full of Christians without their catching on that I had no idea what I was doing? I didn't want to feed these people lies about my spiritual status; I wanted to lie low for long enough to see if they knew anything about taking Jesus seriously.

Gwen introduced me to a few people on the way out. Everyone was friendly, and smart. I was taken aback by their résumés—in twenty minutes, I met PhD's from Harvard and MIT, accountants and entrepreneurs, writers and artists. Dave and his wife were Stanford graduates, I learned; the associate pastors included an investment banker and a chemical engineer. I'd assumed you had to "dumb down" to follow Jesus, eschewing common sense and reason in order to accept what the Bible insisted was right. Instead, I found myself surrounded by people who were certifiably smarter than me—many of whom were cute men without wedding rings. *This might be the best place in Cambridge to meet a husband,* I thought, munching on my bagel. It never occurred to me for a single moment that I wouldn't be back the next week.

Over the next few Sundays, I learned the Proverbial take on relationships, career, family, and friendship. Dave talked about Jesus, considering, "What Would Jesus Say?" about things like "My Desperation to Be Happy," "My Disappointment with God," and even "People Who Annoy Me."

"What if the universe is relational?" he posited one Sunday. "What if our highest level of happiness and satisfaction is found by getting rid of the things that keep us from the relationships we were created for, with each other, and with God? And what if Jesus is the key to making that happen?" Dave's suggestions and ideas helped me, making me feel better about myself in ways I didn't necessarily understand.

I was drawn to this church, counting the days to the next Sunday, the next sermon, the next infusion of guidance for applying the Bible to my life. I still watched Joyce Meyer every morning on TV, but Sundays at the Vineyard were different. There was something about being surrounded by hundreds of people—all experiencing the same talk, the same music, the same prayers—that seemed deeper than watching television from the seclusion of my couch (although it's possible that this something deeper was simply the mind-blowing presence of single men who also made the effort to show up to church on Sunday morning). As divided as my attentions were, I soaked in Dave's suggestions like a sponge. His sermons excited me about what might be possible in life, living this Bible way.

I still didn't get the fixation with Jesus, though. They—Dave, the singers—made it sound like it was Jesus who did the work, rather than each of us climbing our own mountain of spiritual understanding; it was like they believed we could all just stand around singing and expect Jesus to change our lives. I knew better. There was, I knew, spiritual *work* to do, as I'd been taught by my endless reading and seeking. I didn't understand why these people spent so much time thanking Jesus instead of doing the work.

BURNED BY MY lack of due diligence in previous spiritual endeavors, I read everything I could find about Vineyard churches. I wanted to make sure this church was supported by something stronger than the voluminous hallucinogenic experience of a single college professor. I read a biography of the movement's main leader, a man named John Wimber. Wimber had been an atheist. He was a musician who played with the Righteous

Brothers, enjoying incredible professional success while his personal life fell apart. He'd opened the Bible in an attempt to save his failing marriage. After a few weeks of reading and attending a local church, he cornered the pastor and demanded, "So, when do we do the stuff?"

"The stuff?" the pastor responded, "What do you mean, the stuff?"

"You know!" Wimber replied, exasperated, "The stuff in the Bible—healing the sick, making the blind see, raising the dead . . . the stuff that Jesus did—when do we get to do that?"

"We *don't* do that," the pastor informed him. "We don't believe that happens anymore."

"For this," Wimber responded, "I gave up drinking?"

Determined to "do the stuff," Wimber spent the rest of his life praying for the sick to be healed, the blind to see, the dead to be raised, and people to receive the supernatural gifts and power Jesus said his followers would walk in. Shockingly, after weeks and months where nothing happened, he had years of success praying for healing in the name and power of Jesus. The Vineyard movement, I learned, evolved out of his belief that people today, like the people in the Bible, were more likely to believe Jesus' claim to be their personal messiah if they experienced a personal miracle, if Jesus met them in a personal need. The key to spreading the good news of Jesus, he believed, was in what he called "Power Evangelism": calling on God's supernatural power to reveal Jesus through signs and wonders in our midst.

From the Vineyard Web site, I learned that Dave and Grace Schmelzer started their church on this same core belief: that God is alive today, that He acts in our lives, and that Jesus' promises of healing, deliverance, and infilling of the Holy Spirit are just as applicable today as they were two thousand years ago. Starting with thirty people at an Easter service in 1998, their church had doubled in size each year, moving from a living room to a room at the Y to a high school cafeteria—which inspired them to post an ad on the T bragging "Matt Damon ate lunch in our sanctuary!" Now they met in an elementary school gym, unpacking hundreds of chairs, building a stage, and setting up a sound and projection system every Sunday morning for anyone who decided to wander in. Their motto was *Practical. Spiritual. Fun.* I wasn't sure I'd found any of those three in a spiritual practice before, certainly not in combination. It sounded too good to be true.

As I watched Dave and Grace each Sunday, they also seemed too good to be true. I was captivated by their interactions with each other, how they seemed to speak from the same playbook; it was like they were two halves of a larger whole. They didn't compete for attention; one wasn't alpha dominant while the other stood in the background nodding submissively. They worked as a team. I noted the affectionate way Grace touched Dave's back to get his attention, and how he leaned down and listened to her—ignoring everything else around him—and adjusted his comments to take her suggestions into account. I'd never seen that in spiritual leaders; I'd never followed anyone whose romantic life wasn't a disaster. I wanted to get to know them, ask them questions, find out if what I saw was for real.

I was impressed by this church, but wary. I'd heard so many

other great promises of how *more* was possible in life if I did this or that or some other thing. I decided to stay detached, to proceed carefully rather than jumping in. But some part of me surged ahead, hopeful that this Jesus-ey church—and maybe even Jesus himself—could make good on all these claims.

Chapter Thirteen

One New Sheep, Grayish Black in Color

Other than Jesus, what Vineyard people talked about most was small groups. I had no idea what a *small group* was—I imagined little pockets of people gathering in secret to dissect the Bible, judge one another, and perhaps engage in a bit of self-mortification. I'd seen the word "accountability" bandied about in my perusal of popular Christian books—it made me think of the indoctrination groups the Chinese used during the Cultural Revolution to make sure everyone engaged in Chairman Mao's version of "right thinking." For all I knew, small groups were the place where trained church leaders oversaw our Jesus indoctrination, ensuring that our behavior synched up with the Golden Rule and the Ten Commandments.

Bizarrely, I *loved* this idea. I longed to be part of a secret spiritual movement, shepherding wayward souls toward God like

Harriet Tubman moving slaves to freedom along the Underground Railroad. That I was a passenger on this freedom train wasn't lost on me; I wanted to learn the rules of this Jesus thing so I could be sure to do it right (I didn't want to lose out on my husband due to a technicality). And I still had a fair amount of anthropological "come see the Christians live in their natural habitat" fascination going on, which made it all seem like a grand adventure. I couldn't believe I had the list of all their secret meeting places right there in my hot little hand.

My first experience with a Vineyard small group was, to use a favorite word from my feng shui days, "inauspicious." I walked into the living room of a first-floor apartment to find a random assortment of people eating spaghetti and talking about the Red Sox.

So these are the Christians, I thought, surreptitiously glancing around to take it all in. They were, I noticed, an unusually attractive assortment of humanity—lots of cute guys, pretty girls. We looked like a casting call for an Old Navy ad, all earnest and multicultural. There was a noticeable absence of identifying Christian paraphernalia: no Jesus tattoos, no black T-shirts with a cross outlined in front of a huge wall of fire, declaring "*This* is the only thing standing between you and hell!" like I'd seen at other churches. It didn't even look like people brought their own Bibles. *They're too normal,* I thought. I'm not sure what I expected—special costumes, a mandatory password, perhaps. I tried to hide my disappointment as I walked in and found an open spot on the couch.

A few minutes later, after people had scraped their plates

and poured themselves fresh cups of Diet Coke and ginger ale, a tall woman in a MIT sweatshirt called the group to order and announced the agenda for the evening. We were, she said, going to spend the next two hours in confession, admitting our sins to one another and nailing them to the Cross.

Man, they get right to it. Despite my vague awareness of the Christian fondness for accountability, I was unprepared for this. At the very least, I assumed we'd get to know each other a little bit before the contrition started. I'd thought these groups were for outing one another—a place where you were confronted by your brothers and sisters for wearing a short skirt on a dinner date or taking the name of the Lord in vain. I never imagined that we were supposed to fess up to our own wrongdoings when we gathered, or that Christian living meant laying our status as heathen miscreants right out there in the middle of the living room in front of a bunch of strangers. I glanced around the room, checking to see if anyone was as uneasy with this idea as I was. No one seemed troubled by this plan; they all looked fine—happy, even. Apparently, this was an enjoyable way to spend a Wednesday night in the Christian world, far better than sitting at home on the couch watching *West Wing* or *Dawson's Creek* like the rest of the country.

As everyone started to move into little groups, I froze, paralyzed by a flashback from my Catholic childhood. Confession, I knew, was not for me. I'd tried to be contrite and penitent as I searched for God as a little girl—I'd approached my sacramental first confession with great anticipation, certain that entering that little booth for a tête-à-tête with one of God's priestly servants *must* have some sort of special power (I'd watched enough

Superman cartoons to recognize that exciting transformations take place when normal people duck into little booths). But when I got in there on the big day, there was no special energy or secret power; it was just angry Father McNamara going through his script in an absentminded fashion. I don't know if I was overcome by stage fright or disappointment, but from that day on, the confessional booth was one of the few places that left me speechless. I knew I wasn't perfect, that I had *some* things to confess. But when that door closed behind me and I faced Father McNamara's scowling silhouette through the fleur-de-lis screen, I could never remember what those things were.

As a coping mechanism, I always (and by "always" I mean every time I confessed between the ages of seven and fourteen) resorted to my safety sins, the two obvious slipups I knew I *must* have committed at some point since my last visit to the booth.

"Father, I confess that I hit my little sister and I lied to my mother."

"Again?" he'd respond. Sometimes I could even hear him sigh.

"Yes, Father," I'd respond, "*again.*"

Whatever doubts he had about the completeness of my confession, Father McNamara always pronounced me forgiven. I suspect it was the only option in his instruction manual. Two Hail Marys, four Our Fathers, and a Glory Be and I was out of there, absolved from my hitting and lying, free until the next time our Sunday school teachers sent home a parental reminder about the importance of the confessional sacrament.

Two decades later, I realized that if I couldn't negotiate the pressure of confession in a private booth, I had no interest in trying it again in front of this random bunch of strangers. Besides the obvious *normal people don't do this* factor, I still had no idea what I would say. I hadn't hit my sister within recent memory (something I never thought I'd be sorry about as an adult) and while I certainly fibbed to my mother at various points between the ages of fourteen and thirty-three, I wasn't prepared to uncork that bottle here. So I sat there, silent and baffled, trying not to listen to the private things these people shared with God, each other, and (unfortunately) me. That was the end of my first small group. As I said, *inauspicious.*

THE NEXT WEEK, buoyed along by some inexplicable surge of persistence, I took my Bible and my superhero fantasy to another group. At first, the scene was familiar: another living room, another multicultural group of pretty people eating spaghetti and talking about the Red Sox. I declined a plate and settled into the only spot left on the floor, in the back of the room near the fireplace.

The conversation turned from baseball to summer travel, and I learned that the group leaders were just back from their honeymoon. Their names were Paul and Pascha, and they had met at the Vineyard. I took this as a confirmation that men and women in this church found each other somehow, that there was precedent for negotiating the perilous waters of sex-free, Jesus-ey dating and getting to the other side. Already, this group seemed more like what I was looking for in terms of exposure to the details and nuances of Christian living.

Paul called us to attention. He opened with an icebreaker, and we went around the room sharing our names and our favorite flavors of ice cream. This struck me as a much better getting-to-know-you technique than confessing our sins. Subtler, somehow. I relaxed and leaned back against the wall. I was pleasantly surprised to see Gwen—the auburn-haired woman I'd met that second week in church, walk in and sit down next to the door.

"Hi Gwen!" Paul said. "You're just in time—you get to go first,"

"Hi everyone, I'm Gwen," she said, smiling. "I like Rocky Road."

A guy in a plaid shirt and jeans spoke up next. "I'm Will. Normally I'd say my favorite ice cream is cookie dough, but I had a chocolate macadamia nut crunch the other day that may have changed my mind."

"I'm Amanda," offered the pretty Asian girl next to me. "And, oh my gosh—I love pistachio ice cream more than any other food on the planet." She was so thin I couldn't imagine she'd eaten more than an ounce of dessert in any form in her life.

"I'm Trish," I said when my turn came. "My favorite ice cream is Ben and Jerry's Chubby Hubby."

"Ooo, that stuff is so good!" a brunette named Liz exclaimed, eyes wide as she nodded her agreement. I smiled at her, amazed at how even this small connection felt important, like I'd passed the first admission test for acceptance into Jesusville.

At the end of the circle, Paul introduced himself and Pascha, who sat on the floor in front of him, leaning back against his legs. He played with her hair absent-mindedly while he talked, occasionally rubbing her shoulders. They were connected somehow, I realized. They had that intangible thing I'd seen between the guitarist and his wife, and then between Dave and Grace. I stared at their wedding bands, mesmerized. The circles of new platinum gleamed back at me, catching the evening sun shining through the window behind them. Over the course of the night I watched each of them playing with their new rings, twisting them with their thumbs as if they were thinking about each other right there in front of us all. I looked down at my own hand—bare and in need of a manicure. Jealousy and longing wrapped around my chest.

When the icebreaker was done, Paul pulled out a guitar and asked us to stand for worship. I tried not to stare. *Was he going to sing one of those Jesus-ey songs here?* Everyone rose and spread out across the back of the room, transitioning effortlessly from debating the merits of jimmies versus sprinkles to singing to Jesus like this was the most normal thing in the world. Facing the window where a buzzing machine projected song lyrics onto a white vinyl shade, everyone chimed in, "Jesus, you love my soul . . . Jesus, I won't let you go . . ."

I shifted from foot to foot, not sure what to do. This was a little weird, singing in the middle of someone's living room with the windows wide open for the whole neighborhood to hear. I wasn't sure what the song meant, or what this whole worship thing was, for that matter. How could you let go of Jesus? Wasn't he always sort of *there*? Was the God of the Bible co-dependent?

We sang three songs about Jesus—his extravagant love, his wonderful Cross, and the unwarranted forgiveness of our sins. I was okay for the first song. By the end of the second, I was rocking and twitching, and by the third I wanted to bolt from the room. It felt *strange*, standing there singing to Jesus, with people all around me bursting into tears, swaying from side to side, smiling at the ceiling, eyes all glassy. One girl lay prostrate on the floor, mumbling something I couldn't make out, and a guy by the couch sat down, burying his anguish-racked face in his hands. I considered kneeling for a bit to break up the monotony, but was afraid they'd somehow know that it wasn't virtue or remorse driving me to my knees.

The final song broke through my discomfort. It was different—less about how pathetic we are without Jesus, more about why it might be worthwhile to believe: "This is the day of the coming Lord. All the lost years He now restores. He has changed my mourning to laughter; what He has freed, is free ever after. . . ."

That didn't sound too bad. *Where, exactly, is this happening?* I wondered.

"Thank you, God." Paul said when the song ended, interrupting my train of thought. "We ask that you be here with us tonight, and bless us. In Jesus' name, Amen." He lowered his guitar back into the case, and we made our way back to our makeshift seats and perches. Pascha passed out photocopies of a Bible passage, while Paul described one of Jesus' famous speeches, called the Sermon on the Mount. I'd heard of it, but had no idea what it said. "Take a few minutes and read it through," Paul instructed, "and then we'll sort it out a bit and try and get at what Jesus is saying."

I looked down at the black-and-white sheet. "Blessed are the poor in spirit, for theirs is the kingdom of heaven. Blessed are those who mourn, for they will be comforted." I wasn't sure what I was supposed to glean from this read-through. A can of pens circulated around the room, but I didn't have any pearls of wisdom I was in a hurry to jot down. "Blessed are the meek, for they will inherit the earth. Blessed are those who hunger and thirst for righteousness, for they will be filled." I wasn't sure what this meant. I skimmed through the rest of the passage, thinking how the Bible was just as vague and unhelpful as I'd always assumed it would be. I didn't follow much of the discussion after that—too many opinions I had no way to sort out, too many paragraphs of blessings and admonitions to cover in an hour. I was left with a vague sense that Paul knew Jesus' words were important, but wasn't going to tell us why. We were supposed to work that out on our own.

When we finished, Pascha asked if anyone who was new to the group would like Newcomer Prayer. "Newcomer Prayer," Paul explained, "is where we try out this thing the Bible calls the gift of prophecy. None of us knows you, so we'll ask God to give us pictures, impressions, sayings, or some other type of message that He wants to communicate to you that we couldn't know any other way. We'll write everything down for you so you don't have to try and remember it all. You don't have to say anything, but if something one of us says strikes you as relevant, let us know and we will pray more into that." It seemed like a fun party trick, like a Christian psychic game, only without the Ouija board or crystal ball. Always game for a spiritual adventure (and liking to be the center of attention in a context where I didn't have to confess my sins), I raised my hand to volunteer.

"The Bible tells us three important characteristics of

prophecy," Paul explained, "things we look to as signs that the senses we get are, in fact, coming from God." This struck me as odd; it hadn't occurred to me that my senses could come from anywhere else. "Who remembers what these characteristics are?" he asked.

Gwen answered, "In First Corinthians, it says that prophecy should be strengthening, encouraging, and . . . some other very important thing I can't remember," she trailed off as the group giggled.

"Prophecy should be comforting," Paul finished for her. "Good job," he said with a smile. "Okay, so, Trish, what we're going to do is pray, asking God to give us something for you. Take what seems right and forget about the rest. And remember, we're all learning, so if something seems weird or off, disregard it. Okay?"

"Sure," I said. "Um—wait." I stalled. "What should I do? I mean, should I close my eyes or pray, or what?" Suddenly, I felt very conspicuous. This whole sitting in the middle of the circle thing seemed a bit untenable.

"You don't have to do anything," Paul answered, confirming my worst fear. "You can close your eyes if you want to, or if you feel more comfortable seeing what goes on, that's cool too. There's no wrong way to do this," he reassured me. "I'll start us with a prayer," he said. "Jesus, thank you that you speak to us. We ask you to come right now and give us words of strength, encouragement, and comfort for Trish . . ."

Silence.

More silence.

Maybe God won't speak to them about me, I thought, mortification creeping up my spine. *Maybe He's telling them awful things, things they're too polite to mention.*

More silence.

They're embarrassed, I decided. *Too nice to give up and move on to someone else.*

Just as I was about to call the whole thing off, a girl blurted, "I see a picture of a wheelbarrow next to a windmill." I turned to see her squinting off into the distance, as if God were projecting this picture onto the kitchen door. "I think it means that you're carrying a heavy load, but that you're close to a place where things will go easier for you."

I smiled at her, unsure of how to respond. A wheelbarrow. Okay.

The blond guy piped up from his perch on the edge of the couch. "I keep hearing that Billy Joel song *Just The Way You Are,*" he said. "It seems like something Jesus would say to you; that he doesn't need you to change before coming to him—that he wants you just the way you are."

He's kind of cute, I thought, nodding. *A little mushy, though—Jesus singing Billy Joel? Please.*

Next to him, a guy with a Russian accent spoke up. "I see a fish that's all different colors—all of them very, very bright. It's like you're that fish. You're going to attract attention everywhere you go, and you don't know yet what to do with it. I think maybe you're supposed to keep swimming."

Pascha jumped in. She looked like she was going to burst with excitement; my eyes widened as I wondered what God had told her. "I'm getting this picture of a crown," she began. "It's a false crown, like something an evil leader or false teacher would wear, and you're smashing it to pieces. I feel like God is going to use you to smash new age lies; that he will use you to bring people the truth about Jesus."

Whatever, I thought. Suddenly, I was ready for this game to be over. This antispirituality stuff among the Jesus people was getting on my nerves.

Then Paul chimed in, "I'm getting a picture of you being launched out of a cannon," he said. "It's like right now you're waiting to be launched, but when it happens, it's going to be huge." I wasn't sure if that was good or bad, this idea of sitting around waiting to be shot out into the world. I needed some sort of "launch" to get my life going, and it did feel like I was sitting around, waiting for something to happen.

After a few more moments of silence, Paul called my Newcomer Prayer to an end: "Lord, we thank you for these words. Thank you that you speak to us and through us. We ask that you protect and nurture any seeds that were planted here and we claim your best for Trish and her life. And anything that was not you, God, we ask that you wipe it away. In Jesus' name. Amen."

"Amen" we echoed. I opened my eyes and blinked, then noticed everyone staring at me expectantly.

"So how was it?" Paul asked. "Did anything resonate?" Liz handed me a sheet of paper with everything written down: *Windmill. Billy Joel. Bright fish. Smashed crown. Cannon.*

"It was great . . ." I said. "It was . . . um . . . inspiring. I'm not sure what else to say. I think I'll go back to my seat by the fireplace and wait for my cannon to go off." As I hoped, the levity broke the serious tone in the room, and I was allowed to leave the prophecy chair and slide back into obscurity. I folded the piece of paper and slid it into my back pocket, unsure whether or not I'd look at it again later.

It was after eleven when I left that night. (Apparently, this small group business was not for the faint of heart.) I didn't understand most of what I saw, but the group met my standard for spiritual viability: people were friendly, there were several cute men, and no one demanded that I kneel down and give my life to Jesus. I wasn't sure what to make of the whole prophecy thing, but as I thought about it later, what stuck with me—what *resonated*—was a sense of astonishment that a bunch of strangers would stay so late on a Wednesday night just to pray for me. That, I had to admit, was pretty amazing. I couldn't wait to invite these nice people to my next spirituality lecture. *I bet they'll like it,* I thought on my way home.

WHAT SURPRISED ME most over the next few weeks as I immersed myself in life among the Cambridge Christians was the upswing in my social life. My e-mail in-box filled with invitations to movie nights, birthday dinners, and kayaking adventures in nearby states. As a member of this not-so-small group, I now had a staggering array of fun social options to choose from, none of which involved discussing God's wrath or monitoring each other for biblical obedience. Following Jesus, in this group at least, was fun.

I met a great girl named Amy who picked me up for church on Sundays so I wouldn't have to take the train. She quickly became my new best friend, making me laugh with her comical perspective on life. She also sprinkled a healthy dose of

Jesus into our conversations. "What is God talking to you about today?" she'd ask. Suddenly, this seemed like a valid question.

One weekend, Pascha organized a group of us to volunteer for the Special Olympics. We helped coach a softball game, cheering on our players, giving them high-fives and hugs. My team lost badly (even by Special Olympic standards) and I prepared to console my players, dredging up stock "better luck next time" lines.

"Twish!" one of my players called, running up to me, face glowing with excitement. "Guess what? Guess what? Guess what?"

"What, Joey?" I asked, putting an arm around him to stop him from jumping so I could understand what he was saying.

"We came in *second!*" he yelled, doing a victory dance right there next to the pitching mound. His entire body writhed in glee, his upper limbs flailing with joy as he reveled in the satisfaction of a job well done. "That means we won the *silver medal!*" It never occurred to him that second place, in a contest with two teams, is last; there were no losers in Joey's Olympics.

I told Pascha and the rest of the group about this afterward as we made our way back to the car. "You know," Pascha said, "that's why I love the Special Olympics. When I'm messed up and I've blown everything, I think Jesus sees me like a silver medal, not last place. Your dude Joey reminds me what that looks like."

That gave me something to think about.

PEOPLE IN OUR small group talked about God all the time, but in interesting ways I'd never heard before. There was no judgment, no grandiose political proclamations, just lots of wonder and hope and awe. I thought more about Amy's Sunday morning question: "What is God talking to you about this week?" No one had ever asked me that before. What *was* God talking to me about this week? For a spiritual junkie like me, this was nirvana. And in the midst of these people, I felt like I found the secret connection: the miraculous portal I'd searched for as a little girl, that special link to God. I was amazed by the way my supernatural efforts were multiplied—exponentially, even—when our group prayed together, or even when we just hung out, talking about Jesus and what he was doing in our lives. There seemed to be power in this group thing. I wondered if this was what Jesus meant when he said, "Where two or three come together in my name, there I am with them."

I recalibrated my prayer style, lining up with what I heard around me on Wednesday nights and Sunday mornings. Vineyarders didn't pray like me, I noticed. They didn't approach God with long, ellipsis-filled soliloquies of blessing and requests, terrified of leaving something or someone out. They didn't affirm the universal good of our common life force, or higher power, or most enlightened manifestation of being; they didn't chant self-selected affirmations. They talked to God like a friend, only with a bit more hope and reverence. They expected Him to respond when they prayed in Jesus' name, whether it was a prayer for healing, help with a difficult roommate, or a parking spot in Harvard Square on Sunday afternoon. It was different from what I'd heard before. Easier, somehow.

In those first few months, church and small group felt like Christmas every week, as these new friends handed me the gifts of God's Holy Spirit one by one: Peace. Love. Joy. Patience. Kindness. Generosity. Gentleness. Faithfulness. Self-control. All these were mine, they said, because of Jesus; I could unwrap them, take them home. "It comes with the package," Paul assured me. "This is how you know Jesus is working in your life." I didn't quite get what he meant, but it seemed like one heck of a deal.

I didn't know what Jesus was doing in my life—I still couldn't pin down who or where he was. But I watched and listened, begging God to bring me the sense of roots and spiritual belonging I saw all around me. I liked how Dave and Grace and Paul and Pascha lived, how they built their lives together around each other and their friends and Jesus. I liked the idea that this kind of love might be possible for me.

The only ant at my little picnic was that I didn't understand what my new friends meant when they described how Jesus *saved* them. I got all vague and foggy when they talked about their *personal relationship* with him, and how he freed them from their sins. I didn't ask them what they meant, though. I liked my new life, with the prayer and the singing and the Saturday night dinner parties. I was afraid that if my new friends learned that I wasn't sure about Jesus—that I was winging it, trying to figure everything out on the fly—they might have to kick me out.

I was living a bit of a spiritual double life, trying to keep a handle on all this information. My morning reading took hours now, as I sat on the couch with Kylie, drinking my coffee and seeking spiritual ballast to get me through the day: I was back reading the *Course*, certain it could help me take Jesus seriously, along with Jayme's books, which I unearthed to explain what the complicated language of the *Course* said. After that, I'd reach for one of Joyce Meyer's books on making the most of my life. Finally, I'd open the Bible to whatever prophet or Gospel story Joyce mentioned in that morning's chapter to make sure she wasn't exaggerating, that her claims weren't too good to be true (because it seemed like they must be, all those promises about victory and joy and overcoming obstacles to get to the promised land). Satisfied that she wasn't embellishing, I'd close the Bible and ask God to make something good of my day. Then I'd set to work revising my "Feminine Magnetic Power" lectures, weaving Bible quotes and Jesus-isms in among the other principles comprising my philosophy of love.

I invited the group to my next event: "As a few of you know," I announced one Wednesday night, "I give lectures and classes on spirituality. Mostly I talk about astrology and the biblical revisions Jesus made through a book called *A Course in Miracles*." Pascha stared at me, eyes wide. "But lately," I continued, "I'm finding some exciting stuff in the Bible, so I'm adding that to my teachings. Anyway, my next lecture is this Friday night at the Unicorn Metaphysical Bookstore, and I'd love it if you all came!" I smiled at the group, excited by how my attendance numbers would skyrocket once word of my work got out. (It would be years before I understood that the metaphysical smorgasbord of confusion and half-truths I brought to the group was the spiritual equivalent of showing up with a raging case of the smallpox, offering to give everyone a hug.)

Paul and Pascha offered me a ride home that night. "So, Trish," Pascha asked as we got in the car, "what do you talk about in your lectures?"

"I talk about metaphysical principles," I gushed. "You know—how Jesus shows us how more is possible in life; how we all need to actualize our highest good so we can manifest fully in the world."

"You mentioned that you find the Bible helpful," Paul asked. "What do you like about it?"

"I like Jesus' pep talks," I responded, eager for the chance to let them in on what I knew. "All you ever hear Christians talk about is the Crucifixion," I complained. "But if you read the Gospels, Jesus spent most of his time making promises about how abundant our lives should be."

Paul missed the point. "The Crucifixion bothers you?" he asked.

"It's not a big deal," I said, a little exasperated. "Honestly, the Resurrection is what matters, because that shows us that we too can overcome death—that it's all just a lie and an illusion. But beyond that, the Crucifixion isn't important." I explained how, according to the *Course*, Jesus is our divine elder brother sent to teach us to overcome the illusion of evil. "I believe in Jesus, he's our role model," I clarified. "If we try hard enough, each of us can *be* Jesus. And when that happens, we'll realize that things like misery, sickness, unhappiness, and disappointment are imaginary, that only the love is real."

I WAS SHOCKED, and a little hurt, that Paul and Pascha didn't come to hear me speak that Friday night. After our great talk, I'd really thought they'd be there.

Chapter Fourteen

Spiritual Monogamy

Our small group read portions of the Gospels—the four books at the front of the New Testament chronicling Jesus' thirty-three years of life—over the course of the next several weeks. At first, I was thrilled at the prospect of a guided tour into Jesusland, with real people to answer my questions and point out the important sights along the way. But my enthusiasm waned as we dug into Jesus' words and I learned that my years of spiritual training conflicted with every second or third thing he said.

I was amazed, and infuriated, to discover his claim, "If you want to have a relationship with God, the only way to do it is through me." *I've had a relationship with God for years,* I fumed. *What can Jesus add to that?* To my utter consternation, Jesus also claimed to be the only path to abundant life and the only way to get to heaven. As maniacally devoted as I was to the idea of romantic monogamy, it hadn't occurred to me that spiritual monogamy might be a good idea, as well. ("If Jesus dated," a friend suggested later, "wouldn't he have dated exclusively?") Worst of all, though, was Jesus' claim that he was the only one who could forgive us of our sins. *Why would I need forgiveness?* I wondered. No other path talked about forgiveness in these terms, like something we need to receive. Forgiveness was something you *gave*, like compassion; it was a sign of your spiritual evolution.

This forgiveness thing was tied somehow, I realized, with the Christian obsession with Jesus' death. I was still baffled by songs like "The Wonderful Cross" and "Victory at Calvary" that made it sound like this was the site of a great battle rather than the location of a gruesome murder. Somehow, the songs suggested, we were supposed to come to the Cross (metaphorically? physically? through some sort of prayer-induced astral projection?) and leave our sins there, after which Jesus would give us abundant life here on earth and eternal life with him in heaven. It sounded like a sorority ritual combined with some sort of metaphysical timeshare, the chance to buy a piece of a multiroom vacation house in the afterlife. I stared at my new friends wide-eyed as they described this like it was the most logical thing in the world.

I scoured Christian bookstores and Web sites for some reasonable explanation of these claims. I found pamphlets featuring "irrefutable laws," illustrated with stick-figure drawings indicating that in my current state I was going to hell. The stick-figure flames were daunting, but I couldn't figure out *why* this was certain to befall me, or what on earth Jesus had to do with this predicament. Several sources quoted C. S. Lewis (of *Chron-*

icles of Narnia fame) who, they alleged, proved that in light of Jesus' claims about himself, there are only three possible conclusions anyone can reach. They called them "The Three Ls": Jesus must be either *Lord*, a *liar*, or a complete *lunatic*. This was served up as an evangelical *fait accompli*, as if there was no possible way one could contemplate this truth and not capitulate immediately and beg for membership in the Christian Coalition. But to me, it made no sense at all. I read and reread these claims, but couldn't figure out how they applied to my life. It reminded me of the way people tried to figure me out over the years—my single state, my failure to make relationships work. From my track record, there were only three possible conclusions anyone could reach: I must be a *loser*, a *lesbian*, or a complete *lunatic*. But it's not as if deciding on one of these helped you understand me better, or even made it true.

Honestly, when I thought about Jesus, I didn't care about the details of what happened on the Cross, or even what fabulous afterlife party he might be inviting me to. What I wanted to know was could he help me? Was he the spiritual leader who could explain why, despite all this effort, I kept making the same mistakes over and over again? If I got some forgiveness along with the package, well—so be it.

BUOYED BY THIS new perspective, I decided to read the Bible in its entirety. I was tired of other people's conflicting opinions; I wanted to know the truth, who was right—the people who insisted that the Bible was a flawed document designed to repress us, or the people I met at the Vineyard who told me it was God's personal message of hope and possibility.

Intimidated by Genesis, I started with the book of Acts, in the middle of the New Testament. After that I read letters by Paul, Timothy, James, Peter, and John, struggled through Revelation, then circled back to Genesis and, "In the beginning . . ." I waded through tales of miraculous healing, vicious persecution, family turmoil, Jewish dietary laws, generations of plight and plenty, kings and villains I couldn't keep track of, prayerful Psalms, wise Proverbs, a racy book about sex, dizzying prophets, and the four Gospels of Jesus. Every few hundred pages, I found a story I knew—Noah and the ark, Jonah and the whale, Joshua and the walls of Jericho. It was like running into an old friend in a new city, a bit of comfort in the midst of unfamiliar surroundings.

My crash course in the Word of God took five months. By the end, I still mixed up Moses (who lead the Jews out of captivity in Egypt to the promise land of Canaan) with Abraham (who fathered all those Jews in the first place) in my mental time line. I didn't emerge from my reading binge as anything close to a theological expert, yet, mysteriously, I felt like I knew a whole lot more about God. The Bible was different than other spiritual books I'd read: the more I studied it, the more I "got" the whole God thing—who He was, what He wanted from me. "For God knows the plans He has for you," it said. "Plans to prosper you and not to harm you, plans to give you a hope and a future."

The Bible, I discovered, was a hotbed of pithy advice on romance: "Do not awaken love before its time," "Do not throw your pearls in front of swine," "Delight yourself in the Lord and He will give you the desires of your heart." *Why didn't anyone tell me this was in here?* I thought. I read story after story of God bringing great husbands to single women—Isaac and Rebekah, Boaz and Ruth. *Who wants a man from Mars,* I thought scathingly, recalling one of the books I'd labored over trying to decipher why I couldn't make my relationships work, *when you can have a man from heaven?* The Bible was like a father's letter to his daughter, encouraging her to trust that he has her best interests at the forefront of his mind. In a way, it was almost like the preface to a fairy tale. I was stunned by how much I liked it—how the words spoke to me, how hopeful they made me feel even as they said, essentially, "You've been doing this all wrong; it's time to recalibrate!" As I read the stories and poems and passages, I considered the outrageous possibility that maybe God was more interested in my life than I'd thought; that perhaps all He wanted from me was to sit still, trust Him, and let Him sort things out.

As excited as I was about this new understanding, the Bible posed a whole host of theological problems, forcing me to confront irreconcilable differences between what I always thought of as "the truth" and what the Bible said.

By far, the toughest thing I found was the idea that we human beings aren't inherently good. According to the Bible, we have a human propensity to *sin* (miss the mark, screw up, be selfish and demanding and miserly and mean, hurt the people we love, disobey God) and *that* is our inherent nature from birth. No amount of effort or good intention will save us from our own personalized cycle of missteps and mistakes, it said; the only way to overcome it is through faith in Jesus Christ. This idea was as foreign to me as if it were written in the original Greek. Sure, I'd heard of Adam and Eve and the incident with the snake and the fruit tree. But I'd been told for so long, by so many sources, that our inherent nature is *good* (and that any evidence to the contrary is simply our personal failure to manifest as God designed us) that all the Christian rhetoric about "sinners in need of a savior" blew right over my head. The *Course* taught that sin was an illusion, "a moment when we forget that we are children of God." That sounded so much *nicer* than all this inherent sinfulness stuff, so much more like how it should be, if the world was perfect. Unfortunately, however, reality didn't bear witness to this *if you ignore it, it will go away* approach. For me at least, the baggage from my mistakes didn't go away. It accumulated, stacking up around me until I practically needed a stack of affirmations and a staff of bellboys to get me up out of bed in the morning. The Bible told me that without Jesus, I might as well just lie there. There is, it said, no hope of being good on my own, and no point in trying, really—there is no continuum between good and bad to wiggle along, no scale of justice to influence with my choices, no point in doing nice things to tip the balance toward the "good person" side. Rather, it implied, the scale is permanently tipped, and we are all piled in a heap on the side away from God, wallowing in a mess of fear, shame, and regret that keeps us from the lives we want to live. None of our efforts, however well intended, can get us up out of that pile. According to the Bible, God sent Jesus to sit on the other side of this teeter-totter, to lift us out of the pit. And for those of us who want to, we can defy this spiritual gravity and slide up into his arms and get off this scale once and for all, trusting that no matter what we do, if we slide back to Jesus, he'll lift us out of this cycle. This is, the Bible said, the mystery of God's grace.

As if anticipating that I'd balk at this strange assessment of my hopeless state, the Apostle John laid out three types of sin I'd find if I gave myself an honest look: a preoccupation with gratifying my own desires, the urge to acquire and accumulate, and an obsession with status and importance. *Do I do that?* I wondered. I was so accustomed to affirming my universal perfection as a beloved child of God, it never once occurred to me to root around inside myself for evidence of my inherent selfishness. But there it was, clear as day:

— Preoccupation with getting my own way? Check.
— Stockpiling material things, yet still wanting more? Check.
— Obsession with status and how people perceive me? Check.

Unbeknownst to me, I'd been living out the sin trifecta, thinking I was a regular nice person walking around. Which, according to the Bible, I was, as nice as any of us could be, anyway, on our own without Jesus. But if I synced up with Jesus, John said, my life would be different. *Different how?* I wondered.

For starters, John promised, if I said yes to Jesus' offer, I'd somehow have the ability to avoid making the same mistakes over and over again. I'd know how to shake loose from my endless selfishness, insatiable desire, and concern over how the rest of the world saw me, and live a happier, better life. That sounded good. And yet, I didn't get why Jesus was necessary—couldn't God just forgive me?

The Old Testament prophets went on for pages, I noticed, about God's justice and righteousness, and how sins require a sacrifice to make things right again. I read gruesome instructions in Leviticus about how under the Old Covenant, Jews were to slaughter bulls and goats and sheep and doves to atone for various transgressions. This was God's old system of substitution to allow people to make it up to Him when they blew Him off and went their own way. There was a set price for various sins, a number of animals to be brought to the priests and killed as an atoning sacrifice. It wasn't pretty, and it was relentless—anytime you made even the smallest slip or error, you weren't right before God and needed more blood to restore you. Life was a constant struggle against a system you couldn't conquer. Kind of a hell on earth.

This was, I realized, what happened after Adam and Eve accepted the serpent's offer and ate that fruit from the forbidden tree, the one that gave knowledge of good and evil. Before, they knew only good; evil they chose on their own. And now, my inability to stay out of the mud or steer clear of bad decisions was a direct result of this, the Bible implied—because of their choice, I was born cursed with a bent away from God. It might not be a profound, serial killer–style bent; I might be just a few degrees off course. But it was there nonetheless, leading me step-by-step away from the life God created me for. For every mistake, I learned, there was a consequence—something was needed to atone, recalibrate, set me right again before God, something more substantial than my own feeble "Gee, I wish I hadn't done that." My heartfelt regret, the Bible implied, didn't do any good. Blood was required, as I'd literally sold my life to the devil to get what I thought I wanted.

Crap, I thought. *No wonder no one talks about this stuff.* I didn't know what else to do, so I read on, hoping to get to the "good news."

The tangible atonement—the blood—the Bible said, comes from Jesus' death on the Cross. Because he was innocent, without sin (like all those bulls and goats and doves), he could offer his blood in our place, literally dying so we can live. This is what it means when we call him "the Lamb of God Who Takes Away the Sins of the World." (Reflecting on this, I immediately forgave all the people who tried to form me as a Catholic child; I never realized what they were up against, trying to convey this grisly message via coloring books and craft projects.)

Jesus' death put an end to all the sacrifice and bloodshed, the Bible said, paying the price for my mistakes, bad choices, and moments of willful disregard. This was the New Covenant: we still can't help but sin, but God so wants to forgive us that he gave Jesus as the atoning sacrifice for all of our screwups—past, present, and future.

This was a lot to swallow. All I needed to do to get back on track was say yes to Jesus, repent, accept forgiveness, and move on? It seemed too easy. The new age/enlightenment path taught that I needed to struggle to overcome my past mistakes, that it would take *work*. (Spiritual people love to talk about their *work*; my new age conversations often sounded like a self-improvement edition of *This Old House*.) Jesus seemed to say that all it would take is *him*. I didn't know what to do with this, but there it was, in black and white: "If we claim to be without sin, we deceive ourselves," John said. But "if we confess our sins, Jesus is faithful and just and will forgive us our sins and purify us from all unrighteousness." Okay then.

BEFORE I COULD sort that out, things got even stranger. The Bible also said that God was not the only player in the spiritual drama going on around us. Indeed, the same evil being who convinced Adam and Eve to eat the fruit was alive and in the world today, it said, tempting, taunting, and lying to us in order to lure us away from God. The Bible described the devil—a fallen angel, not a cartoon with horns and a spear—as a spiritual being whose sole goal was to ruin our lives, tempting us with things that aren't God's best for us, the same way he tempted Eve. It called this being Satan, a serpent, the Deceiver, the Accuser, the Enemy, and the Prince of This World. The Apostle Peter described him "prowling around like a roaring lion, looking for someone to devour."

I had no mental grid for the notion of a Kingdom of Evil actively seeking to thwart God's best for me, or the suggestion that we were all warriors in a cosmic spiritual battle. The warlike imagery synced up with my childhood sense that *something* big was going on around us, though, and explained why there were so many inspiring movies about good triumphing over evil, none of which involved the hero turning his back on the villain and saying, "You're just not real."

I spent hours dissecting these passages with Amy, begging her to make sense of this craziness. "Do you believe this stuff?"

I asked, wondering if her business colleagues knew about this prowling lion thing.

"Yes I believe it," she assured me. "I've seen it; it's real."

"What's real?" I pressed, baffled that this seemed so natural to her, that she woke up each day believing that Jesus could protect her from mistakes and regret and shame.

"Jesus is real," she started. "And Satan is real, too. The Bible tells us there's a war between them going on all around us here on earth, and that the only way to win it is through Jesus."

"What about the people who don't know Jesus?" I countered. "What happens to them?"

"They get caught in the middle—in the crossfire," she acknowledged. "It sucks, because they don't even know what's happening to them. Why do you think some believers can be so obnoxious in sharing their faith? It's because the stakes seem so high and they want people to know that Jesus is the only way out of hell—eternally, but also here in everyday life."

I stared at her, wide-eyed. I had no idea what to say to that. Here was a girl I respected: she was smart, normal, gainfully employed. There was no reason for her to fall back into some crazy religion to make her life work; her life worked fine. And yet she believed this stuff. *How?* I wondered. *Why?* I thought back to that day at Kristen's house when I'd tried to meditate; how I'd been chased from the room by that vision of a giant man with a sledgehammer, then overwhelmed by the feeling I was being shot through with poison. Was this the kind of evil Amy was talking about?

•

IF THE BIBLE was true, I faced some major changes in how I thought about life. I had always believed that spirituality was about mastering my positive thinking and burnishing my personal wholeness and self-esteem. I had never imagined it would be about Jesus, admitting that I was entirely sin-prone, and fighting off an evil being who wanted to devour me. Suddenly, this Christian thing seemed like a bizarre *Star Trek* episode where I had to master the hidden forces of some new galaxy in order to survive. But as I read the Bible, I felt God saying, *This is the self-help book you've been looking for.*

Chapter Fifteen

Another Notch in the Bible Belt?

I still wasn't sure I wanted to be one though—a "Christian." The word carried so much baggage. Gandhi once said something to the effect of "I have no problem with your Jesus; in fact I rather admire him. It's his people I can't deal with." As I explored Jesus from the safe confines of my seeker-friendly Vineyard church, and my "Yay, I have a life!" small group, I couldn't help but notice that our gentle approach to salvation wasn't the norm in other parts of the country. I read in the paper about a group of midwestern Episcopalians who drove a bus all the way to Maine to stand in a town square with signs reading "God Hates Fags!" Christian television was rife with proclamations about who was going to hell, offering lists that categorically included almost everyone I knew. People with gruesome placards lined the streets in front of Planned Parenthood, multivolume novels about how unbelievers will be left behind dominated bestseller lists, and a girl in church leaned over to me one day and whispered, "Do you think Jesus could love a Democrat?"

I prayed about this. A lot. "*These* are your people?" I asked, incredulous. "These are the ones you picked to spread the news that you're the one true way to God?" I read the hysterical declarations of Christian leaders like Jerry Falwell, who claimed that the attacks of September 11 were caused by "pagans, abortionists, feminists, gays, lesbians, the ACLU, and the People for the American Way," and Pat Robertson, who told his television audience that feminism caused women to "kill their children, practice witchcraft, destroy capitalism, and become lesbians." *Southern feminism must be quite a movement,* I mused. (Admittedly, I had my own doubts about feminism, but more because I couldn't see how flinging my bra into a tree would help me succeed in the workplace.) The idea of aligning myself with these fundamentalist wing-nuts made me want to spend my days as a follower of Jesus hiding with my dog under the couch.

The more I studied Jesus' words in the Bible, though, the less the rhetoric of his most strident supporters made sense. These fundamentalists and their coalitions were always battling some other group's agenda—the liberal agenda, the gay agenda, the feminist agenda. And in a certain way, I saw the connection—Jesus busted everyone's agenda; it's kind of what his life was about. He threw the money changers out of the temple, he berated the religious experts for their legalistic attempts to manipulate God. He told all of us that the most important thing we need to do is to love one another (which rarely stays on my agenda for long when tested by someone who bugs me). But the thing I noticed about Jesus that I didn't see in many of his front men was that he really got in there and loved people. He loved them in a personal, relational, *helpful* way, not in that arms-length, "love the sinner–hate the sin" kind of doublespeak that any sane person recognizes as Christianese for "I don't know you, but it's clear that you're doomed, and I have to at least try and make you change." Jesus, I found, rarely drew these types of distinctions.

Perusing the new arrivals section at the library one day, I came upon a book called *When Bad Christians Happen to Good People*. What I read in its pages was daunting. Following through on this Jesus quest, I learned, meant aligning myself with not only Falwell and Robertson, but with legions of culturally disconnected believers across the country whose idea of fun evangelism was giving gifts like flip-flops that leave Jesus Loves You footprints behind in the sand, or a tie tack in the shape of fishing fly so you can tell curious friends, "Like Jesus, I'm a fisher of *men*." I read about everything from golf balls to "testa-mints" breath fresheners inscribed with scripture passages, all the better to share the gospel while duffing or combating halitosis among the unsaved.

A month or so earlier, I would have found the book hysterical—one more example of how Christians are the silliest people around. Honestly, how many people find salvation through a breath mint? But now I read with a different perspective—I had one foot in this crazy camp; I was in line to be sized for my flip-flops. *Jesus needs a new public image campaign if these are his top representatives*, I thought, reading page after page of ridiculous stories. *He might be the way, the truth, and the life, but honestly*—*who wants an offer of salvation from a middleman sporting weird accessories and raving about the fiery pit of hell?* Tacky *is not a witness for the boundless love of Christ.* I wondered if I'd been duped —if my Cambridge church was a bizarre anomaly, a gathering of the only normal Christians on the entire planet.

I was saved from my despair by a CD Amy gave me on the way home from church one day. "Take it," she said. "Let me know what you think." The girl on the front cover was pretty, and normal looking, so I decided to give it a try.

The singer's name was Nicole Nordeman, and her lyrics pierced me like a needle as she sang about colliding with a new agey girl who sounded an awful lot like me. The girl was reading a yoga magazine, talking about the healing power of her crystals, and wondering about her past life, in which, she was certain, she'd been the wife of a plantation slave.

I was mortified. That could have been me, waxing poetic about my advanced spiritual exploration to a baffled stranger. But the song's chorus surprised me, changing the whole direction of the song. Nicole admitted that she'd dismissed this girl, until God reminded her, *I created her in My image . . .*

Nicole *was* talking about me, I realized, but she wasn't saying that I sucked or that I was doomed the way so many other people had. She was speaking to them—the others—reminding them that no matter how off track I might be with my crystals and my curiosity about past-life regression, God made me. Which meant that they were charged by Jesus to love me, and when they couldn't (which might be often) they were supposed to ask him for help, not dismiss me as one more purveyor of some evil agenda.

I bought Nicole's next CD, and listened incredulously as she asked Jesus, "Help me believe . . . don't let me miss any miracles." Her words made me feel like perhaps it was okay if I didn't "get" this Jesus thing automatically. I'm not sure why I needed someone famous—and far away—to tell me this, why I didn't believe Paul and Pascha when they assured me of this very thing. Despite their efforts, I couldn't shake the feeling that *they* got it, and *I* didn't, and this discrepancy created an insurmountable barrier between us, an ever-widening chasm I couldn't cross. But if Nicole—a *professional Christian*, for Pete's sake—put out an entire CD that said things like "Help me believe," perhaps it was okay if I didn't understand quite yet. Her music gave me hope that not all of Jesus' people outside of Cambridge were crazy; that some were thoughtful and sophisticated and talented and open about their lives. In my mind, I followed Nicole around like a pesky little sister, traipsing through her songs again and again trying to learn the way to Jesus.

At the Vineyard, I found people more like Nicole and less like *those other Christians*, people who spent their time wondering what Jesus was leading them toward, rather than obsessing over the wayward direction of others. They reassured me about a thousand things—that followers of Jesus can wear cute shoes, that I could still love my gay uncle, that it was okay to go home for Christmas dinner without asking my parents if they wanted to pray the sinners' prayer. Armed with this, I made it my goal to be the most normal Christian nonbelievers ever met (knowing full well that here in New England I might be the *only*

Christian they ever met). I couldn't stop the bad press, or the busloads of agenda-fighting believers whose approach to Jesus differed from mine. But if Jesus was real, I decided, he could come up with results that overcame that other stuff. My life, pre-Jesus, was a disaster. *If following him makes it better,* I thought, *who cares if people think I'm a Jesus freak?* And yet at the same time, I wasn't sure this was what I wanted to be; I still didn't know what it meant, exactly. But I was sure I was faking it well enough to fool the true Jesus freaks around me.

OH HOW WRONG I was. I was hanging out with Paul and Pascha a few nights later, when Paul asked me, point-blank, "Trish, do you understand what happened when Jesus died on the Cross?"

Shame filled my body like hot black sludge, and I sunk down low in my chair, waiting for them to chastise me, to send me home in disgrace. For the first time in my spiritual journey, I was being called out as a fraud. "No. I don't get it," I admitted quietly. "I'm so sorry. I've tried. But I don't. The blood, the death—what does any of that have to do with God? What does it mean?"

"It means," Paul said gently, "you can make a mistake and it doesn't have to cut you off from God. It means that for all your 'stuff'—your baggage, your issues, the times you've tried and failed—you can say, 'I'm sorry. I don't want to do that again, I don't want to be stuck with this forever. Jesus, help me . . .' and Jesus will take it all and give you another chance."

"Like a mulligan?" I asked. "You mean like in golf, when you hit a shot that's so bad everyone lets you start over?"

"Sort of," Paul conceded, breaking into a smile. "I think for tonight we can think of it as a mulligan. It means that when Jesus died on the Cross, he took all the mistakes that feel like they'll dog you forever with him; his death cancels them out. When he died," Paul explained, "they died, too."

"So if it's done," I asked, baffled, "what does that have to do with me? And why do I still feel like garbage if my mistakes aren't supposed to count anymore?"

"Because you have to opt in," Pascha explained. "Jesus doesn't just take over your life; he waits to be invited. We have to let him take our sins—we have to *ask* him to save us." I stared at the carpet. I had no idea what to do with this information, or where I'd go on Wednesday nights once they locked me out.

"Why don't you try it?" Paul suggested. "Tell Jesus you're giving him all the things you've been through and that you want him to take them. See what happens."

I took a deep breath. "Okay. I'll try." I looked at them both, then bowed my head. My nose overflowed and I swiped at it with tissue. "Jesus," I began, "I give you my asshole ex-husband. Oh crap," I stammered, looking up. "Am I allowed to call him an asshole?"

"That's okay," Paul assured me.

"Sorry. Okay. Anyway," I continued. "Jesus, I give you all the ways I'm disappointing and terrifying my parents with my life choices. I give you all those relationships that didn't work out. I give you my relationship with Mark, which isn't working out. I give you my pathetic life, with no job, no husband, and a gross apartment. I give it all to you, Jesus. Have at it. Amen." My effort felt half baked, but it was the best I could do. I was exhausted—

tired of fighting for the right to do things my way, tired of defending spiritual adventures that left me facedown in the mud, tired of getting up every morning to face my scraps of a life. If Jesus was willing to take on this type of renovation project, the least I could do was warn him what he was getting into.

As I finished, Paul and Pascha surrounded me in a giant, reassuring hug. Shockingly, they didn't seem to be judging me for my swear words or my reluctant trudge toward Jesus. They seemed happy to see me hanging in, like the people who stand alongside a marathon course long after the winners have past, offering the stragglers cheers and encouragement. I didn't feel any different, Jesus-wise, but I felt loved.

At the end of the night, Paul suggested that I abandon my smorgasbord approach to spirituality: "Why don't you put aside the new age teachings," he proposed. "You know—feng shui, astrology— and just do Jesus for a while? Think of it as an experiment," he said, "see what happens." This might have been a major turning point for me, if I'd understood what Paul was asking. I was still clueless, though, thinking, *Yeah—it would be good to read the Bible more,* the true nature of his suggestion whizzing right over my head.

NEWLY IMMERSED IN my Jesus experiment, I started to miss my other spiritual friends, the ones I knew from my life before the Vineyard. And I worried about them, that they might be missing out on this Jesus thing. None of their lives was going all that well either—like me, they'd all spent years trudging along various paths, always believing they were getting closer to the top of some mountain, but never stopping to notice that for all that effort, the view was still pretty bleak. But when I talked to them about this Jesus thing—about my Fabulous New Discovery—they didn't seem all that interested.

"Um, yeah. That's nice for you," Reina told me one day after our Unity Yoga class. "But, yanno, I've tried that whole fundamentalist deal. I'm just not into some guy in a suit thumping a Bible and telling me what to do."

I didn't know what to say. I was so accustomed to people jumping on the bandwagon whenever I found a new spiritual path to wander; I was shocked by her outright dismissal.

"But it's not like that," I stammered. "Dave—the pastor— he doesn't even wear a suit . . ."

Jonathan was the same: "I've done too much work getting my chakras aligned," he insisted. "Why would I surround myself with all that negative Christian energy?"

Okay then.

Jessie—whom I knew was a long shot to begin with— berated me for forty-five minutes, insisting that my very act of considering the Bible suppressed struggling women around the globe. Her eyes gleamed with pleasure and fury as she ranted, pouring out the frustration of a generation of lipstick lesbians who didn't have the benefit of a real-live Christian to yell at. (I hadn't considered how few opportunities an angry feminist has for these kinds of encounters in Cambridge.) *It's true,* I thought later. *People hate Christians.*

Chapter Sixteen

Weeded and Pruned

I once read a passage by Madeleine L'Engle in which she explained how it was possible to crash through a plate glass door and emerge unscratched. The damage doesn't come from the breakthrough, she said, but from our instinctual urge to pull back afterward, trying to return to the other side. If we go with the momentum and let it carry us, we'll be okay. But if we pull back, we end up sliced and bloodied by broken shards we could have left behind.

I crashed through an awfully big window on my way to becoming a Christian. I landed in an extraordinary world of exceedingly friendly people who think it is normal to wait until they are married to have sex, but abnormal to read their horoscopes in the daily paper; a world where prayers are lifted up in Jesus' name (as if, it seemed to me, everyone needed reminding of whom we were praying to), and people talk about deliverance and prophecy as if they are gifts similar to athletic talent or the ability to draw a still life that actually looks like fruit. Faced with this strange new world, I desperately wanted to pull back. But smashing through this glass and landing in life as a follower of Jesus was like choosing the red pill in *The Matrix*, I learned: it took me into a place few people know of, a world of spiritual battles and forces larger than life. But once you know, I discovered, you can't un-know; I was committed to staying the course, even if I wasn't loving the trip.

To put it bluntly, I wasn't loving the trip. Here's the thing: when God told me he had a husband for me that day in Buffalo, I thought He meant right away; I thought He understood that time was of the essence. I'd been going to church, I'd given up sex—by all accounts, I'd held up my end of the bargain. Accordingly, I expected a handsome man to come up to me at any moment and announce, "Hi there . . . God sent me," after which we'd hop into his chariot, ride off into the suburbs, and live happily ever after.

But that wasn't how it went. Sure, I had one or two guys ask me out—an earnest insurance salesman who told me on the first date that he'd belonged to a cult and still chanted to his guru, a second-year student from Harvard Business School searching for a willing partner to continue his genetic line. Not exactly what a girl thinks of when she imagines a dream man handpicked by God.

"Have you lost my file?" I asked Him one day, stomping through the woods while Kylie bounded through the piles of fallen leaves, "Because overall, this doesn't seem to be working. What if I opt out?" I asked suddenly, raising the stakes of our transaction. "What if I decide *not* to be a Christian?" I taunted Jesus with the things I'd heard he hated most: "What if I'm still a feminist?" I asked. "What if I vote for Democrats? What if I'm . . . what if I'm *gay*?" I half expected to be struck down, right there in the woods. As I stomped through the leaves and watched Kylie tree a squirrel, I almost wanted Jesus to kick me out of his little club so I could cobble together some sort of a life from the few pieces he hadn't ruined. Instead, he said to me:

I can give you—and anyone else who wants it—a life that defies your definitions. I can empower you more than feminism, I can make the world work better than any political party. I can bless you to live in the best romantic relationship you've ever had. But I won't do it unless you want me to—it's your choice.

"I want that," I admitted. "All of it . . ." I decided not to pull back.

Night after night I had nightmares of snakes. I saw huge constrictors hiding under every pillow and dangling from every tree, waiting to wrap themselves around my head and engulf me. I woke up sweating, the words to that childhood song about being swallowed by a boa constrictor echoing through my mind. I pored over books on dream interpretation and animal symbolism trying to figure out what these images meant. The general consensus of both the psychics and the Freudians was that snake dreams represented emerging sexuality: *the stirring of my kundalini energy,* as one eloquent yogi put it. Clearly, that was not it. Besides the obvious fact that I'd given up premarital sex for Jesus, there was nothing sexy about a dream where a python ate my dog.

I asked Paul and Pascha about my dreams. And Amy. And anyone else who might have some reasonable explanation for this nocturnal reptile torment.

"It's Satan," they told me as if reading off the same cue card.

Oh—*it's Satan*. Well then, that explained everything. I stared back at my friends, perplexed.

"Satan is fighting back," Paul explained. "He doesn't want you to follow Jesus, he wants you to be miserable. His whole goal is to scare you, annoy you, bug you, and otherwise push you away from Jesus, and from anyone else following Jesus. So he's hijacking your dreams to freak you out."

"It's working!" I blurted. "What am I supposed to do?" It was exasperating that not only was I having this absurd conversation, I was having it repeatedly.

"You fight back," Amy told me.

"You pray," said Pascha.

"You renounce all the ways you've given Satan a foothold, then tell the snakes to leave in Jesus' name," recommended Paul.

"You read Ephesians 6:10," Pascha added. "That will tell you what to do."

I went home that night and read the Apostle Paul's advice to the beleaguered Ephesians about what to do in times of spiritual battle. I read about how I should dress myself with the "belt of truth," the "helmet of salvation," and the "breastplate of righteousness," taking up the "shield of faith" to quench the fiery darts of the enemy and the "sword of the Spirit" which was, somehow, the word of God. But while the Bible assured me I had all these protective garments at my disposal, I had no more idea how to put them on—how they *worked*—than I would an Indian sari or the complicated obi of a geisha.

Paul loaned me a book on fighting evil, which I hid behind my copy of *Prozac Nation* as I rode the train. I didn't care if people around me thought I was depressed; when you're on the T that just makes you normal. But I wasn't ready to field the puzzled stares of people wondering why I wanted to fight demons. There were still many questions I couldn't answer.

ONE OF THE surprising things I noticed about Jesus was how much he talked about gardening. For a carpenter whose unofficial job description was "Save the world," he exhibited an unlikely preoccupation with seeds and soil. Some of his gospel messages read more like turf management lectures than spiritual direction: plant on rocky soil, and you can't expect much to take root. Toss those seeds haphazardly in the middle of a thorny patch, he warned, and they'll be choked out long before they have a chance to grow. It was essential, he suggested, to cultivate the soil—to soften up the hard places and clear out the weeds—before you could expect to produce anything. If you want to plant seeds, he said, you need to loosen up the ground, otherwise it's all wasted effort. And by the way, he added: those branches that look pretty and leafy but don't bear any fruit? Those have to go.

ONE DAY AS I was subjecting Amy to yet another explanation of why Mark would be a better husband for me than one of the cute guys in our small group (Mark was a Taurus—the perfect counterpart to my Capricorn-Leo, while the other guy was an Aries, which made for the worst combination imaginable) she broke her posture of patient spiritual correctness and said, "You know you're not supposed to be doing that, right?"

"What are you talking about?" I asked.

"Astrology," she said. "God specifically told us not to look to the stars and planets to guide us. That's looking to the created for guidance instead of the Creator, and the Bible is pretty clear that God doesn't want us doing that."

"But astrology is in the Bible," I replied, feeling defensive. "The three wise men were astrologers, following the star to Jesus."

"They were astronomers," she clarified, "they studied the stars. There's no indication they looked to the planets to make decisions about their love lives."

I wasn't sure what to say.

"You know, don't you," she continued carefully, "that not every spiritual message you hear comes from God?"

"But God made the planets and the stars," I countered. "Why can't He use them to tell us things, to communicate with us?"

"He could," she conceded. "But He didn't set it up that way. When God says 'Seek me,' or 'Ask and I will answer,' He wants us to pray, not consult a chart of planetary alignment. God doesn't make it that complicated—He wants a relationship with us, not a science project."

I didn't know what to make of this. Astrology was still the basis of every decision I made, my way of negotiating the world. It didn't seem contrary to my "Just Do Jesus" project, but rather complementary. I couldn't imagine functioning without the information astrology provided, or why this might be necessary.

"I'll tell you what," Amy said after a lengthy silence. "Why don't you ask God how He feels about this stuff? Ask Him what you should and shouldn't be doing, and trust Him to tell you. We'll leave it up to Him."

COULD AMY AND Paul and Pascha be right? I wondered—was there really a problem with my "many paths to the top of the mountain" approach to spirituality? I thought of one of my law professors, a theatrical septuagenarian who had warned us endlessly of the importance of recognizing "red herrings"—facts or evidence that look important but are really distractions, false leads designed to pull you off course and take you down the wrong path. His exams were filled with such temptations, sentences leading us to believe we were dealing with a certain type of case, except for a word or two buried in the next paragraph negating that conclusion. "That's it!" you'd think, excited and proud to have recognized the issue so easily. Puffed up, you'd blow right by that next paragraph, already drafting your brilliant answer. If you fell for one of these red herrings, you could spend the whole exam time analyzing the facts from the wrong perspective, miss the real issue, and fail the class. And the kicker was that you wouldn't realize what had happened until it was too late. Red herrings were the most dangerous part of his tests. *Could the Course, astrology, and all my other practices be spiritual red herrings?* I wondered. Amy's words echoed through my mind: "You know, don't you, not every spiritual message you hear comes from God?" What did that even mean?

I e-mailed Pascha for advice. "It's true," she wrote back. "Not everything we pick up on comes from God. But don't worry—there are ways to get rid of the funky stuff, and ways to sort it out.

"Essentially," she explained, "there are three places messages that seem spiritual come from: some are from God, some are things we make up in our own mind, and some are from Satan. It's like you're a TV antenna," she continued, "and you pick up a wide variety of stations: great programming, static, porn—the key is to learn the distinguishing characteristics of the great programming channels so you can filter out the rest."

Are you kidding me? I thought. *Is this possible?* But even as I chuckled at how preposterous this sounded, my brain clicked away, registering the twelve billion little experiences this explained about my life—nightmares, senses about people, creepy feelings when I entered certain places or picked up certain books. I'd never had any way to work with this information, no inkling that it meant anything in the larger scheme of life. (I'd always thought this sensitivity was due to the placement of my moon sign on the cusp between Aquarius and Pisces.) *What if,* I wondered, *in all my wandering around, I somehow made a deal with evil forces, aligning myself with them in exchange for little snippets of information, taking myself off of God's path for my life?*

"How do you sort this out?" I wrote to Pascha, trying not to panic. "How do I realign myself and make sure I'm hearing from God?"

"Don't worry," she assured me. "Jesus can sort you out." I wasn't sure what this meant. She described how God's messages are always consistent with what He says in the Bible, and that they bear good fruit: they are encouraging, and the choices they lead to bring good results. I thought about the *Course,* and its "fruit": how no matter how hard I tried to apply its principles, the results were bad. My astrology planning also failed: my ex-husband was a Virgo, Mark was a Taurus; my "perfect" matches weren't viable in any of the ways that mattered.

Digging deeper, I remembered the time I went with Kristen to see a psychic three months before leaving my marriage. Knowing only the first letter of my name and my date of birth, the woman used tarot cards to reveal a shocking level of intimate knowledge about my life: how my husband controlled me, how it would get worse before it got better, and how I'd soon live in a giant house filled with valuable antiques. She was deadly accurate; clearly she was getting supernatural information from somewhere. But there were none of the hallmarks of God in her message—nothing encouraging, no advice for what to do next or how to make things better. I'd left that day feeling awed, but grim. What she said was true, but her recitation only served to underscore my misery and make it seem endless and inevitable. Was that bad fruit? Had I been making little deals with the devil all this time, trying to find supernatural information without going to God? If so, how could I get Jesus to sort me out?

"The kingdom of heaven is like a merchant looking for fine pearls," I read in Matthew. "When he found one of great value, he went away and sold everything he had and bought it." I felt like I'd been that merchant, collecting a wide assortment of spiritual paths. *Was Jesus the big-kahuna pearl?* I wondered. This parable suggested that while my accumulation of spiritual insights might contain bits of truth, Jesus was more valuable than all of them put together; the only path to God that was *entirely* true. And the merchant in the parable didn't just add the new pearl to his collection, I noticed. Rather, he sold everything he had in exchange for that one pearl. Almost like choosing a spouse. *Omigosh,* I thought, *does this mean I've been unfaithful to God?*

I thought back to a story that had caught my attention when I read the book of Acts, about a bunch of spiritual seekers who decided to follow Jesus. They confirmed their new allegiance by gathering all the paraphernalia from their previous practices—statues of other gods, books of spells and ways to manipulate the universe, sources claiming to give knowledge of the future—and burning them. The Bible didn't say these other paths weren't "spiritual"—just that they weren't God's best. They were counterfeits—good enough to convince people they *might* be the real thing, but of far less power and value. When you see the real thing, the story implied, you'll be more than willing to give up the others.

I asked Amy about these passages. "It's true," she said. "Getting rid of other spiritual alliances loosens Satan's holds on us, and gives Jesus authority to force the devil to leave us alone," she explained. "That's why Jesus says, 'No one sows a patch of unshrunk cloth on an old garment. If he does, the new piece will pull away from the old, making the tear worse.' You can't just add Jesus into whatever else you're already doing."

This was my problem—I was using the Bible like a patch, trying to cover up the gaping holes in my ripped-up life with a little Jesus iron-on, hoping the frayed edges wouldn't show and that the adhesive would hold.

When I got home that night I scanned my bookshelves, which were crammed full of different recommendations for negotiating the spiritual world: everything from existential philosophy to mystic poetry to meditations designed to awaken my inner truth. I remembered the Bible's warnings about false teachers—how they promise light but deliver us to darkness, how they lead us in circles, saying what we want to hear, leaving us always studying but never acknowledging the truth. That sounded a lot like me. I was a fanatical customer at the local spirituality store, dashing in like a strung-out junkie whenever another mood swing hit, searching for a new author, a new path, a new spiritual perspective to make my life worthwhile. I read voraciously. I was always studying, but never came to the truth; none of my spiritual hits ever lasted for longer than the time it took me to read the most recent opinion on what would fix my life.

God doesn't want me to add a few Jesus books and tchotchkes to my shelf, I realized, *He wants me to start over.* I decided that I, too, would burn some books.

I wasn't sure of the logistics: our house was not exactly flame-retardant, and I wasn't convinced God wanted me to take down the entire neighborhood to purify my reading habit. I couldn't bring myself to call the Cambridge fire department to request a burn permit to facilitate spiritual cleansing (I flirted with throwing the word "exorcism" in for a little flair, but decided against it). I wasn't sure how to proceed.

I looked at the painting of Isis hanging over my bed, a souvenir from my pilgrimage to Greece (I'd never understood why the tour company had chosen to commemorate our time in Greece with a symbol of Egyptian mythology). *This is as good a place to start as any,* I thought, taking it down from the wall. I threw away my gold pendant of Athena and my school ring with the picture of Pan. I gave Mark back his lucky Buddha statue and tossed the pile of rose quartz crystals from my romance corner into the backyard. My room looked pretty bare.

When I woke up the next day, it was raining. Not a light drizzle or a springtime shower, but sheets of rain coming sideways through the air. I wondered if I shouldn't revisit that section in Genesis about Noah and get the specifics for building an ark. Then I realized: I could put the books out in the rain; that would destroy them almost as well as fire. I boxed them up: *The Psychic Pathway, The Celestine Prophecy, The Spiral Path, Conversations with God* (volumes 1, 2 and 3), *The Tenth Insight, Your Guide to Casting Runes, Feng Shui for Business, Feng Shui for Romance, A Beginner's Guide to Feng Shui, The Guide to Intuitive Healing, Everything You Need to Know About Astrology, The Invitation, The Dance, The Way of the Peaceful Warrior, Your Heart's Desire, True Balance, Finding True Love, The Seven Spiritual Laws of Success, The Path to Love, Anatomy of the Soul, The Four Agreements, Goddesses in Everywoman, Women Who Run with the Wolves.* (*Why,* I wondered, *did I ever want to run with the wolves?*) I piled them in on top of each other, hauled them out to the alley beside our house, and set the boxes in a giant puddle. Leaving nothing to chance, I left the boxes open, ensuring the contents would be drenched beyond repair. The last thing I needed on my conscience was to have someone wander by and pull one of these useless books out of the box. If someone was desperate enough to pillage my garbage in search of life direction, I certainly didn't want to lead the person down the same dead ends I'd traveled.

Walking back into the kitchen, I stopped cold at the sight of the giant framed poster on the back wall. The five-foot Toulouse-Lautrec print—left behind by one of our house's former inhabitants—had hung on that same wall since the day I moved in, but somehow I had never noticed its subject matter: a woman wrapped head to toe by a snake poised to strike her in the face. *That can't be good,* I thought. I wrestled it down from the wall and out to the alley next to my boxes.

I thought of this day three years later, when I read two books in the same week that each contemplated this provocative observation by French philosopher Simone Weil: "One has only the choice between God and idolatry. If one denies God . . . one is worshiping some things of this world in the belief that one sees them only as such, but in fact, though unknown to oneself imagining the attributes of Divinity in them." I wasn't quite so oblivious to my idolatry; I'd imagined divinity in all manner of inanimate objects, believing what people told me—that my manipulation of these objects could control the way my little part of the planet rotated. It was an enticing lie, but that didn't make it any less untrue. It was unsettling, though—then, and even now—how quickly I could turn a nothing into my something and inadvertently deny God. That seemed like a habit I should kick.

As I purged my life of idolatrous un-Jesus-ey items, I was still leading my weekly classes and lectures at metaphysical establishments around greater Boston. It was my only source of income, and I liked having this chance to talk to people outside of church about spirituality. But now, in a growing and undeniable way, the haphazard beliefs of the people I taught started to drive me up the wall. Things that had always vaguely irked me—the lack of masculinity in the men; the abject refusal of people to take personal responsibility for their choices; the slavish insistence that various authors were paragons of spiritual virtue, despite glaring character flaws that came out with each new book—now drove me bananas. It seemed ridiculous, all of a sudden, all this gazing at crystals and trying to suck in the energy of the moon.

One Sunday I was the featured speaker at a Unity Church in New Hampshire. After my talk the female minister flew down from the choir loft wrapped in—I'm not kidding—gossamer. She led the congregation in acting out a closing song of prayer she was sure the universe had channeled through her. We formed a circle and they sang:

"I open my heart to the warmth of the sun" (the congregants flung their arms high above their heads like enthusiastic preschoolers taking their first class in creative movement) "and abandon my desires to the waves of the sea" (frantic, flailing hand motions mimicking waves fluttered all around me as I struggled to keep up, wondering what we were doing). "I yield my heart to the lu-u-*uv* of all humanit*eeee*," we affirmed, smiling benevolently around the circle. Some people took this opportunity to hug one another. "Thank you, Universe, for surrounding us with angelic light" (now we hugged ourselves). "I promise to love my brothers" (*"and sisters,"* two women added pointedly) "with all my m*iiight!*" Everyone around me jumped into the air with what appeared to be an attempt at glee.

All of a sudden my Christian friends seemed like the most normal people I knew.

THE UNITY DANCE of Angelic Light was a bit of a turning point for me. I rewrote my lectures, replacing all the quotes from the *Course* with words from the Bible, and giving them jaunty New Testament–inspired titles such as "Get Out of the Boat! It's Time to Walk on Water!" I was certain that if I introduced it gently enough, my audiences would soon realize, as I had, that the Bible was the perfect addition to every spiritual search.

One evening as I prepared for my lecture at Unicorn Books, a strange thought crossed my mind. Most of the places where I spoke worked on a fifty-fifty split with speakers, keeping half the proceeds. I'd never questioned this—I was building an audience, and this arrangement was the industry standard. But it suddenly occurred to me that half of the money I earned went to places that were rather anti-Jesus (and certainly anti-Bible), supporting a whole host of alternative paths I'd never even gotten around to: witchcraft, paganism, Christian Science (I was *terrible* at science), tarot, dragons, talking to the dead, celebrating *womyn* and our monthly cycles (not to mention bad singing and awkward interpretive dance). Considering the other lectures at Unicorn Books, and the titles on the store's spiritually expansive shelves, I wondered how God felt about my working so hard to support this other stuff. I might be talking about Jesus and taking him seriously, and tithing ten percent of my earnings to the collection basket at church, but I contributed five times that amount to new age establishments, some of which hated Jesus. This seemed like a potential problem.

"God," I prayed that night, "if this is an issue, show me. I don't want to use my talents to support things that aren't about you, but I have a full calendar of appearances booked for the next three months. Show me what you want me to do."

That night, for the first time ever, not a single person showed up for my lecture. That weekend's workshop at Open Circle Spirit Center was empty, as was the following week's feature event at the Upside Down Yoga Studio. I'd opened the door for God's input, and just like that, my budding career as a spiritual speaker was over.

Finally, I got it—I understood what Paul meant that night he suggested that I "just do Jesus." I renounced the *Course*, astrology, feng shui, psychic knowledge, and every other spiritual path I'd wandered down. It was a longish list, so this took a while. (I even went on Amazon.com to find the names of all the books whose tenets I'd blindly followed, seeking some sort of psychic or spiritual hope.) I asked God to forgive me for these things, acknowledging that even though it didn't feel like I was doing anything wrong at the time—I didn't rebel against Him on purpose—my choices took me off track for His best for my life, and I wanted to accept Jesus' offer to help me back on. I canceled the rest of my speaking schedule and told God that since this whole thing was His idea, it would be nice if He'd help me pay the rent.

Three weeks later I was sitting in a cube at a venture capital firm, making photocopies for a small hourly wage, certain that becoming a Christian was the worst thing that could happen to a person.

THAT'S WHEN MARK moved out.

"I don't know who you are anymore," he complained. "Or what you want from me."

"I told you what I want," I said. "I want to be married."

"Then I'm not the man for you," he said, dragging his duffel out to the car. "I hope you find him there among your Jesus people." I'm not sure why, but I'd always thought Mark would come around. It would have been so easy for God to do it that way, to transform Mark at the same time He was transforming me—it would be like a fairy-tale ending. Somehow, I thought there would be less heartache once I got on board with Jesus.

"WHAT IF THIS Jesus stuff is crap?" I asked Amy on the way to church that Sunday. "What if it's all just a big story and he *can't* make things better? What if he doesn't have any power and it's just a big hoax?"

"What are you talking about?" she said.

"I'm talking about my life! I had an okay life before Jesus—I had a boyfriend, a career, a plan. Now they're all gone. Where is the *abundance* stuff he promised? Where is my Impossibly Great Life?" Before she could respond, I added: "And don't give me that garbage about how the grass always looks greener on the other side, because that's not the case here. My life was good, and now it sucks, and Jesus hasn't fixed it."

"You're right," she conceded. "Your grass is pretty brown."

Chapter Seventeen

Total Immersion

I didn't know what to think about God's Only Begotten Son after this, so I declined to think of him at all—until a few weeks later when I wandered into an art installation at church and was won over by a seven-foot Jesus made entirely of chicken wire.

Chicken Wire Jesus was the final stop in a Good Friday exhibit of the Stations of the Cross. He was preceded by paintings and performance art and even a minimalist wood sculpture representing how he bore the Cross alone (or something like that; to be honest, I didn't quite get it). I wandered through the installations much like I'd wandered through the last year, ignoring the things I didn't understand, agreeing where I could, and wondering when God would fix my life.

As I approached this final station—thinking about how my feet hurt, looking forward to meeting Gwen and Amy afterward for a glass of wine—I was struck by the emptiness of the giant figure; He looked unfinished, like the early stages of an enormous papier-mâché. A small plaque explained the display, offering instructions for interaction: *Write down something that has been said about you, or something you've said about yourself, that you want Jesus to set you free from. Leave it here, and be free.* We handed around scraps of recycled paper, and little pencils like the ones you use to keep score in mini golf. Then our curator John, a real-life Jewish carpenter, declared: "If anyone is in Christ, he is a new creation; the old has gone, the new has come!" People around me scribbled words on paper, then stuffed them into Chicken Wire Jesus and walked away. Holding my crumpled piece in my palm, I wrote "NO ONE WILL EVER MARRY ME" and crushed it into a ball. Tears welled up in my eyes as the weight of all my hopelessness—my terror of being unwanted, unchosen, alone—pressed down on my chest. I hung back, trying to go last, wanting my paper to be on the top of this Jesus pile, as close to his attention as possible. It felt a little bit like hocus-pocus, this symbolic abandonment of my deepest fear. But if the Bible was true, this act would have real power (not just the power of my positive thinking or unstoppable human potentiality); this act was backed by the word of God, and His promise that giving my fear to Jesus would somehow set me free.

John's voice echoed through the room, repeating, over and over again, "If anyone is in Christ, he is a new creation; the old has gone, the new has come!"

That's when I got it: Jesus stood there, willing to take my garbage. But I had to give it to him, and I then had to leave it there and walk away. If I did, some miraculous work of God would follow, and that thing I left behind would be vanquished:

it would have no more power, it couldn't haunt me anymore. I could have a relationship with Jesus, instead of with my worst-case scenario. But to get that, I had to turn it over.

I stuffed my wadded-up paper ball in at the top of the Jesus heap, then turned and left the room. As I walked the few blocks to join my friends, I said it aloud, trying it on for size: "I am a new creation. The old has gone, the new has come!"

LATER THAT WEEK, I went to Paul and Pascha's house to talk about how confusing my life had gotten since I started following Jesus. My mind swam with all this new information, terms like "spiritual warfare" popping up all over the landscape of my life like so many weeds taking over my mental lawn. I was doing everything "right," but now that the high of having a new fun group of friends had worn off, I felt myself sinking back into the same pit of depression I'd slid into so many times before—walking down the street longing to be hit by a truck, wondering if anyone would notice if I hopped a train and moved to the West Coast. I was right back in the middle of the insatiable need to get away from myself, to stop piling pointless day upon pointless day, looking with disdain at everyone around me who soldiered on with no tangible hope that life might get any better. At my core, I was done soldiering on.

I described this to Paul and Pascha, and our friend Will who came to pray with us that day. I braced myself for a rousing pep talk about my unlimited potential and the need to keep my eyes on the prize, or (worse) a reminder of the streets of gold I'd walk in the afterlife as a reward for slugging through my mediocrity in this one; I didn't give a damn about their streets of gold.

But instead of pelting me with nuggets of biblical positive thinking to counter my angry soliloquy, Paul simply said, "Why don't we pray for you?" The phone rang and Pascha went to grab it. It was her parents, calling from California. "Let's go into the bedroom," Paul suggested. "Pascha needs to take this call."

Will, Paul, and I went into the bedroom, and my stomach began to churn, frustration stirring up inside of me like the early rumblings of a long-ignored volcano. It was too much to take, being there in the middle of their bedroom. The intimacy of their marriage—intimacy I couldn't seem to get to no matter what I did—surrounded me and I felt trapped by the walls, the giant bed, the love note taped on the wall; it was as if God was taunting me, reminding me of how empty and cold my life felt.

Paul and Will stood on either side of me, and Paul began to pray: "God," he said, placing a hand on my shoulder, "thank you that You love Trish. It sounds like she's pretty tormented right now, and so we ask You in Jesus' name to show us what the root of that is—reveal what's going on—and help us pray through that." Then, without warning, both of my hands—which had been clasped in a prayerful fold in front of me—formed hard fists and flew out to either side, punching both Will and Paul in the stomach.

"Omigod," I gasped. "I'm so sorry!" I wasn't, really. Something about punching them felt good. Suddenly, I was a little afraid of myself, wondering what I might do next.

"Well, God," Paul said with a wry smile, "I don't know all the details of Trish's story, but I'm going to take a wild guess and say that the problem here might be anger toward men. Trish, does that sound possible?"

"Ye-yes," I stammered, stunned by his good humor. How could he laugh when I just punched him? How could Will? I looked up at them slowly, astonished.

"I get the sense that you've been pretty badly hurt by some of the men in your past," Paul said, "and that it might be really helpful for you to forgive them."

"How do I do that?" It seemed odd that forgiving someone I'd dated ten years ago might help me *not* want to punch my guy friends now, but what the heck? It might be worth a shot.

"It's pretty straightforward," Paul explained. "You simply say, 'In the name of Jesus, I choose to forgive *x* for doing *y*.' You can add anything that comes to mind."

"Okay," I agreed, taking a big breath. "In Jesus' name, I choose to forgive Chip for cheating on me. I choose to forgive Josh for breaking my heart. I choose to forgive Tim for leading me on when he never planned to marry me. I choose to forgive Drew for being a selfish bisexual hedonist. I choose to forgive Mark for planning a future without me even while he said he loved me. I forgive them all. Amen." I looked up at Paul and Will, wondering what came next. The urge to punch them hadn't subsided.

"Um, Trish," Will said. "You were married before, right? Did you include that guy in your list?"

The muscles across the back of my shoulders stiffened. "Why would I ever do that?" I asked. "You don't know what happened. He doesn't deserve forgiveness."

"It's not about him," Paul said gently. "You don't have to feel all warm and fuzzy about him—or any of these guys. All you have to do is be willing to be free of the effects of what they did to you—you know, the stuff that left you wanting to punch other men. You have to trust God to avenge you, rather than hold on to all that hurt yourself."

"Fine," I spat at him, looking down at the floor. "God, I forgive my ex-husband for lying to me and forcing me to do whatever he wanted." Saying the words out loud was like puking foaming lava, the shame burning its way from my gut to the edges of my lips as I choked out each betrayal. "I forgive him for all the times he accused me of cheating on him, and the times he said no other man would ever have me," I continued. "I forgive him for telling me over and over again that I was the reason his life was so miserable. I forgive him for not being any of the things he promised." The lyrics from that song pulsed through my head: "How can I forget the times you lied to me? How can I forget the times you said no one would want me? What about that?"

"Why should I forgive him?" I demanded angrily. "He doesn't deserve it. He's the one who did all this stuff, why should I let him off the hook?"

"Because you can't punish him," Paul said gently. "But if you give this to Jesus, all those things you mentioned—they can't hurt you anymore; they'll heal. God will still know what happened," he assured me, "but you won't have to live with the aftermath."

Could that be true? I wondered, doubtful that I'd ever be "healed" (whatever that meant) from the ravages of my marriage. If I forgot, wouldn't that mean I could just go out and make the same stupid mistakes again? Didn't I need to remember to keep myself protected in the future? But nothing I'd tried in the past to protect myself had worked.

"In Jesus' name," I prayed, pushing deeper into this Jesus thing than I ever thought I'd go. "I choose to forgive my ex-husband. I'm counting on you, God," I continued, "to make sure I don't ever do something as stupid as that again."

"Do you think maybe you need to forgive yourself for being with him?" Will asked.

"I wonder," Paul added, handing me a wad of tissue, "if perhaps you need to forgive God?"

I stared at them, dumbfounded. When would this be finished? Did I have to forgive *everybody* who had ever known my ex-husband before I could move on? *"Fine,"* I said again. "In Jesus' name, I forgive myself for marrying my ex-husband. God, please forgive me for being so stupid," I added spontaneously, my words connecting with genuine feeling for the first time all night. "I'm so sorry I did that. I'm so sorry I tried to force you to make it work. And God, I forgive You for letting it get so bad. Thank you for rescuing me. Amen."

"Trish," Paul responded, placing his hand back on my shoulder (but still standing, I noticed, beyond the reach of my strike zone), "as your brothers in Christ, we pronounce you forgiven, in Jesus' name. We bless you to know that you're fully free of all you have confessed. And we bless you to know that the things you have forgiven are in your past; we bind any power they may have had over you and bless you to live as a new creation. In Jesus' name, Amen."

"Amen," Will and I echoed.

I thanked them awkwardly, then followed them back out to

the living room where Pascha was setting out dinner for some other members of our group who had come by. I cringed, expecting an embarrassing blow-by-blow of my transgressions, for either Paul or Will to say, "Man—we didn't know what a mess you were!" But nothing at all was said. Nothing. And in the days and weeks to come, neither Paul nor Will mentioned anything I'd said or done that day, or treated me any differently. It was as if the minute we finished praying, they'd forgotten the whole thing.

On my way home that night, for the first time in weeks, I didn't wonder what would happen if I walked in front of a bus. That, to me at least, seemed like progress; a bit of a miracle, if you will.

AT AMY'S PRODDING, I decided to get baptized. Publicly, in one of those total immersion tanks Evangelicals are so fond of. I wasn't sure I was ready to step—or sink, as the case may be—further into this life with Jesus, and Amy knew it. But she insisted, over and over, that there was power in baptism, that making a public declaration of my faith would help me, even if I didn't understand how or why.

"But I've already been baptized," I told her. "Remember—I used to be Catholic."

"How much do you remember about that day?" she asked.

"Exactly nothing," I admitted. "But I'm sure my parents have a picture."

"That doesn't matter," she said, laughing. "It's not about producing evidence; it's about making a decision and backing it up with action. If you stand up for Jesus, that's like standing up to the bully on the playground, a way of telling Satan to back off and leave you alone. You only have to do it once, but you have to do it."

"Fine," I conceded. "I'll get dunked." I didn't believe her in the least that it would make the slightest bit of difference.

THEY ANNOUNCED THE next baptism, and I signed up. In the required preparatory class, Pastor Chuck joked about how we all had great timing and told horror stories of unheated water in the trough during the previous winter's ceremony. I expected the class to be filled with Bible verses we needed to memorize and a harsh scrutiny of our sins (I'm not sure what made me think this—nothing at the Vineyard thus far involved either memorization or harsh scrutiny—I guess I was still waiting for the other shoe to drop). But after Pastor Chuck explained a few Bible passages and why the Vineyard believes in baptism (none of which we needed to commit to memory) he handed out a sheet covering the major topic of our class: what to wear while immersing oneself for Jesus. There was a long list of things to be avoided: white clothing topped the list, followed by bikinis, sheer fabrics, and (incredibly) macramé.

ON THE MORNING of my baptism, I was in a foul mood. I hated everyone, and I was quite sure everyone hated me. I was also sure that I didn't care, that I'd just as soon spend the day holed up in my bedroom, reading the latest John Irving novel and trying not to kick my dog.

Amy called at noon to tell me she'd pick me up at two o'clock; I told her not to bother. She told me she was coming anyway, that she didn't care what kind of mood I was in, and that I was being dunked in the name of Jesus today if she had to kidnap me and wrestle me into my tub herself.

"It won't work," I told her. "We have no spout. The only way to fill our tub is via the tiny shower head, and if you planned to do that you'd have had to start yesterday."

"I don't care," she said. "I'll stick your head in the Brita if I have to. I'm coming there at two—you're going to be ready, and you're going to be baptized. *Capice?*"

"Fine," I conceded.

When we arrived at the Baptist Church whose sanctuary we borrowed for such events (the school gym not lending itself to adult dunking that didn't involve a softball tossed at a target), I was still in a bad mood, and Amy was oblivious, as if God promised her a puppy or a new car if she got me into the building and under water on schedule. She ignored my scowl, and the litany of snarky observations I kept up as we made our way into the building. We were told to head down to the basement to change clothes, then break off into pairs to confess our sins and receive prayer. I had been such a snot all morning that I was rather certain I wouldn't be able to fit in all my confessing in the allotted half hour; Amy assured me that God was quite efficient when need be.

First, though, I headed into the bathroom and changed into my baptism clothes: a one-piece bathing suit, covered by my gray Wheaton T-shirt and denim shorts. I looked more like I was headed to a beach volleyball tournament than to receive a blessed sacrament, but that seemed to be the case with everyone around me. I saw two guys in Hawaiian-print trunks, and a girl wearing a bathing suit and overalls. I broke my first reluctant smile of the day at the sight of a man who paired his bathing suit with a dress shirt and tie; he wanted his pictures to look a little formal. "It will make my grandmother so happy," he explained.

Amy and I found a quiet corner, and as she promised, we got through my confession of negativity rather quickly. Then she prayed blessings over me the likes of which I'd never heard before, quoting passages I vaguely remembered from the Old Testament about coming under God's covering and being blessed going in and blessed going out. She asked God to command His angels concerning me, and thanked Him for the good work He was finishing in my life. I didn't understand what she was saying, but it sounded so good that the knot in my stomach loosened for the first time in what felt like weeks. I still didn't think this baptism thing would do any good, or that it would make any discernible difference in my life. But praying made Amy so happy that it was worth it, just to hear her words flying in the air around me and to see how happy Jesus made her.

We finished praying, and I fell in line with the rest of the about-to-be-baptized, following them into the church sanctuary, where a crowd of friends and well-wishers filled the pews, singing a song about the glory of the Lord. My mind drifted off as two guys and then the girl in overalls offered brief explanations about why they were here today and how they came to follow Jesus, then waded down into the pool and went under. I wasn't paying attention; I'm not sure why. I wasn't bored, just disconnected, like I was sitting in a school assembly on first aid or the importance of not drinking and driving, trying to look attentive while my mind wandered.

"My name is Trish," I said when my turn came. "I've always

believed in God, I guess, in some way or another. But I always made it clear that I didn't think of Him the way you do; that I wasn't one of *those* Christians who believed that Jesus is the only path to God. Well I guess I'm here today to publicly change my mind; to say to the world, 'Yes, I believe that now.'" It was the truth, I realized—whether I "felt" it in that moment or not. I'd seen enough to believe that Jesus was the real deal, that he had the answers I'd been searching for. I still wasn't sure what this meant for my life. But it was refreshing to realize that my spiritual state wasn't dependent on my emotions, that my relationship with Jesus wouldn't crumble just because I had a mood swing or thought Amy's insistence on my getting baptized was a little silly. It was nice that finally the truth wasn't dependent upon how I felt about it.

I waded into the pool. Despite Chuck's promises, the water was pretty cold. Chelsea, our women's pastor, stood on one side of me, Amy on the other. Chelsea asked me a series of questions: "Trish, do you commit your life to the leadership of God the Father?"

"I do."

"By believing in his sacrifice on the Cross, do you receive the forgiveness of your sins by way of Jesus Christ, God the Son?"

"I do."

"Do you ask for empowering for a God-pleasing life from God the Holy Spirit?"

"I do."

"Then, Trish," Chelsea continued, "I baptize you in the name of the Father, the Son, and the Holy Spirit." She and Amy put their hands behind my back and lowered me into the water; I grabbed my nose at the last minute so I didn't come up choking and spitting. Then I was up again, soaking wet. A quick glance at the clapping crowd, and I was out of the pool and wrapped in a towel in the back room, with dozens of people hugging and congratulating me. This I didn't get at all; it wasn't like I had done anything special, anything any one of them couldn't or hadn't already done. I accepted their warm wishes the way I'd accept the autograph of some obscure Scandinavian actor, thinking, *I'm not sure why you're giving me this, but I guess the polite thing to do is play along.* As soon as I could extricate myself from the soggy mob, I grabbed my bag of dry clothing and ran to the bathroom, anxious to be warm, dry, and somewhere—anywhere—else.

But my baptismal duty was not yet fulfilled. After we were dunked and dried, we were supposed to go back to the basement, where members of the church prayer team would be there to pray for us to receive a second baptism—the baptism of the Holy Spirit. I'd been around long enough to know what this was, how people's bodies twitched and some prayed in tongues. I was ambivalent about this; it didn't scare me, but I didn't much care if it happened. I couldn't see any upside to praying in some garbled language. And as for the shaking and falling over, there didn't seem to be much point in it. I'd seen people writhing on the floor at various times over the past year, but none of them seemed any different when they got back up again. If being knocked over by God didn't *change* you somehow, I thought, what was the point?

Nevertheless, I headed down to the basement. Anonymous people came by and prayed for me, touching my shoulder, my forehead, my feet. One person even prayed for my eyes and ears, asking God to open my senses so I could see and hear Him. Then Juan, one of the more enthusiastic members of the prayer team, prayed for me to receive the baptism of the Holy Spirit. I stood there, eyes closed, starting to sway from fatigue as much as anything supernatural. Suddenly I fell, someone caught me, and then I was lying on the floor, surrounded by people mumbling in tongues and thanking God. "More Lord," they said. "More Holy Spirit." My right leg started to bang against the floor, and I felt like I was doing crunches, my abdominal muscles clenching and releasing like a garbage disposal, chewing me up from the inside. I heard voices praising God and I thought about how much I wanted to get out of there, how much the leg banging and ab crunching hurt. It didn't feel like God; it felt like I'd landed in some bizarre hazing ritual. When the prayer team moved on to greener pastures and the coast was clear, I got up, gathered my wet clothes from the table, and headed upstairs to beg Amy to take me home.

Nothing profound happened that day, at least from what I could tell at the time. But I was committed, officially on the Jesus team. The snake dreams dwindled, and that alone seemed worth it. When I look back, it's clear that, somehow, that dunking gave me new ammunition against the depressing thoughts that had dogged me. It was as if I upped my coverage under Jesus' spiritual insurance program and now was protected and assured reimbursement when I had a spiritual fender bender or even a head-on collision. My faith was still shaky, but it had substance. I watched carefully, waiting for Jesus to rescue me.

PART III

Enduring

Chapter Eighteen

Tending the Flock

Paul and Pascha's small group grew to over thirty, and they announced that the time had come for us to break up into subgroups that were actually small. Unbelievably, I was asked to colead one of these offshoots. I wasn't sure I was ready for such an undertaking, but my ambivalence was overcome by my inherent love of leading things. The truth was, I'd spent my whole life cheering on groups of people who were far ahead of me in understanding and talent: I was elected captain of our state champion high school gymnastics team despite the fact that I couldn't do gymnastics, and president of my college dance company even though I hadn't taken a single ballet class until I was almost nineteen. And if my years of new age practice had refined any of my inner qualities, it was the ability to wing it when I didn't know what I was doing. I assumed that if I worked hard to catch up and showered our new group with enthusiasm, things would work out fine.

I was paired with our friend Will (the guy who had prayed for me with Paul the day that I'd punched them). A lifelong Christian who had studied the Bible since kindergarten, Will knew not only my deepest secrets, he knew the Bible like the back of his hand. He quoted verses from memory, whereas I was forever saying things like "Isn't there someplace, in one of the Gospels, maybe, where Jesus says something like 'things tend to work out for good people'?"

"You mean, Romans 8:28?" Will would respond. "Where Paul says, 'All things work for good for those who love God and are called according to his purpose'?"

"Yeah," I'd reply sheepishly. "That's the one."

Despite my lack of Bible savvy, our small group exploded. Will and I soon had over twenty members crowding into our host's living room on Wednesday nights, each with a dazzling array of personal and interpersonal crises besieging us, vying for our attention, and stretching our faith. My friend Kevin, who attended another church, marveled, "Let me get this straight: you're divorced, unemployed, living in a tenement-quality apartment under an assumed name, and people are coming to *you* for advice on how to run their lives?" He had a point. It amazed me that so many people thought my advice might somehow help them in their situation; even more amazing was how often, when I opened my mouth to admit I had nothing helpful to say, something profound emerged: an idea or suggestion or encouraging word I never would have thought of on my own. It might not be raising the dead, but it was something.

WILL AND I met every Monday night to plan that week's group and pray. We'd face each other on two rolling office chairs in his lab at Harvard and talk about our group. It felt a little bit like we'd adopted twenty kids, and were learning on the fly how to parent them. We developed an unofficial agreement over the course of those weeks: I pastored our group members—meeting with them for coffee, finding out how their lives were going—and Will pastored me. He spent hours answering my questions about how this Jesus thing worked—calming me down when I was hysterical about American soldiers taken hostage in Iraq or a family friend whose husband was killed in a car accident, helping me figure out one could believe in the saving power of Jesus in the midst of that kind of suffering.

"You realize, don't you," my friend Heather asked me one day, "that in the history of our church, every guy and girl who have led a small group together have gotten married?" I hadn't realized. This was the most difficult part of the whole adventure for me—this undefined teamwork Will and I jumped into, leaning on each other with no architectural plan for the relationship we created. We were joined by this small group in a way that was unlike any relationship I'd ever had; after all, how many friendships involve the spiritual care and maintenance of two-dozen other people? I had no grid or blueprint for how to make it work. I just knew that Will and I were somehow supposed to keep each other afloat, and get our flock of sheep across this lake of spiritual questions we were all bobbing around in.

When I prayed about our unorthodox relationship, I always got the same picture: a television with a screen filled with static. Beyond the static, I could just make out the show playing: the NBC hit *Friends*. *Underneath all the distracting static,* I told myself, *we're just friends.* That didn't make it easier, but at least it was a definition.

On the flip side of all this angst was the rather astonishing way God showed up in our group, working miracles in our midst. They tumbled out one after another, almost too fast for us to process:

A few months after we started meeting, Amy was diagnosed with a severe colon disorder. We prayed for her for the next few days, after which her doctor called her to say, "I'm sorry, we made a mistake diagnosing your tests. Your condition is treatable; expect to feel better soon." And she did.

Four months into her second pregnancy, my sister, Meg, showed signs of premature labor. I told her we'd pray for "Baby Lumpy" (as my nephew called the baby)—and ask God to make this pregnancy go well. We prayed that little Lumpy would settle in for the long haul and enjoy her comfy surroundings. To her doctors' amazement, Meg not only reverted to a normal pregnancy, carrying Lumpy to term, she went *past* her due date. Finally, exhausted by gestation and fearful she might burst, Meg phoned me one day, begging, "Call your people off!" Two days later Lily came into the world, healthy, happy, and miraculous in that new-baby kind of way, shrieking whenever anyone dared to call her Lumpy.

We saw things like this all the time. When we prayed for Jennifer's knee, she wasn't just healed—she ran the Boston marathon the following spring. When we asked God to stop the pain of Pete's chronic kidney stones, he felt them dissolve. Some weeks felt like a miracle fest as people reported what happened to them that week—family rifts healed, roommate problems solved, impossible tests passed with flying colors. Coming together on Wednesday nights was like watching the Book of Acts (the one describing all the miracles that happened as the Apostles traveled around talking about Jesus) in real life, as Jesus changed our lives in tangible ways, encouraging our faith in him and our connection to one another.

And praying in our group wasn't some odious, mandatory chore—it was fun. Everyone brought different levels of "churchy-ness" to the group, and each of us prayed in our own unique manner: Madeline prayed in her native French when she was particularly impassioned about a subject; Keith (who was a "PK"—preacher's kid) prayed words from scripture; Sean prayed anatomically correct prayers for physical healing based on his years studying muscular systems. The rest of us chimed in as God prompted, filling in around the edges.

"Jesus, heal Will's trapezius," Sean prayed one night, laying his hand on Will's aching shoulder.

"Yes, Lord," Kai agreed in his distinctive Korean accent. "Heal the . . . the . . . upper back!"

"Heal the *latissimus dorsi*," Sean asked.

"Yes, Lord, heal the middle back—the middle back!"

"And the *thoracolumbar fascia*," Sean finished.

"The lower back, the lower back, Lord! Heal it!" Kai implored. By that time we were all laughing so hard at their comedic tag-team effort, it was hard to continue.

"I'm not sure what you guys were praying back there," Will said, "but my back feels a little better."

We also saw personal transformations, as people came out of the various levels of pain and turmoil that had prodded them into church in the first place: a shy woman named Jane wandered into our group one night and sat right by the door, clutching her coat and purse to her chest like one of us might wrestle it from her. She could barely say her name during the icebreaker, her eyes darting around the room under a heavy cloud of bangs that obscured a good portion of her face. I wanted to reach out to her, but she looked like she might bolt if we so much as spoke in her direction. Will and I prayed for Jane after the group that night, and for months afterward. Over time she grew more comfortable and would even laugh when someone cracked a funny joke. By the time our group ended, she was an integral part of every joke, every fun event, and every group picture. Eventually, Jane headed up our church's outreach program at the Cambridge housing projects, speaking in front of huge crowds, running her own small group, and even dressing up in costume from time to time to act out stories in the Bible to make them come alive.

Kelly came in racked with emotional pain, tormented by nightmares and voices in her head. She was overweight, hated her job, and drove a car without heat that leaked exhaust into the cabin and required her to drive with the window open all year long. We prayed for Kelly. For the longest time, it seemed like nothing happened, but we kept praying, asking God to improve her life, set her free from depression, lead her to a new job and a car that would pass inspection. Slowly, things improved.

Kelly found a mentor who helped her with her eating, and she lost over fifty pounds. Her moods lifted as she caught a glimpse that more might be possible for her, and her doctors found a medication that worked for her depression. A new job opened up. A year after our group ended, Kelly walked into church and I didn't even recognize her. Her eyes glowed. She smiled. I heard her laugh and saw a guy walk by and check her out. She was an entirely different person; *a new creation*, as they say.

There were also profound answers for people we barely knew. One night, a quiet girl named Gina raised her hand. This was Gina's fourth week in our group; to my knowledge she hadn't spoken to anyone for more than a minute. She was so skittish she looked like she might disintegrate if you touched her; we were never sure from one week to the next if she'd come back. "When I first came here," she said, "I didn't have any friends. I was wondering why I should bother living, and even thought about killing myself but I was afraid I'd mess that up, too. I asked God for help, and He sent me here. You all have been so nice to me, I feel like maybe God wants me to live." She smiled out at us as we stared back, stunned by her confession. Neither Will nor I had suspected that she might be suicidal; we didn't even know her last name. Our group was so big that it was impossible for us to keep up with everyone, and the squeaky wheels were definitely the ones getting the grease. That Gina floated among us for almost a month, deciding whether or not to end her life without our noticing was mortifying; I wanted to curl up in a ball and weep with shame. But then God swooped in to rescue me from my mental self-flagellation, reminding me, *But, Trish, I knew.*

Oh yeah. God. He knew. That seemed like a good thing. As Gina spoke, making eye contact with her fellow group members for the very first time, I realized that it was God who made her feel safe here, who made her feel loved. Had I known what she was wrestling with, I would have freaked out—we had no training in suicide prevention, we didn't know what she needed. But God knew, and He took care of it. That was how, I remembered, Will and I prayed for the group to operate. Sort of a *Field of Dreams* vision, believing that *if we build it, He will come.* I lifted up a silent prayer of my own, thanking God for taking care of us.

I didn't have time to process much of what went on in our group. It all happened so fast—crises and miracles piling up on top of each other like so many unread issues of the daily paper—I didn't have time to form a theory or opinion about why or how this was all taking place. It felt a bit like I'd landed in a secret Jesus subculture, dramatically different from the world going on all around us. But everyone around me—Paul and Pascha, Will, Amy—seemed to think that all this praying and seeing miracles were normal events in daily life with Jesus, and my reading of the Bible backed this up. So I believed them, diving into the deep end of faith again and again, trusting that someone would teach me how to swim if I got in over my head.

But still, in the middle of all these miracles, when my family or roommates asked what we did on Wednesday nights, I stuttered and stammered, having no idea how to describe this new world I'd entered. "We read the Bible a bit," I'd say. "And sometimes we eat cake." Then they'd look at me kind of funny, unsure why I devoted so much energy to what sounded like a

Christian book club. I never quite got the hang of translating our little world of prayer and miracles into everyday language. I sensed somehow that this strange new world I'd entered had to be seen to be believed, and I wasn't brave enough to chance the bizarre, awkward looks people were likely to give me if I admitted that my new best friend was Jesus. I needed to get used to the idea a bit myself, first. "I'm a Christian," I practiced saying. "I read the Bible, I follow Jesus." It sounded a little odd, even to me.

Chapter Nineteen

Forty Days of Faith

That February, I went on my first church retreat, where Pastor Dave announced an expanded version of Lent we'd undertake together in the spring: he called it "Forty Days of Faith." For forty days, he explained, we would pray and fast together, asking Jesus to answer the deepest desires of our hearts and bless us in tangible, personal ways. Noting that the Bible is clear that God likes it when we pray specific prayers (rather than mumble vague requests that life somehow work out), Dave asked the provocative question, "What do you want Jesus to do for you?"

My answer was crystal clear—and embarrassing. While I was sure everyone around me would ask Jesus to bring world peace, that's not what came to mind for me. What I wanted Jesus to do, more than anything else, was bring me a husband. I hadn't asked him for this specifically before this; after our conversation in Buffalo, I figured that he knew. But now the question was on the table: What did I want Jesus to do for me? And there was only one answer.

Dave passed out sheets of paper on which to write our prayers, and I etched HUSBAND into the page in the tiniest letters possible, covering it with my hand. It felt good to admit—even if only to God—that this was what I wanted, that this was, in fact, the single biggest hope/fear/worry/dream of my thirty-something life. I imagined a handsome prince walking through the doors of our church, making a beeline straight for me . . .

I was jolted from my reverie when Dave told us to partner up with someone, share our responses, and pray for one another. *You must be kidding,* I thought. The blood drained from my face as I looked around the table at all my cherished friends and thought, *No way.* I didn't want anyone to know how much this bothered me, and besides—this just wasn't the done thing in church circles. I thought back to a show I'd seen once on Christian television about singleness, led by a woman who said that wanting a spouse was like wanting dessert after dinner: sometimes you get it, often you don't. "It's not for everyone," she said. "It's not something God promises or that any of us need to survive." She encouraged us to look to the glorious work of the Apostle Paul, how he delighted in his gift of celibacy and labored fruitfully for the Lord. If we were truly spiritual, she'd insinuated, we wouldn't even need a workshop like this; all we'd need to be happy was Jesus. Then she smiled at us with a beatific smile, satisfied to have set us straight about what was and was not okay to ask for in her version of the kingdom of God. She,

I couldn't help but notice, was married. I wanted to rip her face off.

I knew what she *meant* to say: don't make an idol out of marriage, don't use it as a litmus test for God. I understood that God was not a vending machine or an online prayer delivery service. But I couldn't ignore the promise in the Bible that Jesus came to give us abundant life, or the compelling stories of how God brought men and women together: Adam and Eve, Abraham and Sarah, Jacob and Rebekah, Boaz and Ruth. In the book of Ecclesiastes, King Solomon even pointed out that two are better than one: "a chord of three strands is not easily broken." *That* was what I wanted—a marriage uniting me, my husband, and Jesus: strong and unbreakable. I had a hard time believing that God looked at Adam and said, "It is not good for man to be alone," yet looked at me and said, "But you, on the other hand . . ."

Slightly panicked, I grabbed Amy, the one person I could count on to humor me—knowing that even she might advise me to use this opportunity for something bigger than whining about my love life. I fully expected to be reprimanded for my selfish prayer; I hoped Amy, at least, would be kind. Dragging her off to a far corner where no one could overhear, I blurted, "IwantJesustobring meahusbandandIwantthatmorethanworldpeaceandIknowit'snot coolandthatitprobablymakesmeanawfulpersonbutthereitis."

She looked at me wide-eyed and said, "Me too."

That day, as Amy and I prayed, we felt something unexpected—Jesus' enthusiastic reception of our request. It's as if he said, *I know this is what you want . . . thanks for including me in the process.* Encouraged by this, we made the most of it. We told

Jesus that if he was in charge of bringing our husbands, we had a few suggestions for characteristics our Mr. Rights might have.

"Jesus, we'd like handsome husbands," I began.

"And fun husbands!" Amy added, grinning at the absurdity of presenting Jesus with the prayer equivalent of an online dating profile.

"Bring us husbands who are wise and loving..." I continued.

"... and sexy!" Amy added.

"... and single," I finished, "with no weird habits!"

"Jesus, we want husbands who love you, men who recognize us as the wives you created for them and who think that's the best news ever. Amen."

"Amen." I agreed. We closed our prayer in a fit of giggles, feeling like we'd stumbled on the holy grail of romantic happiness. For the first time in months, I was sure, beyond a shadow of a doubt, that my husband was on his way; all I needed to do was pray him in.

FOR THE NEXT forty days, Amy and I believed. We brought our request for husbands to God each morning (and each afternoon and evening, during every lunch break, at every stoplight...) waiting for Him to answer. I walked to work each morning thanking God, telling Him of my great expectations:

"Lord, thank you that you have a wonderful husband for me. I know that you'll bring us together at the perfect time—you won't let us miss each other or end up with other people. Thank you for our fun time dating, our romantic proposal, our beau-

tiful wedding, and our intimate, passionate honeymoon." I'd
pause when other pedestrians passed me on the sidewalk; they
didn't need to know about my intimate, passionate honeymoon.
"God, thank you for the children we'll have," I'd continue, "and
our amazing life together. Thank you in advance for all of
this—you are an awesome, miracle-working God, and you can
make this happen. Amen." Then I'd look around the train station, wondering if any of the men I saw might be my husband.

In addition to all our prayers, we fasted, as if giving up something for Lent. I fasted from coffee, Amy fasted from ice cream;
we told ourselves (and Jesus) that we wanted our husbands more
than we wanted a grande mocha latte or a Blizzard. On Fridays,
we—along with the rest of the church—fasted from food, not
eating from dinner Thursday night until dinner Friday evening.
At first, this felt a bit new agey to me, one more way of modify-
ing my behavior to try to force God to bring me what I wanted.
But as the weeks went on, I saw it differently. In the Bible, Jesus
talks about fasting and prayer as two parts of a greater whole,
mutually dependent ways of seeking God's presence and His
favor. But God wasn't, I realized, obligated to do anything in
response to my hunger. As I squirmed through caffeine with-
drawal on weekday mornings and hunger pangs on long Friday
afternoons, I realized that my real craving, my real hunger, was
for a relationship with the living God who cared about my life,
the God who created me with this urge to be a wife and had
the power to fulfill it. And sometimes, I realized, I needed to
clear out all the other little stuff that clamored for my attention—like wondering what and where I'd eat next—to focus on
what I really wanted, what would satisfy me for more than a few

hours. The Gospels described how Jesus told a woman standing by a well, "Everyone who drinks this water will be thirsty again, but whoever drinks the water I give him will never thirst. Indeed, the water I give him will become in him a spring of water welling up to eternal life." When I fasted, I got a glimpse of that *something more* Jesus spoke of, a sense of satisfaction and wholeness I didn't find anywhere else. I started to look forward to Fridays; in some inexplicable way, they brought me closer to God. It sounds hokey. It felt hokey. But these Fridays brought me a hope I'd never felt before, a sense of partnering with God to bring about His will for my life.

WHEN THE FORTY days ended, our church had a big party, celebrating Easter and spring and all Jesus was doing in our lives, after which Amy and I went home—both of us alone, dateless, and entirely single. We should have been devastated. But it was clear God was doing *something*, edging both of us closer to what it might look like to be somebody's wife.

Amy, a quintessential tomboy, felt an unprecedented compulsion to wear skirts and jewelry, even to get her nails done. She called me one day, exasperated, "Where do you go to buy one of those girly bags?" she demanded.

"You mean a *purse?*"

"Yes," she replied, disgusted. "God told me I need to buy a purse."

I, on the other hand, did not get the makeover–shopping spree path to wifely readiness. I needed an internal makeover—a complete overhaul of how I thought about myself, men, and relationships. Amy's life was redecorated; mine got a down-to-the-studs remodel.

In the Gospel of Matthew, Jesus warned his followers, "Do not give dogs what is sacred; do not throw your pearls to pigs. If you do, they may trample them under their feet, and then turn and tear you to pieces." This line haunted me. I was forever throwing my pearls (my body, my mind, my heart, my soul) in front of pigs, hoping against hope I wouldn't be trampled. I'd spent the past decade in front of a swine stampede, begging God to *change* whatever pig happened to mow me down. This was not, Jesus told me, how things were supposed to work. The time had come to raise my standards.

The very idea of *standards* regarding whom I would and would not date was new to me. Aside from my astrological considerations, I'd had no definitive parameters to rule some men in and others out in the quest for my hand (too judgmental, my spiritual training argued); the truth was, I didn't think it was much of a quest. I'd read too many magazine articles about the shortage of available men, their reluctance to commit, and how my chances of spinsterhood loomed closer with every passing birthday. At thirty-four, I felt like I was caught in a game of relationship musical chairs, terrified of being the hapless unchosen woman left standing at the end of the game. Scared of being "out," I assumed that any man interested in me *must* be sent by God, even if he showed up looking more like swine than royalty. I didn't know how to fix this.

For starters, Jesus said, *this is* not *musical chairs.* He was displeased, it turns out, with my assumption that marriage was a crapshoot in which he had only a passing interest. After all, in musical chairs, it doesn't matter which chair you end up in, just that you're not left standing when the music stops. This was pretty much how I'd approached dating—any chair would do. But Jesus suggested the radical idea that not any chair would do; that he had a special, specific chair, just for me.

"That's fine," I told him, exasperated. "But what do you want me to *do?*" My previous spiritual endeavors had kept me busy—moving furniture, worrying about what might happen when Mercury was in retrograde, affirming my unity with the divine flow of the universe. Now that I'd given all that up, I had no idea what to do all day, or even how to think of myself. My old goal was to become a "Fascinating Woman"—Jayme's phrase for the ultimate manifestation of feminine power. I'd struggled to be witty and sophisticated, alluring and seductive. I thought these were good things, qualities men enjoyed. Looking back, though, I realized how on the prowl I'd been all that time, how subtly aggressive my choices and actions were: scanning the left hand of men to determine their eligibility; dressing, acting, thinking seductively; working to draw male attention my way. *Ick.* At the same time, though, I didn't know who I was without the flirtatious sexuality or the sparkling repartee; I was terrified that this Jesus plan would make me into one of those Utah women in a prim flowered dress with a long braid down my back. I didn't want to be that woman. But I also didn't understand why I could never close the deal—what was better than fascinating?

Exquisite, Jesus told me. *Like the pearl of great price.* The pearl parable again. Over the next few days, Jesus told me that I was like that fine pearl—precious, unique, crafted by God, a gem that the right man would search for and esteem. *Pearls don't start out that way,* he reminded me, *they submit to a process. Pearls are made exquisite, and they are worth everything a man has once they're done.*

A few days later I saw a catalog from Tiffany's, featuring a string of pearls for $95,000. And I heard Jesus say, *Someone will buy those pearls. They will walk through those vaulted doors, count the cost, pay the price, and treasure those pearls forever.* I thought of the "faux" pearls a friend bought for $4.59 at the mall to wear as a bridesmaid—how piles of the plastic replicas fell onto the floor, where anyone could pick them up, try them on, put them back, or steal them. They were worth almost nothing. Thinking of my years of dating, I was appalled at how close I came to permanently ending up like those plastic fakes—easily replaceable, untreasured. "Lord," I prayed, "make me a real pearl."

THE MOST ROMANTIC story in the Bible is the Old Testament book of Ruth. It is *the* fairy tale of scripture, a whole book about God miraculously bringing a man and a woman together against almost impossible odds. The story reveals how a good man acts when he is interested in a woman—taking the initiative, making his intentions clear, pushing obstacles out of the way like so many pieces of red tape.

When we first meet her, Ruth's life is in shambles. Her husband is dead and her country is in famine. Her mother-in-law, Naomi—also a widow—plans to return to her homeland of Bethlehem. They have no family and face the bleak prospect of trying to survive with no protection or support. Against Naomi's urging, Ruth decides to go with her to Bethlehem. She makes a promise of fidelity to Naomi, declaring, "Where you go I will go, and where you stay I will stay. Your people will be my people and your God my God."

They arrive in the new land as the barley and wheat crops are being harvested. It was traditional in those times for the harvesters to leave a certain amount behind in the fields for the poor to gather. So Ruth goes out to glean what she can behind the harvesters and ends up in a field owned by Boaz, a wealthy relative of Naomi's deceased husband. Boaz notices her in the field and inquires about her to his foreman, who reports that she is gathering food for her widowed mother-in-law. Impressed by this, Boaz approaches Ruth and blesses her. He gives special instructions to his workers to leave extra for her to gather. When Ruth returns to Naomi with their food, she tells her how kind Boaz was, how he took special care of her.

"That man is our close relative," Naomi exclaims, "he is one of our kinsmen-redeemers." In that day and age, a kinsman-redeemer was the nearest relative of a deceased husband who could marry the husband's widow and thus save her from a life of poverty. Naomi tells Ruth to stay in Boaz's field for the duration of the harvest, knowing he will watch after her.

After the harvest, when the men are threshing out the wheat and barley, Naomi suggests to Ruth that she ask Boaz to act as her kinsman-redeemer. She sends Ruth to the threshing floor in her finest attire, with instructions to hide there until the men have fallen asleep. When Boaz is asleep, Ruth lays at his feet. In observing this custom, Ruth was asking Boaz to fulfill his role as her kinsman-redeemer, either by marrying her or by finding someone else to do so.

"Who are you?" Boaz asks when he wakes up.

"Spread the corner of your garment over me," Ruth responds, requesting his covering and protection. "You are my kinsman-redeemer."

Boaz is thrilled. That very day, he goes to the one other man who is a closer relative to Naomi than he. The other man does not want to marry the widow as it will endanger his own estate, so Boaz redeems Ruth, taking her as his wife. Their son, Obed, is part of the lineage of King David, and, ultimately, Jesus.

I read this story over and over and over again—underlining, highlighting, searching for clues about what Jesus wanted me to know. It was like a new type of husband wish list, but instead of physical qualities and random interests, this list focused on the *kind* of man God would send to save the day, the qualities of his nature and character. I wanted this kind of man—a man who had his own life together. A man who recognized me as wonderful, precious, and desirable, who acted with clear intention to earn my respect and love. A man who saw beyond my past and wanted to build a new life with me; a man who made his intentions known to the whole community and claimed me as his own. I prayed about this, begging God to make good on His word. This story was in the Bible for a reason, I believed— to give me a tangible example of God providing a spectacular husband for one of his daughters. I wanted to make sure God knew I was taking my place in the "prepare me for my husband" line.

IN THE MIDST of this self-analysis, I realized that I still hadn't done much to sort out my biggest question about the Bible's teaching on relationships—God's supposed prohibition against premarital sex. I still didn't understand why it was such a big deal. If two people were in love, committed to one another, and wanted to sleep together, I reasoned, why wouldn't God bless that?

Now that I'd read the Bible, I had to admit that God doesn't equivocate on the matter—in the sixty-six books of the Bible, He is remarkably consistent: *I created sex for marriage. That's it.* The whole first section of Proverbs warns of the dire consequences of extramarital intimacy, admonishing each man to marry young and enjoy his wife: "May her breasts satisfy you always, may you ever be captivated by her love." In Deuteronomy, God decrees that newly married men should stay home from battle for a full year to learn how to pleasure their wives. *Is this how Christian couples make up for all those months of premarital chastity?* I wondered. Throughout the Bible, God equates marital sex with satisfaction and happiness, while unmarried sex "leads down to the grave." King Solomon cautions, "Do not awaken love before its time," repeatedly in Song of Songs, and almost every chapter of the New Testament warns of the dangers of sexual immorality, equating it with spiritual suicide. God's solution to our sexual urges, the Apostle Paul said, is marriage: "Each man should have his own wife, and each woman should have her own husband." That sounded good to me. I just wasn't sure how to get there, or what to do with all the choices I'd made before. I was too embarrassed to ask anyone directly—it wasn't something I could bring up in our coed small group, or discuss one-on-one with Will. And I couldn't ask Paul and Pascha, either, because, well, they were married. I wasn't sure my new faith was strong enough to withstand married people who were having all the sex they wanted telling me how and why I couldn't have any.

One night after our small group, I asked Pascha to pray for me. I didn't tell her why. Silently, I asked God for guidance. I wanted to know what the parameters were on this no-sex thing, and how much of "not quite sex" a Jesus follower could engage in before it became a problem. I'd read a passage in the book of Isaiah where God promised, "Never again will foreigners drink of the new wine for which you have toiled . . . those who gather the grapes will drink in the courts of my sanctuary." This struck me as applicable to my love life, somehow; I didn't want any unauthorized gathering of my grapes.

Pascha prayed silently for a few moments, then said, "I feel like God is saying, *Keep the banana away from the rest of the fruit. Otherwise, the whole thing will rot.* Does that mean anything to you?" I stared at her wide-eyed, then burst into giggles. *Keep the banana away from the rest of the fruit*—that was certainly clear. Pascha gave me a hug and sent me on my way, having no idea about the nature of the message God had just sent through her. This seemed like some rather amazing grace.

A FEW MONTHS later, the topic of sex came up in a class at the Vineyard. Someone braver than I asked *the question* about why God says sex between two committed yet unmarried people isn't okay, and Pastor Dave gave the first reasonable explanation I'd ever heard.

"First," he said, "it's important to acknowledge that God created sex. If you read the Bible, it's clear that God is pro sex—He thinks sex is great. But it's also clear that sex has a spiritual component; it's not just another random activity in our day. Something happens in the spiritual realm when we join our body together with someone else." Dave called this a *soul tie*, describing how sex forms a bond between people, linking them together in a way that is not casual or without consequence. "It's similar to how glue fuses two pieces of paper together," he said. "When the glue dries, the pieces are now one, and it's almost impossible to get them apart." This was God's design for sex, Dave explained—sex was the glue in a marriage, linking couples together through God's supernatural power. I thought about my past relationships, how I'd hoped sex would create an unbreakable bond that would make the relationship last. It felt good to have my theory confirmed. But why hadn't it worked?

"When we sleep with people we aren't married to," Dave continued, "we form ties that aren't supposed to be there. We become glued to that person, spiritually, in a way that is deeper than the rest of our relationship. We might *feel* committed," he acknowledged, "but if that commitment doesn't include marriage, then it's not the level of commitment God created sex for. And the Bible suggests that eventually, these relationships crack under the stress of supporting this imbalance.

"Then when we break up," he continued, "it's like tearing the glued paper apart—we rip and stick to one another. Neither party comes out whole, or free from leftover debris. When we do this repeatedly over the course of adult dating, we end up feeling like a mere shadow of ourselves, with pieces and bits and baggage from each past relationship stuck to us, haunting us in a way we can't seem to get away from."

Wow, I thought. *That's exactly how I feel: covered in chunks from all my disappointments, awkward bulges that pop out to torment me when I least expect it.* I couldn't remember ever *not* feeling like a weary veteran of love's front lines. But what was I supposed to do?

Seeing our discouraged faces, Dave described how Jesus could help: "Believe it or not," he said, "God has good news for us in all of this. He wants to take away the baggage from our past, and give us a chance to start fresh. If we repent, and ask Jesus to break the soul tie binding us to a person, he will. We can be free: of the debris, and of issues that resurface and ruin new relationships. It can be that simple."

I was sold. That night, I told Jesus that I was sorry for every man I'd been intimate with, every man I'd allowed past first base, every man I'd seduced to try and make him love me. It seemed audacious, but I asked Jesus for the chance to start over. "Please forgive me, God," I prayed. "I don't want to be tied to these old relationships anymore; please break these ties binding me to them—dissolve the glue; I don't want to be stuck anymore." I expected to feel dirty, riddled with failure and guilt; I assumed there was a shame-filled price I had to pay, a moment of reckoning where God would rub my nose in my pile of mistakes to ensure I understood how badly I'd screwed up. But instead, I felt clean. And free, like the load I'd assumed was just part of the weight of being me had been lifted off my back. Telling these things to Jesus, laying them out without hype or drama, admitting, *I did this. And this. And this. I am so very sorry. Please forgive me,* felt good. Really good.

A few days after Dave's sex talk, I read the letters written by the Apostle Paul (the Epistles, my study Bible called them), the words of encouragement he sent out to help early Christians understand how to live once they said yes to following Jesus. I was touched by Paul's hopeful prayers for new believers, how he beseeched God to show us how much He loves us and how much power we have in Jesus—to help us understand that living in us, Jesus is able to do "exceedingly, abundantly, above all we ask or imagine." Some of Paul's other teachings confused me, though, like the one that seemed to speak directly to dating: "Do not be yoked together with unbelievers."

"What's up with that?" I asked Gwen one day. "Why would followers of Jesus only date other Christians?" This narrowed the pool of available men considerably, particularly in greater Boston.

She smiled and answered, "Oh, honey, Christian guys have way more to offer. Think about it—if you call your boyfriend after a bad day and he's not into Jesus, all he can say to you is 'I'm sorry, that sucks.' There's nothing he can do to help. But a guy who is into Jesus can say 'Let me pray for you' and that changes everything. He can support you in ways no other man can."

I couldn't imagine a man I was dating saying "Let me pray for you"—it sounded so intimate; sacred, almost. Later I saw a tiny article in *Reader's Digest,* confirming Gwen's words: "Seventy-five percent of people who pray with their spouses often describe their marriages as 'very happy,'" it reported, citing a study by sociologist Andrew Greeley. "Those who pray are also more likely," it added, "to rate their spouses as skilled lovers." *Sign me up for that!* I thought, tearing out the article and slipping it into my wallet.

But I still wasn't clear how this mysterious way of dating

worked. How did Christians find each other? How did they start dating? I wondered about the practical side—how could you spend so much time with someone you're attracted to and never do more than kiss? It sounded impossible. I couldn't imagine what it would feel like to have a man love me, propose to me, marry me, knowing he wouldn't be "getting any" until after the wedding.

"This is so hard!" I cried to Pascha one night after our group. "I want to do this Jesus thing, I want to obey God, but I'm so afraid I'll screw it up!"

Pascha hugged me tighter and whispered the most reassuring prayer I'd ever heard: "Trish, in Jesus' name, I bless you not to screw it up."

A FEW WEEKS later, Dave's wife, Grace, gave a sermon on motherhood. She told us about a snippet of scripture she kept taped to her closet door, words she prayed for herself each day: "Her children arise and call her blessed; her husband also, and he praises her: 'Many women do noble things, but you surpass them all.'"

At home that afternoon, I cut that passage out of the program and taped it to the front page of my Bible. *I want that*, I told God. I looked up the full verse—the very last Proverb, dedicated to "the Wife of Noble Character," and appropriated it as my own. *I can't make this true about myself*, I told God. *On my own I'm none of these things. But you can make this true about me.* I prayed this Proverb, substituting "I" wherever the Bible said "she," believing God could make it true. I wasn't even sure what some of it meant, like the imagery of churning butter and sewing clothing. I had no idea how to import food or plant a vineyard (unless selecting a nice Australian cabernet to go with dinner counted). But it wasn't up to me, I realized. God knew what it meant, and He could make it true.

The next morning, as I opened my Bible and wandered into celibate Paul's teachings on marriage, I understood why I'd need all that intimate prayer and great sex Gwen had told me about.

"Wives, submit to your husband, as to the Lord," Paul began, in one of his most controversial passages. "For the husband is the head of the wife as Christ is the head of the church, his body, of which he is the Savior. Now as the church submits to Christ, so also wives should submit to their husbands in everything."

You must be kidding, I thought. There it was—the misogynistic, women-squishing mandate everyone warned me about. *I must have seen this passage before,* I thought—*why didn't it register?* I scanned the surrounding paragraphs for softening language, something to reassure me that this passage was taken out of context to support the belief that husbands are in charge in marriage; that couldn't possibly be what God intended. But there was no comfort to be found. If the Bible was true, then God's plan for marriage was for my future husband to have final say in all of our decisions, with the ability to rule over me like a tyrant if he wanted to. I flashed back to a Promise Keepers rally I'd seen on the news a few years back, where thousands of men marched on Washington, then vowed to return home to "take back our rightful place as head of the household." I didn't like that idea *at all.*

I went back to the woods to rant at Jesus.

"*What,*" I demanded, "is the deal with Paul? He isn't even married. Yet he's the guy you use to tell us all how wives are supposed to behave? What about all that 'I have come to give you abundant life' stuff you wooed me with earlier? What about 'exceedingly, abundantly, above all I could ask or imagine'?" I shouted at Jesus as I stomped through the foliage; there's a chance I even shook my fist in the air. I was furious, convinced I'd been sold yet another bill of goods that looked like one thing at the beginning, and then turned out to be something altogether different once I got it home.

I didn't hear anything from Jesus that day; he let me rant. I went home and took a long, angry nap. The next night Will and I met to plan that week's small group. We'd already agreed about what we were going to do, but suddenly Will changed his mind, veering off in a different direction. I was furious. *I have more experience with this,* I fumed. *I've led seminars and conferences and meetings of all sizes. He should listen to me!* I realized that if we were going to have this battle every week, this partnership would quickly become a nightmare. I prayed for guidance about what to do, how to change Will's mind.

Don't do anything, God said. *Do it Will's way.*

"But Will is *wrong!*" I protested.

Pray for him, God said. *Tell Me, don't tell him. See if I don't take care of you.* My personal lesson in Submission 101.

From that point on, I tried not to disagree, taking my frustrations to God in heated prayer. To my astonishment, almost every time I prayed, Will changed his mind, or we reached some miraculous compromise neither of us would have thought of on our own. I was blown away by how effective it was to take my concerns to God, to nag Him when I was frustrated, rather than nagging Will. *Would this work in a real relationship?* I wondered. I returned to Paul's teachings newly humbled, and told Jesus that if he had something new to tell me, I was ready to hear him out.

Read on, he suggested.

"Husbands, love your wives, just as Christ loved the church and gave himself up for her. . . . For this reason, a man will leave his father and mother and be united to his wife, and the two will become one flesh. . . . Each one of you must love his wife as he loves himself, and the wife must respect her husband."

Under this system, I realized, wives got off rather easy. I recognized that my fear about these passages—about submitting to a man and letting him call the shots—was based on the assumption that the man I married would be a jerk, that he'd make bad decisions that I'd be stuck with. Paul's command suggested a new standard, though: that respect was a means by which to evaluate a potential husband. Paul suggested the fantastic possibility that the man I marry *wouldn't* be a jerk.

This was my *eureka!* moment—I saw how I'd approached this backward for most of my dating life: I dated men I loved but didn't respect, men who respected me but didn't love me. That was why it never worked. Men don't naturally *love* women, I realized; it's a rare response, a sign of something special. In the same way, women don't naturally *respect* men—a man has to earn our respect, that's how God designed us to work together. God puts the onus in relationships on the men—to pursue us, to earn our respect, to love us faithfully once we're won. Suddenly, Paul's alleged misogyny seemed like one heck of a great deal. "If I don't respect him," I repeated with glee, "he's not my husband!"

I read a Christian book about dating that explored this theme, called *The Unspoken Rules of Love: What Women Don't Know and Men Don't Tell You.* It was an eye-opener, declaring in no uncertain terms that if I wanted Jesus to bring my husband, I needed to raise my opinion of myself and the man who would one day marry me. The authors offered a tangible way of evaluating "respect" (which was helpful, as my previous definition was something like "He showed up and asked me out"). They asked, "If you fell into a coma, and the man you're dating was put in charge of your life—your bills, your house, your kids, your dog—for six months, what would happen? What would you find when you came to? Would things be in better shape than if you'd been awake or would everything around you be in shambles?"

That paragraph stopped me cold. It had been years since I'd dated a man I'd trust with the details of my life. There were only a few I'd trusted with my dog. And yet I'd been willing to attach myself to each of them—to any man willing to marry me, really—to escape the stigma of being single. Like Esau in the book of Genesis, who sold his birthright to his younger brother for a single bowl of gruel, I'd been making long-term choices that gave short-term results.

"God," I prayed, "if You'll help me, I'll wait for Your best for me: a man I respect, who loves me as Jesus loves his followers. Someone I can, without resentment or worry, submit to." Suddenly, I thought of the vows I'd made that fall day two years ago in Connecticut—when I said I'd never marry again, never let anyone control me, never trust, never have children. "I don't mean that anymore!" I cried. "I take it all back!" I couldn't believe I'd ever said all that; it felt like I'd cursed myself. "I'm so sorry for saying those things, for believing they were the only way to stay safe and not end up in another dangerous situation," I prayed. I remembered a recommendation I'd heard Dave mention in a sermon, about "coming in the opposite spirit." I wasn't sure exactly what this meant, but it occurred to me that if my negative words had power, perhaps my positive words might be helpful in canceling them out. "God, with Your help, I *will* get married again." I said. "I *will* trust the wonderful husband You send, because You will make him trustworthy. And we *will* have children together, and build a life and a legacy. Thank you God," I concluded, feeling oddly buoyant and hopeful. "In Jesus' name, I pray."

The next day, still excited by this revelation, I boldly said to God, "Okay—we're clear now, right? Is there anything else I need to do so You can bring my husband?" Almost as soon as the words were out of my mouth, I felt a bizarre compulsion to read the Ten Commandments. I was certain I hadn't murdered anyone, or even coveted their livestock; I assumed this was God's way of reassuring me of how well I was doing.

I flipped back and forth through the Old Testament, unable to remember where in the narrative Moses came down from the mountain. Finally, I found the passage and ran through the laws like a checklist. *You shall have no other Gods before me:* Check. *You shall not worship idols:* Check. *You shall not take the name of the Lord in vain:* Check (my expletives were typically of the unblasphemous variety). *Observe the Sabbath:* Check. *Honor your father and mother:* Oh.

The truth was, I realized sheepishly, I'd been kind of crappy to my parents; to my entire family, for that matter. The map of our relationship over the course of my adulthood was an awkward series of zigs and zags: I'd storm off into some ill-fated adventure, determined to do things my way, then stumble back home to receive their comfort when my way failed. Time after time, they'd patch me up and encourage me (and not infrequently foot the bill for my mistakes), then off I'd head again, still certain I knew better than they did what would make me happy. I'd missed birthdays and funerals and even my nephew's birth, all because I was far away, figuring out my life. My parents and sister and brothers had been wonderful to me—fanning out like a safety net, catching me each time I tumbled down from whatever hill I'd tried to climb. And yet I'd never really listened any time they'd tried to help me.

They love you, God reminded me. *Let them.* I thought about how lucky I was—how much I actually *liked* the members of my family, how honoring them wasn't a burden, but merely something I'd been too selfish to pay attention to. I didn't want to elope again without them there, I didn't want another marriage without them in it.

"Help me do better," I asked God.

A WEEK OR so later, as we visited my parents in Maine as part of my new endeavor, Amy and I made a side trip to Wal-Mart. We took our usual detour through the book section, and the title, *The Power of a Praying Wife,* caught my eye. I felt that familiar longing welling up inside me as I imagined how amazing it would be to *qualify* for that book. "I want that," I told God for

the nineteen hundredth time that day. "If you give me a husband, I'll pray for him, I promise."

Buy it now, God replied. I was horrified. I had no husband,
not even an engagement ring, and it wasn't as if I was there alone
and could pretend to be buying it for a friend.

Amy saw me staring at the book. When I told her what God
said, she responded, "I'll tell you what—if God told *me* to buy
a book like that, I sure wouldn't leave here without it!" That
was all the push I needed. I bought the book, hiding it on the
checkout counter between a six-pack of Vanilla Coke and some
kitchen towels I didn't need. I wandered out of Wal-Mart that
night feeling like I'd purchased my first bra—excited, but not
sure what I'd do with this new grown-up thing once I got it
home.

I read the book every night after that. *If God told me to buy it,* I
figured, *He must want me to pray the prayers for my future husband.* So
I did. I prayed for his faith and his health and his life purpose.
I asked God to protect him from temptation, to surround him
with awesome friends, and to build his relationship with Jesus
so he would be the man God designed him to be. I prayed for
him to find me, and for God to make me into the woman he was
praying for. Gradually, I saw myself in a new way: as someone's
intended, chosen wife. I wasn't just another single girl waiting to
be taken off the shelf, I wasn't a puppy trying to win someone's
affection and love. I was this man's future. This changed something in me, causing a subtle shift in how I thought of my life. I
loved the idea that God was working in our relationship already,
even if I couldn't see what He was doing from where I was.

"Faith is being sure of what we hope for and certain of what we do not see," the Bible reminded me.

At the same time, though, a fresh crop of fear sprouted up to counter my new perspective: *What if this man meets me,* I wondered, *and doesn't want a wife who was married before? What if he thinks I'm damaged goods? What if he won't have me?* I was haunted by Jesus' words in Matthew, where he said, "Anyone who marries the divorced woman commits adultery." I hated this passage, with its condemning, hopeless tone. I didn't know what to do with it. Yes, I was divorced. But God had told me—specifically, unequivocally—that he had a husband for me if I took Jesus seriously. I was terrified to talk about this with anyone, certain they'd fall back on the hackneyed suggestion that perhaps *Jesus* was my new husband, and wasn't that exciting? No, I'm sorry—it wasn't. That's not what I agreed to, and God knew it. Unfortunately, I'd been around long enough to recognize that you're not allowed to say, "But I want a *real* husband" in most Christian circles, and that the whole "Jesus isn't enough for me" idea didn't sell in a culture oddly convinced that if knowing Jesus didn't fill you with perfect bliss (or at least the ability to fake it) 24-7, you had yourself a problem.

But I'd read the Bible, and it seemed to me that Jesus offered us tangible good things in life—the desires of our heart, as the Psalms so eloquently put it—not just some vague semi-satisfied state where we'd learn that we really could do without. When faced with a hungry crowd and only a few loaves and fishes, Jesus didn't tell the people to fill up on his words and presence, he *fed* them. Actual food. When he attended a wedding where the host ran out of wine, he didn't bless them with a sudden urge for temperance; he made more. Jesus didn't make people satisfied with their disappointing lives when he walked by; he changed things in a way that erased the past and opened up a new future. And that's what I wanted him to do for me: to work miraculously, through tangible means.

I found a bit of solace repeating the promise from Chicken Wire Jesus: "If anyone is in Christ, he is a new creation. The old has gone, the new has come." That's what I was banking on: that Jesus had washed the slate clean of my mistakes—including my first marriage and divorce—and that the husband he had for me would cherish me as his bride, perfect, shiny, and new.

I forgot the key plot structure of any good romantic story: the hero doesn't ever show up until something really bad has happened, something that convinces you that all hope for a happy ending is lost.

Chapter Twenty

Allegiance Encounters

My friend Kevin and I were at a restaurant, enjoying a beer outside by the water. He was teasing me about my sudden rise to superstar status at the Vineyard, joking about how I was leading the masses to abundant life in Jesus while my own life languished in squalor. "Isn't there something in the Bible about fruit?" he asked laughingly. "Some insinuation that if you're on track with God, life should look somewhat better than yours does?" I laughed along with him, wincing at how his words stung. Despite my months of prayer, fasting, and diligent Bible study, even after getting baptized and purging my bookshelves of blasphemy and idols, I had nothing at all to show for it. No man, no career, no life. Even I couldn't figure out why I was allowed to lead other people—I had no proof that the things I talked about each week worked. But everyone told me what a fabulous job I was doing, so I kept on keeping on. I was devastated, but I didn't know what else to do.

We finished our beers, paid the check, and headed out. As we passed the bar I saw a guy I'd known in grade school, standing with his brother. Adam and I had grown up together in the same small town, and even dated for a few days in sixth grade after he penciled our names together in a heart on the top of his desk. *True love forever*, it said. (In his defense, three days is a lifetime when you're struggling to learn decimals and sentence structure as a tsunami of hormones wrecks your inner world.) I hadn't seen Adam for years—I'd heard through the grapevine that he'd become a tennis pro, and that he'd married at some point and then divorced a few years later. And now here he was having a round of Bud Lights, catching my eye as I gave Kevin directions back to the highway.

"Hey there!" he said, touching my arm. "Haven't seen you in a while—how are you?" He enfolded me in a friendly hug as we exchanged surprised pleasantries, and his brother Joe made some nice comment about how the water must be good wherever I lived because I looked great. At their invitation I pulled up a stool; Adam bought me a beer, and we exchanged a decade of life information in tasteful snippets that made both of us look good. *This tennis pro thing is kind of sexy*, I noticed as Adam told me about winters in Florida and summers at various resorts across New England. Three hours later, he asked me out on my first official date in months.

We met for drinks the next night, and he invited me to a barbecue at Joe's the following day. His friends teased him about his past marriages (as it turned out, there had been not one, but two) and described how they were planning a new line of re-usable wedding accessories with a fill-in-the-blank format say-ing, "I married Adam (*insert date here*)." I laughed, ignoring the implications about his relationship history. It didn't occur to me that none of the princes in fairy tales (or the Bible, for that matter) had a group of friends warning women to beware of him because he'd already ditched a few damsels in his quest to become king.

A week or so later, I visited Adam at work and discovered that while he was, technically, a tennis pro, his real job was re-stringing rackets and handing out buckets of balls at the local courts, for which he was paid $10 an hour under the table. He was considering bankruptcy, after a stint in the hospital ran him aground financially because he hadn't paid his health insur-ance premium. He kept what little money he had in his sock drawer, as he didn't trust banks, and attempted to double his worth with frequent visits to the local off-track betting club. Did I mention that he had a temper? And yet when I told him I was a Christian, and that I wouldn't be having sex again until after my wedding, he said, "Okay. That sounds a little weird, but if it works for you than I'm fine with it."

It's a sign! I thought, triumphantly, certain that he'd never agree to the no-sex thing unless he was sent by God. I conve-niently forgot about all the other guys I'd dated over the years, nice men who'd agreed when I said no and didn't make a big deal about it even without a divine explanation. I wanted a sign, and I saw one. So I ignored all that stuff about not being yoked with unbelievers. *He's Catholic,* I reasoned, *that's close enough.* I ignored his admission that the last Mass he'd attended was in celebration of his first marriage. *He's interested in spirituality*, I assured myself. *He's just never had a chance to explore Jesus before. I can be his chance!* I pushed aside all the warnings I'd heard about the dangers of "evangelistic dating," and the dismal success rate for women who let themselves fall for nonbelievers on the grounds that loving us will be enough to woo men into the Kingdom of God. "It doesn't work that way," everyone said. *It will in this case* was my determined response, as I dove headlong into Adam's romantic promises. *After all,* I reasoned, *it's not really "yoked" until you're married.*

They say that an alcoholic can be sober for decades, then pick up a drink, and the physiological result is the same as if he or she has been drinking the entire time. That was what it was like when I met Adam—like I was still married to my first husband, and all the bad choices, violent outbursts, lies, and general life mismanagement I'd held at bay for the past three years landed on me again like an avalanche. It was déjà vu, these conversations about scrambling to pay (or avoid) bills, how I'd done this or that to piss him off. Out of all the men in the world, I somehow managed to find one so eerily similar to my first husband that I picked up right where I'd left off. After two years of following Jesus, I was right back in the same place again—convinced this might be my only chance at marriage, having a family of my own, making something of my life. So despite the warning signs, I grabbed onto it with all my might and squeezed, as if my pressure and determination alone could cut off the negativity in his life and keep it from poisoning mine.

All that summer, we went to different churches. He listened

politely to the sermons, then gaped openly as the music played, eyes wide as he stared at our fellow congregants raising their voices and praising God. Sometimes he'd even crane his neck around to take in the full spectacle. I tried—and failed—not to be embarrassed for him, *by him*. He had little moments of breakthrough that kept me hoping he might "get" the Jesus thing—one Sunday he wrote a prayer request on the little card that came in the program, another week he snuck up at the last minute and took Communion. He even asked me if there was a "certain prayer" you had to say to be a follower of Jesus. I showed him a Post-it note in the front of my Bible, where I'd copied some words about telling Jesus that I believe he died for my sins, then rose again to give me new life, and asking him to be my savior. Adam copied the words onto a slip of paper, then tucked it into his sock drawer next to his life savings. That was the last I heard about it. Adam treated my spiritual hopes the way other guys had treated my dreams of marriage—tossing out just enough interest to keep me believing he might come around, without actually committing or changing anything about his situation. And yet, despite the growing dichotomy between who he was and what I wanted, I got more and more hooked into the fantasy life he painted for me during our long talks over cold beers at our favorite bar next to the ocean. We talked of having a family, of the home we'd build and the work he'd do to establish his career as an instructor. "All I've ever needed," he told me, "is someone to believe in me the way my mother did. Neither of my other wives did that, but I feel like you're that woman."

Drawing on years of practice in recasting disappointing declarations just like this, I ignored the thousand-part subtext of Adam's statement: that it was all about his needs, that his first two wives were to blame for his current state of affairs, that *I* was the savior he was waiting for—and focused on the fact that God had promised me a husband, and Adam had shown up. I tried to ignore the nagging sense that I'd expected better, that when I prayed those prayers and went hungry on fasting days, the vision I clung to didn't have this many obstacles to conquer—spiritual, emotional, financial, physical—to get to the life I dreamed of. But then I'd remember Jesus' teachings about not judging one another, and how he loves even the least of us, and assume that God must want me to believe for a miracle for Adam; that if Jesus had changed Peter from a buffoon to a leader, and Paul from a vicious killer to the author of two-thirds of the New Testament, he could do something similar for Adam. I hoped he'd do it soon, as I hated being the only "spiritual one" in our relationship. I'd never thought the princess was the one who rode in and did the rescuing.

Adam asked me to move with him to Florida for the winter. *Why not?* I thought, dreaming of warm February days and drinks at the club at sunset. The cold reality of Adam's economic status drowned out my fantasy, though—he had nowhere to live, and we'd have to shack up with several of his tennis buddies in some hovel near the courts. "Maybe you could get a job as a waitress," he suggested. Desperate for some sort of movement in my life after two years of stagnation, I considered it. But I didn't tell anybody; they wouldn't understand.

•

"I FEEL LIKE God gave me a picture for you," Will said to me the following Monday night as we prayed. "It was a football helmet with the word 'Giants' written across it." I looked at him, puzzled. "You know, like the football team," he clarified, "but I don't think the football part is important. There was also a tree," he continued, "and a big hand that came and picked the tree right up and tipped it over, to show that it had no roots. It was sitting there on the ground, but there were no roots keeping it in place." I had no idea what to make of this. After a long, pause, Will continued: "I feel like these pictures mean that God has big things for you. But you need to put down roots, something to hold you in place long enough to get there."

"How do I do that?" I asked.

"You stay put, I guess." Will replied. "You believe the things God has told you, you believe that He cares, you believe that He's good and that He loves you. And then you wait to see what happens."

"Oh," I joked, trying to ease the intensity of the moment. "Is that all?" But inside, I was churning. *I've never stayed before*, I realized that night as I walked across Harvard's campus to get home. Year after year I'd left, ran, fled when things got hard. Philadelphia, Washington, Connecticut, Cambridge. A big game of hopscotch, each move chosen because it got me out of some regrettable mess or disaster, each fresh new step a geographical cure for the disease of being me. I'd moved eleven times since college graduation, seven of them in the past four years. I wanted roots as much as the next person. But I didn't want *these* roots, or any of the ones I'd considered so far. I wanted different roots, *better* ones. I wanted a husband root, and if God didn't understand that by now, I'd keep moving. On a spiritual level, though, I was rather out of options. I couldn't go back to the *Course* or any of the other practices I'd renounced. Spiritually speaking, I'd reached the end of the line. Geographically, though, I had options. I could follow Jesus in Florida, right?

But when I asked God, He said no. Specifically, He said, *If you stay in Cambridge, I have something for you. But you can only get it here, and only if you stay.* Okay then.

THAT SUNDAY, DAVE and Grace gave a sermon entitled "Destiny-Shaping Experiences: How God Shapes Our Lives to Be Good." It was my first time back at the Vineyard in months. The few times Adam had visited the church with me that summer had been exceedingly awkward, as he stared at people during worship and his eyes glazed over uncomprehendingly during the brief sermons.

"Is he a believer?" asked a woman I barely knew, commenting on his strange behavior. She warned me pointedly not to chain myself to a man who didn't share my devotion to following Jesus. "You'll regret it for the rest of your life," she warned.

I'd been furious. This wasn't what I wanted to hear. Adam *was* devoted to following Jesus, I told myself; he just didn't understand what that meant yet. What I couldn't fathom was why he at least couldn't fake it better. "Can you believe she said that?" I'd asked Amy, furiously, recounting this woman's unsolicited interference in my life. My years of stubbornly demanding the right to do things my way came back full force.

"Maybe she has a point," Amy said. "He doesn't seem to be catching on."

"It's all new to him!" I protested. "He wants to know, he just doesn't yet. He's here, isn't he?" I crowed triumphantly, as if sitting through the occasional Sunday service was hard evidence of a newfound commitment to Jesus.

My friends shied away from confronting me after that, afraid that if they did, I might leave the church—and Jesus—completely. This was my first time back at the church since those conversations, and I sat defiantly alone, not wanting to field more questions or opinions about how I should handle my life.

Dave started his sermon that day by acknowledging that there was a spiritual battle going on around us. "Periodically," he said, "we wander from where God wants us to be and need to be 'wrenched back' onto a path that will lead to God's best." Offering an example from her life, Grace shared about dating a guy in college who was raised in a church but was not at all interested in pursuing spiritual things. He was a talented musician, he drank a lot, and he wanted to move the relationship along quickly on the physical front. Her roommate hated him.

That sounds like Adam, I realized. He was talented, in a certain way. He hadn't pushed my physical boundaries, but he pushed me to move with him, live together, have kids as soon as possible. And while my friends didn't hate Adam, I hadn't given them much of a chance to know him. I kept my worlds separate, convinced they'd clash like oil and water, leaving me struggling to swim through the middle. I dreaded what Grace would say next; obviously, she hadn't ended up with that guy.

"I was part of an on-campus group of people who were

into following Jesus," she continued, "and I went to a work-shop they put on about dating and relationships. I left that day horrified, aware that if my goal was to grow up and marry a man who shared my beliefs, then dating this guy put me on a path away from what I wanted most in life." She went back to campus that night determined to break off the relationship. "When I walked into the party where we were supposed to meet," she said, "I saw him half naked, dancing with two other women. I realized where I was headed if I stayed with him, and it broke my heart.

"It was still a few years before I met Dave," she admitted, "and I had a lot to figure out about how God wanted me to think about myself in relationship to men. But I never regret-ted getting off the path I was on with that other guy, the path marked with such clear signs of danger to the future I hoped for."

Dave came back on to the stage to join her. "Just to wrap up—and at the risk of sounding like the hero," he joked, "how do you see your life now?"

"My life today is a pretty vivid contrast to that story," Grace admitted. "I'm a happily married woman who loves her life. I feel like all my dreams of love, family, and adventure are com-ing true, like God gives me a wide and spacious place to play and dream and act. Trusting God paid huge dividends for me," she continued. "It saved me from the tortuous experience of tossing my heart out before every guy who walked my way, and put me in a position to make my life count for something great. On the whole," she concluded, "I'm grateful."

Why didn't God tell me this? I wondered. *Why didn't He protect me?*

Why didn't He intervene when I threw myself before any man who might be a potential husband, raising the stakes of what I offered in each audition while lowering my standards of who and what my "Mr. Right" had to be? But even as I asked, I knew the answer: God protected me as best He could without violating my free will. It was miraculous, I realized, how the violent men never hit me, the alcoholics rarely got me drunk, the drug addicts never shot up or smoked or snorted while I was in the room, and the men who wouldn't commit always left. God had, I realized, bailed me out time and time again, always making sure I survived no matter how much money I lost or what awful things a guy said on his way out. He protected me in every way I'd allowed, without overriding my grim determination to have things my way. I remembered Pascha's words: "Jesus doesn't take over your life. You have to *ask* him to save you."

As Grace left the stage, Dave suggested that over the course of our lives, each of us faces two types of destiny-shaping experiences in our relationship with God. The first he called a "Power Encounter," where we realize that there is a God—that He is real, and that He acts. I remembered sitting in the front row at church when I was five, certain that God loved me, and sitting at that stoplight in Buffalo so many years later, hearing God tell me He had more for my life if I'd give Jesus a chance.

Next Dave described a second type of experience, which called "Allegiance Encounters"—the events that shape what God can and cannot do in our lives. These encounters come, he explained, as we arrive at decision-making points in life and choose to either follow God's best for us or pursue our own way. "There are four areas where these choices typically appear," he said, "career, integrity, sex, and relationships."

"What would have happened to Grace," Dave wondered aloud, "had she pursued the relationship with the guy in college? Would she have gotten the full life God designed for her? Probably not," he concluded. "God would still love her, of course, and she could still pray and go to church and live a good life. But God's best for her would be off the table because she was partnered with someone who wasn't partnered with God. And without that partnership, God's best doesn't work."

I stared at him, stunned, realizing how heavily I'd gone into wishful thinking about my relationship with Adam, claiming that he was a spiritually viable partner for me just because he came to church from time to time. I'd fallen back into my old model of God, I realized, where I'd do whatever I wanted and assume that God *had* to bless it, simply because He loved me. I'd forgotten that it doesn't work that way. Ignoring the warning signs, I'd believed that Adam would come around, that he'd give his life to Jesus with wild enthusiasm, after which God would *have* to restore his fortunes, his health, his temperament. Suddenly, I saw how close I was to repeating the worst mistake of my life, justifying inexcusable behavior I would never admit to my friends or family because it felt so much easier to be with Adam than to be alone.

This is it, I thought: *my allegiance encounter.* I'd given God my career, worked hard to rebuild my integrity, and even given up sex when He'd asked me. But I still had a stranglehold on my love life, insisting on the right to date whomever I wanted, believing

I could force God to make it work. Now, I had to choose again: God's way, or my way?

As we stood to sing the closing song, I knew that I was going to break up with Adam. I didn't decide; I just knew. For the first time, I was more afraid of missing out on God's best for my life than of being alone. *If God is* God, I realized, *I won't be alone, because He promised me a husband, and a family. Either all my chips are on that card, or I'm not playing at all.* I asked for a miracle—what would I tell Adam to explain my change of attitude?

The next night, Adam called and broke up with me. *He* broke up with *me*. He ranted that he didn't like how I was spending my time, accusing me of not being focused enough on him, on our life together, our future. His tirade came out of the blue, as two days earlier he'd been quite satisfied with our arrangement. He was calling my bluff, I realized later, trying to manipulate me to reassure him of my devotion. But I saw it as my miracle and jumped at the opportunity.

As I got off the phone that night, I saw the situation clearly: Adam offered all of the pain and drama from my first marriage, with none of the perks—no house, no car, no huge diamond to adorn my hand. And yet I'd thought he was God's answer to my prayers, simply because he'd shown up and asked me out. It never occurred to me to consider that the power that sent him might not be God; that Adam might be a decoy, another temptation to settle. It never occurred to me that Adam might be a test of my allegiance. (Later I read a quote by C. S. Lewis, saying that the biggest threat to God's best for us is rarely something bad; it's usually something just good enough to convince us it will do, that we should grab hold of it lest we be left with nothing at all.) It felt like I'd been wrenched back onto God's path for my life, as Dave and Grace described, but in the gentlest possible way. For the first time in my adult life, I felt like God was celebrating, that He was delighted to have me back. *Of course the husband I have for you will know Me*, He said. *How else will he know how to love you?*

Chapter Twenty-one

A Knight in a Shining Honda

Knowing I should probably take some time off from relationships—go back to square one, perhaps, and pray through my dysfunction, *heal* whatever drove me into the arms of yet another Mr. Wrong—I committed myself to some quality time alone with God.

Two days later, a new guy wandered into our small group and blew this plan to smithereens. He had green eyes. His name was Steve. He looked like someone ordered from Central Casting for the part of "Cute Guy to Help Trish Get Over the Tennis Pro in Scene 43."

"He's single," Will told me one night.

"Who is single?" I asked, pretending I didn't know the relationship status of every other male member of our church.

"Steve," Will replied, humoring me. "You know, the guy who matches the description of 'your type' to a T?"

"He's single?"

"Yep. He's single. His mother keeps asking him when he's going to find a wife. Did I mention that he plays hockey? You like hockey, right?"

Despite Will's good-natured teasing, I was determined to remain indifferent, to keep my pearls to myself rather than tossing them out to be trampled. I remembered the wise words my friend Deidre's grandmother told her about how a girl should guard her heart: "Remain cool," Grandma advised. "Not hot, not cold, but cool. Let a man make his intentions clear to you; until then, keep your feelings, and your heart to yourself. Don't give yourself away." I'd never exercised this much restraint in my life, but this time I was determined to heed her wise words and lie low. *When you send the right guy, Lord,* I prayed, *let him make his intentions clear. Protect us from ambiguity. If he's Your man, let him make the first move toward me, and let him want the type of relationship You created us for—exclusive, devoted, contemplating marriage. Don't let me get all worked up again over the wrong guy.*

STEVE BECAME A regular in our group that summer. Little pieces of information leaked out about him as the weeks went by: he'd grown up in Cambridge, he worked for a biotech company, he had season tickets to the Red Sox (back when they hadn't won a World Series in eighty-six years and only genuine fans still cared). He'd been raised by an Italian mother he adored, and had turned to Jesus after September 11 convinced him that something bigger was going on in the world, making him anxious to be, as he put it, right with God. The more we got to know him, the more I struggled to maintain the facade that my interest was merely that of a conscientious small group leader. I felt like Steve was a special exhibit—a sample, so to speak—sent by God to show me that He still had some good guys up his sleeve. But everyone knows that you don't get to take home the sample.

One night at church, one of the associate pastors offered to pray for the singles, asking God to bring us awesome spouses and great marriages. Amy and I scrambled over the chairs to get to the front, grinning at each other and trying not to laugh. We were expecting our husbands to arrive at any moment; this seemed like a move in the right direction. As we gathered in a corner, Steve appeared next to me, his tall frame blocking my awareness of everything around us.

"Weren't you dating someone?" he asked, looking at me with a puzzled expression.

"I was," I blurted, "but I'm not married . . ."

"Oh. I guess that's true," he responded.

Just as I started to clarify my single status, Pastor Val began to pray for us; I gave up and closed my eyes. *I'll tell him when we're done,* I reassured myself. But when Val finished and I opened my eyes, Steve was gone.

After that night, it seemed like Steve was everywhere—sitting in front of me in church, next to me in small group. We had tiny moments of connection—we both read the same online devotional each morning, and Steve brought me a hardcover copy as a gift. We talked about hockey and living in New England, and how hard it was to pray before work when small group kept us up late the night before. In any other context, this would be flirtatious banter, and I'd have dropped hints about how fun it would be if we could get together sometime to talk more, "grab coffee," as the standard non-date suggestion went. But I didn't suggest. Steve was polite and attentive, but that's it. Our conversations were the model of Christian propriety, the perfect supportive, platonic dialogue between a brother and sister in Christ. *That's all this is,* I told myself firmly. *Stay cool.* Over and over, Steve wandered into my thoughts, and over and over, I cast him out, thinking about the latest antics of my adorable nephew or the cute earrings I'd seen at Target. I was tired of conducting relationships in my mind, of living in a fantasy world with no real participation from the subject of my daydreams. *Please God, help me stop this,* I prayed. *I can't handle getting hurt again.*

He was only twenty-nine, I discovered. I was thirty-four. That pretty much settled it.

"Can I talk to you for a minute?" Steve asked one Sunday, grabbing me on my way into church.

"Sure," I said, surprised. We stepped out of the stream of people and I looked up at him expectantly. "What's up?"

"I just finished the Vineyard 201 class," he said. "They told us to discuss the material with our small group leader—can you help me with this?"

"Sure," I said, struggling to hide my disappointment. I was his small group leader—that's all. "Let's meet before service next Sunday."

"Great! I'll see you then." He disappeared into the crowd

and I ducked into the ladies' room, fighting the urge to slam the stall door and hurl rolls of toilet paper against the floor.

Don't make anything of this, I told myself the next Sunday. *You are helping him with his class, nothing more.* I didn't dress up that day, not much anyway. And I used only a little extra lip gloss.

We sat down together in the school cafeteria (the gym was the church sanctuary, the cafeteria the all-purpose prayer and meeting room) and talked about some of the Bible's suggestions for getting the most out of life. He seemed to have a handle on things—financially, emotionally—and I admired the way he talked about his family, his job, his friends. Remembering the coma advice I'd read in that book, I wondered what my life would be like if Steve were left in charge. *If this conversation is any indication,* I thought, *my life might be better if I checked out for a bit and signed things over to him.* Our friend Julie walked by as we were finishing, bemoaning a date that hadn't turned out the way she'd hoped. "He's a Christian," she moaned, "but let me tell you—that alone isn't enough."

As she left, Steve turned back to me and said, "Dating— wow. I don't know how to think about that here in church, where even to start."

Exasperated by months of comforting disappointed women who all thought the same few guys liked them (guys who made frequent vague gestures of interest but didn't follow through), I let him have it: "Whatever you do, whoever you're interested in, can I say on behalf of all the women at the Vineyard—*please, ask her out.* Don't equivocate, don't beat around the bush, don't hint or ask her to some noncommittal event like coffee. If you like a girl, *ask her out!*"

Steve was quiet, eyes glued to the table. The air between us filled with a long, awkward pause as he gathered up his papers. Finally, he looked up at me and said, "In that case, I have something to ask you. . . ."

The next night my phone rang. It was Steve, with plans for our first date. "I thought we could check out the Rembrandt exhibit at the Museum of Fine Arts on the day after Thanksgiving—how does that sound?"

How does that sound? I thought, incredulous. *That sounds amazing.* "Great," I said, fighting to maintain my composure. "The MFA sounds great."

I HEADED HOME for Thanksgiving with an odd mix of anticipation and dread. I despised Thanksgiving. No other holiday so highlighted my abject failure as an adult. Over the years, as my siblings added spouses and children to their lives and our gatherings, I'd shown up alone, taking back roads to avoid the one-dollar toll in New Hampshire, with just enough gas in the car to get me home. It was pathetic. My boyfriends had never invited me to join their families for turkey and stuffing (except for Jewish Jon who relished the chance to shock his mother)— it had always been the day when I'd realize once and for all that me and Mr. Man of the Moment weren't building any sort of a future together. This was why I didn't want to tell my family about Steve: it was too embarrassing. I'd done this so many times before, regaling them with news of some new guy who just might be the one. My sister even joked that she might put together a slide show of all the men who'd sat on my parents' couch, then disappeared into the ether, never to be heard from again: Chip, Josh, Tim, the Bobs, Drew, Mark . . . the list went on and on. When we were growing up, my dad always heralded our young breakups with the declaration, "He's in the book" (presaging, perhaps, this very memoir). By all accounts, my book was a little thick.

But I thought about our upcoming date all day on Thursday, secretly wondering if this time, things might turn out differently. *We're going to the Rembrandt exhibit!* I thought over and over again. I loved the sound of it—so sophisticated, so interesting. I'd always wanted to be the kind of girl who caught the important exhibits when they came through town. I wasn't—in truth, I hadn't been to the MFA since a field trip in the seventh grade—but I wanted to be. I felt like Cinderella, like my life might be transformed by magical things to come. *Which means,* I reminded myself, *that this could all disappear at midnight, and I'll be back toiling in the embers of a burned-out fire.*

"Hi," I said, opening the door for Steve the next day.

"Hi. This is for you." He handed me a flower—a single, perfect, gerbera daisy.

"Thank you," I said, smiling. "Come on upstairs. Let me find something to put this in and then we can go. This is Kylie, by the way," I added, pointing to my beloved pup, who was spinning madly in anticipation, hoping Steve would pet her. "She's our resident guard dog, but it seems like you've passed muster." I left the two of them together in the living room and searched frantically through the kitchen for a vase of some sort. *We're not really a fresh flowers kind of household,* I realized, finally sticking the flower in a plastic iced tea bottle pulled out of the recycling. I promised myself I'd find a better home for it that evening, once I knew for sure if there would be a second date.

I walked back to the living room and found Kylie sprawled on the floor with her paws in the air, reveling in the attention as Steve scratched her belly. *She doesn't do that for everyone*, I observed, remembering the guys she'd snubbed over the years—backing away from them, growling, even stealing food off their plates when they weren't looking. *Score one for Steve*, I thought.

I grabbed my coat and we headed out to the car. Steve opened the passenger door for me with an easy nonchalance, not making too big a deal out of it. *Chivalrous, but not obnoxiously so. Nice.* I glanced around for clues to his personality. The car was clean, but not so perfect as to hint at anal retentiveness. There was no overpowering scent of a "Spicy Vanilla" or "Razzy Raspberry" air freshener masking smelly habits; it just smelled like car. I looked at his CDs and saw Dave Matthews and Blues Traveler—music I had in my own collection. By the time Steve settled into the driver's seat and fastened his seat belt, I was cautiously optimistic.

"I preordered the tickets," he said as we walked into the museum, pulling them from his wallet and leading me past the crowd surrounding the main counter. A man renting tape recorders came toward us, giant black machines swinging awkwardly around his neck. "Do you want a taped version of the tour?" Steve asked.

"Not really," I said, "I don't really like them. It feels too much like the machine puts you in your own little world so you can't talk about what you see."

"I feel the same way," he agreed. "I want to know what you think, not the expert on the machine."

We toured slowly through the exhibit, laughing and talking as the crowd jostled us together. Several of the paintings were biblical—portraits of Jesus, Mary with her cousin Elizabeth when they were both pregnant, different scenes from the Gospel stories. There was no choice but to talk about Jesus, which felt weird on a first date, in such a public setting. *Why is that?* I wondered. *I used to talk about astrology everywhere—bars, at the gym, with random people on the subway. I didn't care if people thought I was crazy. But here I am on a date with a guy I met at a Bible study, surrounded by pictures of Jesus, and suddenly I'm waxing poetic about Rembrandt's use of color?*

I leaned down to make out the details of a tiny drawing, called something like *Farmer at Home with His Wife in the Afternoon*, as Steve looked over my shoulder. Then I realized that the farmer was *in bed* with his wife that particular afternoon, his head buried between her meaty thighs. "Wait until I tell my friends you took me to a porn exhibit for our first date," I teased Steve, trying not to blush. "So much for your Mister Nice Guy image."

"We've seen nine hundred pictures of Jesus—no fair focusing in on the happy farmer," he countered, laughing and following behind me. "Besides—the farmer was taking some time off to be with his wife—isn't that what the Bible instructs husbands to do?" The way he handled this awkward situation was impressive—not making too big a deal of it, not dwelling on it or making lewd comments. He dismissed it with a casual joke, then moved on. *Classy.* I smiled at him, wondering what would happen next. Hyperaware of his every gesture, I waited for him to take my hand, or put an arm around me. Resisting the urge to lean into him, I tried to focus on what I saw: self-portraits, copper etchings. Steve stood beside me, so close our arms brushed from time to time. By the end of the exhibit, I was exhilarated, and not by the intricacies of great European art.

After the museum, Steve took me to a restaurant that had been a Cambridge landmark for almost a century. It was comfortable—not too showy, but a significant step up from the Golden Arches. When the waitress brought our dinners, Steve looked at me before touching his plate. "Shall we pray?" he asked.

"Yes," I said, melting into my seat. *He says grace!* I screamed inside, trying to hide my glee.

"Lord, thank you for Trish, and for our time together. Thank you for this food. Bless our conversation, bless this meal to nourish our bodies, and bless the hands that made it. In Jesus' name, Amen."

"Amen," I echoed, smiling like a three-year-old at Christmas. *He thanked God for me!* No one had ever thanked God for me before, except maybe my mom and dad.

We chatted through dinner, about family and school and church and art. When the bill came, Steve grabbed it, waving off my offer to contribute. And on the way out to the car he reached for my hand, weaving his fingers with mine and assuring me that I was indeed on a date.

"Would you like to come up for a few minutes?" I asked as we pulled in front of my house.

"Sure," he said, putting the car into reverse and maneuvering into a tiny spot. Kylie greeted us at the door, and we sat down on the couch to talk. Before I knew it two hours had passed, and my admiration for him had completed its journey from cautious optimism to warm delight. I listened hopefully for some suggestion of a second date. *Don't force it*, I told myself. *The ball is in his court.*

"I should get going," Steve said, rising from the couch. "I have to help my friend paint his new house tomorrow—his wife is pregnant, so we have to get everything squared away so they can move in before the little one comes along."

"I'll walk you out," I said, disappointed. I admired his willingness to help a friend, but if he was interested, wouldn't he want to spend more time with me? (It was a few weeks before I understood that in Christian circles, a guy leaving early can indicate that he's exceptionally interested in you, and knows to leave because he can't do anything about it until you get married.) I leashed Kylie up for her evening walk and followed him down the stairs.

"I had a great time today," he said, turning to face me on the sidewalk and pulling me close for a hug. He smelled warm, like a blend of shaving cream, fabric softener, and testosterone Kristen used to call "good boy smell." *Steve has good boy smell in spades*, I thought, breathing deeply. That's when he tilted his head until his lips touched mine. His hands encircled my waist; I rested mine on his shoulders, and we fell together into a series of soft kisses that made the streetlights around us blur.

Fast-forward one hour: we were still standing there, still kissing. My roommate came home from work, went to the gym, and returned again. Kylie climbed back up on the porch and lay down, realizing that her walk wouldn't be happening anytime soon. It started to rain, and still we stood there, talking and laughing, enjoying the best ending to a first date I could have imagined.

"Can I see you again tomorrow?" he asked, kissing me one more time.

Chapter Twenty-two

What If Jesus Dated?

And just like that, I had a boyfriend. We watched a movie at his place the next night, and sat together that Sunday at church. He shoveled out my car after snowstorms, opened doors for me when we went out, and called after work to see how my day went. He made plans with me weeks in advance for New Year's Eve. It was like a dream come true, as our dates spilled out over the following days like they'd been predestined since the beginning of time.

As I got to know Steve, it was clear that if I fell into a coma, Kylie would be safe in his hands. He told me, bit by bit, how his life had changed over the past few years: he'd lost seventy-three pounds, moved from a job selling sneakers to a salaried position for a biotech company, started following Jesus, stopped smoking pot. I realized that if we'd met ten or five or even three years earlier, it wouldn't have worked—we weren't the people we were now. I waited to stumble on to the awful part, the caveat or exception that would make him like the other men I'd dated. I was used to glossy surfaces hiding a mess underneath, so I fully expected Steve to look into my eyes one day and confess a criminal past or illegitimate children or underground mob involvement. Instead, on our way home from a Christmas party one night, Steve parked the car on my snowy street and leaned over to kiss me. After a minute, the windshield was covered in white powder, and we were ensconced in our own little world. Kissing my forehead, Steve looked into my eyes and said, "I am so in love with you."

I stared at him. I didn't know what to say—I didn't want to rush things or ruin what we had, and after all we had only been dating for one week. My brain went into a blur: I really did sort of like him, and some people might call that love, but not smart people, because smart people know you can't possibly be in love after only one week, and I wanted to be a smart person, only I didn't know what a smart person might say. I sat there, smiling at him, panicking. After what felt like an hour of silence, I opened my mouth, determined to deliver a neutral, safe response.

"I love you, too," I blurted. And as he hugged me, I knew it was true.

A WEEK OR so later we had another snowstorm. Steve picked me up on Saturday and we rented movies, planning to spend the day hanging out on his cozy couch. We'd been there for about ten minutes when his mom called, asking if he could help shovel out her stairs. "Do you mind?" he asked me, holding his hand over the phone.

"Of course not," I said, reaching for my boots so he could take me home. I was disappointed to see our day together disappear, but after dating so many men who'd *hated* their mothers, Steve's willingness to help his out was rather endearing.

"No, no—you stay here and relax," he said. "This shouldn't take long. I've got a trillion channels you can flip through, or you can use the computer. I'll be back in an hour or so and we can watch the movies then."

A few minutes later, I was alone in Steve's condo. And for the first time in my adult life, I had no desire whatsoever to snoop around. This was a miracle. Suspicion had been a daily reality in my prior relationships, ever since Chip had cheated on me. I'd spent hours of my life searching and picking through various bookshelves and coat pockets, looking for evidence that I wasn't the only woman on the scene. More often than not, I'd found what I was looking for—phone numbers, hair elastics, cards expressing some other woman's hope that my man would call. This led to awful, awkward confrontations: What is this?/ Where did you get that?/Why do you still have it?/Were you spying on me?/Don't you *love* me? /Don't you *trust* me? /What does this mean? Each time, I secretly hoped my boyfriend would rise to the occasion, that he'd play the hero: I waited for him to throw away the offending object, sweep me into his arms, reassure me that no woman other than me existed in his world. But that was never how it happened. Not even once.

I didn't feel the urge to snoop on Steve. Left alone in his condo, I didn't want to pick through his desk, rifle through his dresser drawers, or scan his e-mails for evidence of other women. I wanted to trust him. We'd been careful in what we shared about our pasts, protecting each other and our new relationship—I didn't know the names or stories of his former girlfriends, and he hadn't heard the drawn-out saga of my dating history, either. Neither of us had had a significant relationship since deciding to follow Jesus (Steve had met Adam, but we both agreed that that wasn't significant), and we believed what the Bible said about how once you were following Jesus, "the old has gone, the new has come." Accordingly, we agreed not to burden each other with sordid histories, bucking the pop-psychology tradition that to have "real communication" you need to know everything about each other. We didn't hide from the past, but we made a point not to dwell on it, either. It was stunning how good that felt. Dating Steve was the first time I considered the possibility that jealousy and distrust might *not* be a part of God's design for relationships.

I turned on the television and wrestled with Steve's three remote controls. I checked my e-mail and read a news report about two celebrities eloping at an island resort. And I looked in Steve's Bible, sitting on the coffee table, tabbed, underlined, with a pen sticking out of the book of Galatians. It was the same chapter I'd read that morning. I sat there on his couch and stared out the window, amazed that we looked to the same words to guide our lives.

STEVE AND I agreed that we wanted to follow the Bible's rules about dating, but we had little in the way of clear guidance on what that meant or how to make it happen. Our church discussed vague theories like compatibility at dating workshops, but no one ever came out and said, "Here is a list of dos and don'ts." So we prayed. Here's what we heard: *Don't have sex until you get married.* We didn't realize it at the time, but this would require quite a bit of our attention. It was challenging, we soon discovered, to focus on what we were *not* going to do. When someone says, "Don't think about the Eiffel Tower," suddenly Paris is on your mind.

It was a particularly stormy winter, so most of our dates took place indoors. We watched TV and rented movies, but that was all just a coverup; all we wanted to do was snuggle and make out. We kissed chastely for a while—gentle explorations of the new, intimate landscape of *us*. But eventually things would heat up, and I found myself wanting to do things we'd agreed we wouldn't do. Apparently, we discovered, God didn't protect Christian couples by neutralizing their hormones until they reached the altar—not at all. (To this day, when I think of those evenings, I can remember every detail of Steve's favorite plaid shirt, which I memorized to distract myself. *The thin blue line goes up to the shoulder seam, where it picks up the horizontal bit of yellow. They cross over the green together, making a little square . . .*)

We employed a teamwork approach to chastity, but it was clear from the beginning that Steve was our captain. I agreed to our goals wholeheartedly, but when push came to shove (so to speak) I was always the one ready to sell us down the river for a quick roll on the couch. Steve however, had the strength to say, "No way," and stick to it, which made me love, trust, and long for him even more. We developed strategies to keep us out of trouble: whenever things got hot and heavy, we'd flip to Psalm 119—the longest Psalm in the Bible—and read it until we cooled down. We kept the giant book right in front of us on the coffee table, marked with a bright green Post-it; the prospect of reading 176 lines about how blessed people are who walk according to the law of the Lord was always enough to put us back in check.

We agreed not to spend the night together, reasoning that when the Bible said, "and he lay with her," it didn't mean they merely shared a tent and a little spooning. It sounded quaint, but we wanted to save the intimacy of sleeping together—in all the phrase's connotations—until marriage. So we stayed on the couch. We cuddled, we hugged, we even slid down a bit from time to time into a kind of uncomfortable semi-nap position that we pretended to love because it felt good to be that close. I liked hearing his heartbeat and feeling his fingers in my hair.

Something amazing happened inside me as those days and nights went by and Steve ended our dates with gentle kissing and careful, A-framed hugs: I realized that he loved me. He loved *me*. Not my sexual wiles or flirtatious energy, not my bedroom skills or some new magazine technique I picked up in the checkout aisle at Stop & Shop, but *me*. There were no "perks" to our time together, no secret agenda making me wonder why he stopped by. If he said he missed me and wanted to see me, I could believe him. And as the months went by and he drove me home after every date, never once suggesting that I crash at his place, "just because we're both so tired," I realized that protecting me, and us, was worth something to him—that he valued what we were building enough to spend forty-five minutes in a cold car at the end of the night so that we didn't get into trouble. Most of our dates ended by 10:00 p.m., but this was the most adored I'd ever felt.

Despite all this love, however, I was still haunted by that awful passage in Matthew. Had Steve seen this passage, where Jesus said that anyone who married a divorced woman was committing adultery? I wondered. Did he think marrying me would be adulterous? Of the few people I dared ask about this, no one had anything encouraging to say. "I don't know," they'd mumble. "The Bible says God hates divorce." None of them had been divorced, or worried about such things. They tried to hide it, but the look in their eyes showed that they weren't entirely sure about Jesus' promise that I was a new creation. I tried to remember the words one person prayed for me when I first came to church, a woman who knew nothing of my circumstances: "God will give you beauty for your ashes," she said. "He will redeem what has been taken from you."

God, I prayed, *please let this be true.*

One night when Steve came to pick me up, the look on his face told me he'd found that passage. "We need to talk," he said, his voice grave and shaky.

"I need to know what happened with your first marriage," Steve said without any further introduction or preface. "I need to figure out if it's right for us to pursue this, if Jesus is okay that we're dating."

My heart sank. I couldn't spin this, I had no crafty plan to convince or entice or seduce him. I had prayed for a man who ran his life by God's rules, and here I had one; his decisions were beyond my manipulation. "Can we pray first?" I asked. Part of me was stalling, but mostly I wanted to make sure that if God was about to ruin my life again, He was there to witness my pain.

"Lord," Steve prayed, taking my hands in his, "be with us right now. Show us what You want us to see. I thank You that You brought Trish out of that marriage, and that You brought us together. But we want to make sure we do everything according to Your will, and we need Your help to do that. Be with us here tonight. In Jesus' name, we pray. Amen."

"Amen," I repeated, taking a deep breath. "Okay," I forged ahead, terrified of what would come next. "What do you want to know?"

"Just tell me what happened."

How could I tell him about the awful things my ex had done? The truth was, I didn't really think of myself as "divorced," not often, anyway. I'd put it behind me when I decided to follow Jesus, but now all that talk of being a new creation seemed like nothing more than rhetoric. "I was his third wife," I began. "He was demanding." I told Steve how I'd get in trouble for getting my hair cut without my ex's permission, or folding the laundry in the wrong order. "He'd even yell at me for petting the dog," I said, stroking Kylie's silky ears as she lay next to us on the couch, oblivious to my angst. I described my life in those days—the constant yelling, the fear. I told Steve about the time I met a nice woman at the gym, only to have my ex tell me that he'd had an affair with her, how he went out to bars and brought home women's phone numbers, and went to his ex-girlfriend's house whenever we had a fight. "I don't know where this leaves us," I said at the end. "I took Jesus at his word that my past was put behind me when I said yes to following him, and until tonight it seemed like it was true." Tears pooled in my eyes and I looked away.

"It will be okay," Steve assured me, not sounding sure himself. "I love you so much—you're the woman I've been praying for," he said, pulling me into his arms.

The next day he called. "Can I come over?"

"Of course," I said. *Please don't,* I thought. *I'm not sure I can take it.*

"I spent last night praying," he said when he was back in my living room, back on my couch, arms back around me in that way that felt so right. "I asked God if I could pursue you, if I could think about us building a life together. You should know something, before I tell you any more: I don't care that you were married before. I love you, and that includes your past, your present, and, I hope, your future. If Jesus hadn't mentioned divorce in the Bible, I wouldn't give it any thought at all. But he did, so I have to; it's what following Jesus is all about."

"You're right," I acknowledged. Here Steve was, showing all the character and devotion I dreamed of, right before breaking up with me. *This should put quite a dent in my evangelism,* I thought bitterly. *I'm sure divorcées will flock to Christianity once they discover it dooms them to life alone.*

"So here's what God told me," Steve continued. I sucked in my breath and looked away. "Look at me," he said, moving my chin with his giant hand. "You're free," he began. "Your past has been erased."

"What do you mean?" I asked. Was I free to apply to the convent?

"Your first marriage happened before you knew Jesus, or even understood what God meant when He created marriage. Your first husband wasn't in a position to enter a covenant with you; he'd broken covenant with two other wives already. He deceived you, and it seems pretty clear he was unfaithful to your marriage. Jesus exempted women whose husbands had been unfaithful," Steve reminded me. "On every level," he said, a huge smile filling his face and lighting up his eyes, "God told me you are free, that it's okay for us to pursue this, that I can continue to woo you and try to win your heart. I love you, Trish, and I hope I can make you as happy as you make me."

I collapsed into an exhausted, grateful heap in his arms, crying. Steve fished a tissue out of his pocket and dried my tears, holding me close and teasing me about my puffy eyes. I blew my nose in front of him for the first time, and that's how we began the next phase of our relationship.

Chapter Twenty-three

Good News in the Garden

It would be perfect if I could tell you that I spent the next months of our dating in a state of relaxation and bliss, certain my future was in God's hands and trusting Him to make my life complete. Unfortunately, that would be a total lie. I was still dogged by the vague, tormenting sense that *time was running out*—that if I didn't close the deal and get married soon, the things Steve and I had dodged so far—jealousy, disillusionment, disappointment—would overtake us. I wanted to believe that things with Steve could be different, that things with Jesus would be different, but I wasn't sure I had the faith. Jesus said, "Everything is possible for him who believes." *I believe*, I told him. *Help my unbelief . . .*

Then one morning as I put on my makeup, I heard a voice say, *You and Steve will be married on June nineteenth.* I dismissed it, assuming it was my imagination. My Christian dating books were filled with stories of delusional women who thought God told them when and who they would marry; they were always wrong. *That's impossible,* I told myself. *June is three months away, and we're not even engaged.* I pushed it out of my mind and smoothed a bit more Pink Celebration onto my cheeks.

Three weeks later, Steve suggested a Saturday picnic at the Boston Public Garden to celebrate the first warm weekend of spring. *How romantic!* I thought, but I was confused. We weren't, from what I could tell, a "picnic in the park" kind of couple. I mentioned this to Amy, who pointed out that we'd never dated in warm weather, that we might, in fact, be a "picnic in the park" kind of couple, I just didn't know it yet.

I stared at the grounds of the Public Garden wide-eyed as we walked in that day. I'd never been there before, and I took in the scenes I'd imagined in my childhood as Mom read us E. B. White's classic, *The Trumpet of the Swan:* the lily ponds and paddle boats, the bridge under which mute swan Louis once slept. Steve looked handsome, his maroon waffle pullover falling from his broad shoulders. I smiled, remembering the encouraging words of a woman preacher I'd seen on Christian television a few months earlier, exhorting us not to settle: "Remember, ladies," she said, "God don't bring no shlumpy, triflin' men. If he's shlumpy and triflin', he ain't from the Lord!" Steve was neither shlumpy nor trifling, and I was happy to be starting spring with his hand wrapped around mine.

We found a spot under some trees, spread out a blanket, and claimed our place among the other Bostonians emerging from hibernation. Steve unwrapped turkey roll-ups and fruit salad; we ate as we watched a little boy toddling after a soccer ball. I turned to Steve to thank him for planning such a magnificent, relaxing day. "You're wonderful. I love you for doing all this for us. I can't imagine anything better." I wrapped my arms around his shoulders and gave him a big hug.

"In that case," he responded, pulling back slightly and looking in my eyes, "Will you do me the honor?" I looked down and saw a black velvet box in his hands, holding a sparkling solitaire diamond. I stared at it, astonished.

"Where did that come from?" I blurted. "It's so beautiful!" I felt my heart pounding as my eyes filled up with tears. *Is this really happening?* I wondered, afraid I might be making it up. *Can this be true?* I looked up and saw Steve smiling at me, his eyes twinkling, shining with a love like I'd never seen before. *He wants me!?* I thought, incredulous. *Steve wants me to be his wife!*

"It was my grandmother's," Steve said, turning the diamond so its facets caught the sun. "My mom saved it for me for all these years, and I had it reset last week for you. Do you like it?"

"I do! I mean, yes! Wait a minute," I paused, wanting to draw out this wonderful moment, "I don't think you ever finished your question . . . will I do you the honor of what?" I teased, a huge grin on my face.

"Will you do me the honor of being my wife?" he asked, smiling, but with a serious look in his eyes.

"Yes," I said. "I would love to be your wife." Steve wrapped his arms around me and pulled me to him, my head fitting into the space next to his neck, my chin on his strong shoulder. Then he slipped the ring out of the box and onto my ring finger, where we watched it sparkle for what seemed like hours.

"We should pray," I said, tearing my eyes away from this new treasure on my hand and looking up at Steve. "I feel like we should include God in this."

Steve took my hands in his and bowed his head alongside mine. "Lord, thank you. Thank you for bringing us together, thank you for the promise of marriage and new life. Bless us as we start this new chapter together. Be with us, Jesus, and knit us together. We dedicate our new family to you," he prayed. "Your turn," he said to me, squeezing my hands.

"Jesus," I said, "thank you for coming through on your promise. I'm so glad I took you seriously. Thank you for being the right God, and for bringing me the right guy!"

Steve pulled a tiny bottle of champagne out of his bag and we shared a discreet toast, careful not to draw the attention of the mounted park police. I looked down at his grandmother's diamond, saved by his mother for the woman who would be his wife. I was that woman.

You and Steve will be married on June nineteenth. God's words echoed in my head. *That's impossible,* I thought again. *Yes, it's impossible,* God confirmed, interrupting my thoughts. *But what is impossible for you,* he reminded me gently, *is possible with Me.*

"June nineteenth is just two months away," Steve pointed out when I told him. "Can we plan a wedding that quickly?"

"If God wants us to, I guess we can."

"Then June nineteenth it is!"

BRIEF ENGAGEMENTS ARE a running source of humor at the Vineyard: After all, when a couple isn't fooling around or sleeping together, they get to know each other much faster—what else is there to do but talk? And once a couple is engaged, the prospect of a grand wedding often fades into the background as they contemplate their wedding night, and starting their new life together takes precedence over waiting nine months for a certain ballroom or favorite flower to be available. Never before had I found a community that so "got" my mother's maxim that planning a marriage should take precedence over planning a wedding. But two months was rather fast, even by Vineyard standards.

We shared our date with Brian, the associate pastor we asked to marry us. "June nineteenth is soon," he observed, smiling at us. "Want to tell me what led you to choose that date?"

"Well," I began, feeling foolish and defensive, "my mother has been sick. She's on oxygen twenty-four hours a day and has had some severe bouts in the hospital where we didn't know what was going to happen. We want to make sure she can be there with us, that we don't wait too long."

"That makes sense—" Brian said.

"That's not the only thing," Steve added, interrupting him. "Tell him what God told you," he said, prompting me.

I was mortified. It seemed so silly now, the idea that God spoke to me and told me when we were supposed to get married. "I thought I heard from God a few weeks before Steve proposed," I mumbled, staring down at the table. "A voice said, *You and Steve will be married on June nineteenth.* But that's not the only reason we picked this date, and it might not even be a good idea anyway . . ." I trailed off, not knowing what else to say. Who was I to claim to hear from God?

"I think that's significant," Brian said, surprising me. "If God told you June nineteenth, then you should listen to that. Unless we come across some reason in our premarital talks why you shouldn't get married so soon, then I think that's the date."

That's right, I remembered, embarrassed—*Brian's a pastor. If anyone believes we can hear from God, it's him.* I silently apologized to God for almost bowing out of our "let Him plan the wedding" agreement.

"You won't be able to take the marriage class we offer before your wedding," Brian said, but I'd encourage you to take it this fall. There is valuable material there that will help you that I can't cover in a few two-hour sessions." We promised to take the course that September. That's when it dawned on me that we would be *married* in September, that my life now included plans for when I'd be Mrs. Steven Ryan, when we'd be living together as husband and wife. I shivered in delight.

"Are you getting cold?" Steve asked, concerned.

"No," I assured him with another giant smile. "I'm fine."

As well as that talk went, the rest of our wedding planning was bizarre. There was no rhyme or reason to our approach; we needed everything, but weren't at all sure what "everything" was. We had no idea where to have our wedding, and no plan of what to do. Our guest list reached almost one hundred, and I balked at the idea of catering a meal for that many people. "It will wipe us out!" I fretted. "If our friends love us, they'll be fine with a few hors d'oeuvres!" I dreamed of the simpler days of small-town life, where brides-to-be booked the local Elks' lodge and a committee of church ladies made piles of deviled eggs and ham salad sandwiches.

"I'm Italian," Steve protested. "We have to feed people—it's what we do. I don't know how we're going to do it, but I trust that God will work it out."

The food dilemma paled in comparison to our larger problem, which was that we didn't know *where* we'd be doing any of this. I called the quaint church where my sister had been married ten years before. They wanted $800 to use the sanctuary, $200 to pay an organist we didn't want, and another $100 for a cleanup guy to take care of the mess they assumed we'd leave behind. That prospect grew dimmer still when we received a call from the church secretary, who told us that their reverend would be happy to perform our ceremony, but required an additional donation and three premarital meetings.

I told Steve the grim news. We knew nothing about this pastor—who she was, what she believed. I was sure she was a lovely woman, but she was a stranger. We had no relationship with her. That night we asked God for guidance, after which I called the church office and withdrew our request for their help. "It's up to you now, Lord," we prayed.

We drove north to my home town in Maine the following Saturday with the single goal of finding a place to get married. "The Congregationalists might let you in," my father speculated, "or maybe that Baptist church downtown." We sat in the Baptist parking lot for twenty minutes, working up the courage to go in.

"We're not Baptists," I told Steve. "This feels like a total lie."

"We don't have to lie to them," he pointed out. "I bet they have people ask them all the time if they can use their church."

"I can't do it. Let's go for a ride around the beach so I can pull myself together."

We drove past the library, turning down a winding back road that brought us out on a hill overlooking the river. "Take a right," I said. "I feel like we're supposed to go right." Two hundred yards down the road was the Nonantum Inn, the most elegant wedding site in town. A banner bellowed out from the pristine sign: Wedding Fair Today! I gaped at it, speechless.

As we walked up the stairs, passing rocking chairs and planters filled with flowers, I noticed how charming the main building was. Even though I'd grown up in this town, riding my bicycle and later driving my parents' car down this street thousands of times, there had never been any occasion for me to enter the Nonantum, or even risk trespassing in its outdoor pool (which was far too close to the guest rooms to be suitable for night diving). I was surprised to find it so appealing, even filled with wedding industry experts and hundreds of brides-to-be. Weaving our way past DJs, piles of embossed invitations, and mannequins decked out in yards of tulle and satin, we found the main table in the back and met Dawn, the Nonantum's wedding coordinator.

Not only was June nineteenth the last date available that summer, she told us, but our late-morning time slot was discounted so they could mark their season full. After a whirlwind meeting, we booked an elegant room for our ceremony, the ballroom overlooking the river for our reception, and a catered, multicourse buffet for one hundred people—all for less than one of my friends had paid for her wedding *dress* a few years earlier. The florist was available for the nineteenth and agreed to do my bouquet for free. Dawn even offered us a river-view room for our wedding night, compliments of the house. Honestly, it was as if Jesus had walked into the place ahead of us and told everyone, *Take care of these people, they're with me.*

I SPENT THE next month surfing crazy Bridezilla Web sites, wondering if I was an awful person because I didn't plan to give my bridesmaids hand-studded flip-flops, or velvet hoodies with their initials written out in sparkling Diamonique. "What kind of bride," one poster asked, "doesn't own a glue gun?" I had no answer for that. I had a larger concern looming on my bridal horizon, rearing its ugly head in the form of a pink-and-white Victoria's Secret gift card Gwen bought to help me "prepare" for my honeymoon (Gwen comes from a long line of women who understand the value of some well-placed lace and satin— her mother sends lingerie care packages to missionary couples in third world countries). The card left me terrified. Ever since God had clarified the terms of what following Jesus would entail for me (*You realize, don't you, that this means no more sex until you get married?*) I'd worked overtime to purge myself of every bit of sexuality: I'd checked my outfits carefully to make sure my tops didn't "accidentally" ride up or slip down, skipped over steamy scenes in books that threatened to "awaken love before its time," and thrown away all five of my Janet Jackson CDs once I realized that almost every song she sang either offered, reflected on, or fantasized about some sexual interaction that didn't sound at all like a celebration of monogamous marital intimacy. *Damn,* I'd thought at one point, foraging through my CDs for something safe to listen to, *this Jesus thing is turning me into Tipper Gore.*

As silly as it felt, though, narrowing what I took in had helped me toe the line, sexually speaking. As a practical matter, it was far easier to keep my mind off of forbidden activities once I stopped singing about them every time I hopped in the car or ran on the treadmill. When Steve and I started dating, I veered off even more to the extreme, treating every sexual temptation as poison to our budding relationship. I'd "given the cow away for free" too many times before. I didn't want to do that again, and the only way I could figure out to keep a hold of the cow, so to speak, was to avoid sexual suggestion entirely. So this was how I'd spent the past two years of my life, avoiding all things sensual, trying to be *honest*, rather than seductive or alluring.

If there's one thing Victoria's Secret isn't about, I realized, walking into the store ten days before my wedding, *it's honesty.* Engulfed in a surreal sea of hot pink, my eyes swam. I felt besieged. *What does one do,* I wondered, *to flip back on all the sexy switches I've flipped off?* Giant pictures from the catalog hung around the perimeter of the store, Amazonian models stared down at me, as if taunting, "*This* is what your man wants . . . you can buy the outfit, but you'll never look like me." It was awful. I looked for something pretty, sexy, inviting. I wanted to be me on my wedding night, only better—a little lace, a little satin. Something beautiful in ivory that would feel good against my skin, then puddle delicately on the floor. But all I saw were giant padded cone bras covered with marabou, cotton tank tops with Let Me Be Your Angel spelled out in rhinestones, and a gold satin thong with a string of pearls—pearls?—running up the back. That was *not* where I wanted to keep my pearl of great price. There was nothing elegant, nothing sexy-but-discreet. It all screamed, "We've

done this before—here's something new to spice things up!"
These were not the terms on which I wanted to start my married sex life—assuming we were already bored, trying to wow
Steve with my willingness to climb into yards of elasticized
costuming to keep things between us "hot." At some point, I
hoped to have a nice collection of sexy little items he'd enjoy,
things we'd accumulate together over time, once we figured out
how we worked. But these racks and mannequins and pictures
all told me I should give up now, because I'd never be that tall,
that thin, that curvy; Steve would never find me sexy. I left that
day feeling pathetic—embarrassed that I thought I could be a
sexy woman when it was so obvious I didn't have what it took.

After that ill-fated shopping trip, I found myself paralyzed,
and paranoid. I couldn't watch a movie, a television show, or
even a commercial without hearing a voice in my head, taunting
me that Steve wished I looked more like *her*, whoever the actress
on the screen happened to be. I saw him glancing through my
issue of *In Style* magazine and assumed he was fantasizing about
the woman on the cover. I felt like an idiot. "What's wrong,
honey?" Steve asked, over and over that week. "Are you okay?"

"I'm fine," I lied. "I think I'm nervous about *(insert whatever
wedding detail might convince him my weirdness is all wedding related)*."

By the time our final premarital session with Brian rolled
around, I was a basket case. Steve wanted to see a movie that
night, to take our mind off all the planning. I couldn't explain
to him why this terrified me. What was I going to say—"But,
honey, movies have actresses, all of whom look better than me,
which will only leave you disappointed. Our only hope for a
happy marriage is to never go to the movies again"?

Our sessions with Brian had been pretty low-key up until this point. Steve and I had remarkably parallel lives, and looked to the future hoping for pretty much the same things. Our parents loved each other and loved us, we'd weeded all the skeletons out of the closets before getting engaged, and we both liked the traditional vows Brian showed us from the Anglican Book of Common Prayer. Mostly we talked with Brian about how much we were looking forward to being married as opposed to planning a wedding. At that last meeting, though, I was antsy and miserable. When Brian asked, "Is there anything you need prayer for between now and Saturday morning?" I blurted, "Yes! I'm scared, and I don't know what to do!" Brian and Steve both looked at me wide-eyed, stunned to hear such misery in my voice.

"What is it, love?" Steve asked. "Are you all right?"

"No. I'm not. I don't know what happened. I was so excited about our wedding night, our honeymoon, finally enjoying all the marital benefits we've waited for. I even went to Victoria's Secret last week to buy some things I thought you'd like." I was embarrassed to say this in front of Brian. *He's married*, I reminded myself. *He probably knows about honeymoons and lingerie.* "All they had," I continued, "was stuff like you'd wear in a rap video, and models who looked like they'd give you whatever you wanted. It made me wonder, why would you want me if you could have *that*? And even if you want me because you can't get *that*, won't you be thinking about *that* all the time, wishing *that* was how I looked?" I gasped, smearing my mascara with a lunch napkin, sniffling between little hiccups.

"Honey," Steve said, "I don't want that. What can I do to

show you that you're what I want on our wedding night, and for the rest of our lives?"

"Nothing," I wailed. "That's the thing. You tell me all the time, but I don't believe you."

"I know one thing we can do," Brian said. "We can pray. Would it be all right if I prayed for you about this?"

"That would be great," Steve said, folding my hand in both of his.

"I guess so," I allowed, not at all sure praying would help.

"Jesus," Brian began, "we come before you today and we thank you that when two or more of us are gathered in your name, you are here with us. I lift up Steve and Trish to you and thank you for all you're doing in their lives, preparing them for marriage. I ask you to step into this situation Trish described. We know these feelings of fear and inferiority are not from you. In Jesus' name, I bind the evil spirits behind these taunts. I bind all spirits of seduction, manipulation, pornography, prostitution, and lust off of this relationship in the name of Jesus—I command them to leave this couple alone and go to the foot of the Cross. Trish and Steve, I speak joy and fulfillment into your marriage, particularly the intimacies you'll share as man and wife. In Jesus' name I bless you with passion, satisfaction, and enjoyment of one another. Steve, as the Bible says, 'May you rejoice in the wife of your youth, may her breasts satisfy you always.' Trish, I bless you with freedom, to bask in Steve's love and fend off all the lies of the enemy that would come against your marriage."

I felt something lift off of me then, like a weight coming off of my chest. Suddenly, I was happy. Ridiculously so. Not in a fake way, but in that *life couldn't be better and why does everyone look so serious?* manner that felt like a miracle.

"How are you doing?" Brian asked.

"Great," I replied. "Amazing. Wonderful. I feel like me again."

"Well, praise God," he exclaimed, smiling. "Lord, thank you for answering our prayers. We ask that you remind us all that you are the answer to the problems we can't solve on our own. Thank you for taking such good care of us, and we ask that this freedom hold. In Jesus' name, Amen."

"Amen," Steve and I echoed.

"Do you want to see that movie tonight?" Steve asked as we walked back to his car.

"Maybe," I replied coyly. "But first I have some shopping to do."

THE NIGHT BEFORE my wedding, Meg and Kristen took me out for dinner and chocolate martinis. They placed a giant plastic veil on my head, attached to a crown that had "Bride To Be" on it in blinking red lights. They prayed fervently—humorously—asking God to give my new husband exceptional skill on our wedding night, making jokes about us "unwrapping our gifts."

By this time tomorrow night, I thought happily, feeling my blinking bridal crown digging into my head, *I'll be Mrs. Ryan . . .*

Chapter Twenty-four

I+I+I=I

The next day, as I stood outside the double doors of the little chapel, my father offered me his tuxedo-clad arm. "Are you ready?" he asked with a smile.

"I'm ready." I nodded. And I was. I felt relaxed, standing there next to my father, and delighted in a way I had never felt before, amazed that this was finally (*finally!*) my wedding day.

It hadn't been a perfect morning. The weather was gray and rainy; my hairdresser was hung over. (When she swung my chair around to show me the results of the forty-five minutes she'd spent wrestling with my hair, all I could say was "Well, the veil will cover it.") Honestly—miraculously—I didn't care. I got it that morning, somewhere deep inside: I understood that the details of the wedding were no big deal. The big deal was that in a few hours, Brian would pronounce Steve and me husband and wife, and God would somehow knit the two of us together into one. *When that happens,* I reminded myself, *it won't matter what my hair looks like.*

Dawn adjusted my train and I looked back one more time over the yards of ivory, embroidered with pink and lavender flowers and an intricate pattern of leaves. I felt like a princess, there on my father's arm. Tears welled up in my eyes as I heard the notes of the opening song, the same verses that had greeted me the first time I walked into the Vineyard: "Here, O Lord, is the place where I belong. Now is the time for me to find my place in your design." That's exactly how I felt—finally, I was where I belonged, taking my place in God's design. *Thank you, God,* I whispered under my breath, looking up at the sparkling ceiling. *Thank you for keeping your promise.* I squeezed my father's arm as the doors swung open, and he led me down the aisle to the man who had chosen me—me!—to be his wife.

"We have come together in the presence of God to witness and bless the joining together of this man and this woman in marriage," Brian announced, beginning the ceremony. "The bond and covenant of marriage was established by God in creation. It signifies to us the mystery of the union between Christ and his church, and Holy Scripture commands it to be honored among all people."

Steve reached for my hand, as he did whenever we stood together, and it felt like the most normal thing in the world to be up in front of our family and friends in our finest attire, declaring our love for God and each other to the world. It was like a party, a celebration that things had finally turned out right.

"The union of husband and wife in heart, body, and mind," Brian continued, "is intended by God for their mutual joy, for the help and comfort given one another in prosperity and adversity, for partnership in God's redemptive purposes in the world, and when it is God's will, for the procreation of children and their nurture in the knowledge and love of the Lord."

I hung on these words, savoring them. *There it is*, I thought. *This is what I've always wanted.* The traditional Anglican teaching encapsulated why I'd longed for marriage—the mutual joy, help and comfort, partnership and connection, and family that only God can make possible. I squeezed Steve's hand, not wanting to miss a moment of this ceremony. *All those years I chased the sacred*, I thought. *Now, here, this is it.*

"Steven," Brian asked, "will you take Patricia to be your wife—"

"I will!" Steve blurted. We burst out laughing. My heart swelled with the realization that not only did Steve want me as his wife, he was jumping ahead to make it happen.

"Hold on," Brian said, grinning, "let me spell out all you're agreeing to. Steven, will you take Patricia to be your wife, to live together in the covenant of marriage as the Lord your God commands, will you love and honor her, lay down your life for her, comfort and encourage her, and, forsaking all others, be faithful to her as long as you both shall live?"

"I will," Steve repeated firmly, giving my hand a squeeze. I looked at his shining eyes, amazed that we'd finally reached this moment. I wanted to shout, *Me too!* but I waited for Brian to continue.

"Patricia," Brian asked, "will you take Steven to be your husband, to live together in the covenant of marriage as the Lord your God commands, will you love and honor him, lay down your life for him, comfort and encourage him, and, forsaking all others, be faithful to him as long as you both shall live?"

"I will," I promised, lost in Steve's big green eyes.

Our parents agreed to receive us into each other's family and recognize us as a family in our own right, and the congregation agreed to do everything in its power to help us keep the promises we made. Then Brian gave a wonderful sermon about love and marriage, most of which I missed because I kept sneaking glances at Steve and thinking, *This is it! This is my wedding!* I was jolted back to attention when Brian announced that it was time for us to exchange our vows. He started with Steve, instructing him to repeat the vows we'd discussed in our class, the ones God would use to link us together:

"With God's help, I, Steven, take you, Trish, to be my wife." I stared at him in awe, afraid I might actually *swoon*, like a character in a nineteenth-century British novel. "To love you as Christ loved the church," Steve continued. "To submit to you and lay down my life for you. To have and to hold and, forsaking all others, be faithful to you. To comfort and encourage you. To honor you and communicate with you. To forgive and seek forgiveness. To cherish and delight in you in all circumstances. To strive toward the potential God has placed in me, and to encourage you to strive toward the potential God has placed in you. And to follow Jesus and encourage you to follow with me as long as we both shall live." I exhaled as he finished, only peripherally aware that I'd been holding my breath.

"With God's help," I responded, repeating Brian's cues, "I, Patricia, take you, Steven, to be my husband." *My husband!* I thought, a childish wave of glee sweeping through me. "To respect you and submit to you as to Christ," I continued, knowing deep down inside that the words I spoke were the absolute truth. I wasn't going through the motions; I wasn't saying vows because of the beauty of following tradition. I meant these vows—every word. "To love you and lay down my life for you. To have and to hold and, forsaking all others, be faithful to you. To comfort and encourage you. To honor you and communicate with you. To forgive and seek forgiveness. To cherish and delight in you in all circumstances. To strive toward the potential God has placed in me, and to encourage you to strive toward the potential God has placed in you. And to follow Jesus and encourage you to follow with me as long as we both shall live."

We exchanged rings. Contrary to all the bridal lore I'd heard about puffy stressed-out wedding fingers, these outward symbols of our inward covenant fit perfectly, and I twisted the thin band of platinum with my thumb—just as I'd seen Paul and Pascha do when they were newlyweds and I first came to their small group, all those months before.

"Now," Brian pronounced with a smile, pulling me from my reverie, "I declare you husband and wife. Steve, you may kiss your bride." Steve took my face in his hands as he kissed me, the clapping and cheers of our family resounding in the background.

He loves me, I realized, and this time I knew for sure. It was just as the Bible promised—*exceedingly, abundantly, above all I could ask or imagine.*

PART IV

Happily Ever After

Chapter Twenty-five

Learning to Roast a Chicken

My sister and I had a longish conversation the other day about the best way to roast a chicken—it felt like a bit of a miracle. I'd never roasted anything; my life was always more of the "grab a bologna sandwich" variety. But now that's changed. I'm married. Happily married, that is. I cook chicken for my husband, which means I have a husband to cook for. To me, that simple fact is proof that God is real, that He acts in our lives today and follows through on His promises.

Steve and I faced some transitions in our first days of marriage, to be sure. After months of staying vertical and monitoring our kisses for heavy breathing, waking up in bed next to my new husband each morning took a bit of getting used to. As did his strange conviction that green beans and granola bars don't constitute a full dinner. We learned a lot that first year: We discovered that when you combine a man who is effortlessly punctual with a woman who is chronically early, you somehow end up with a couple who is ten to fifteen minutes late everywhere they go. We learned that sometimes you don't know you're "in the mood" for something until you say *Sure, why not?* and go for it. We learned that the freshman fifteen is nothing compared to the newlywed ninety (I think I started to gain weight the minute we said, "I do," as if my body relaxed and stopped feeding off of itself for the first time since I was fourteen). We learned that when those feelings of indignation, irritation, and frustration well up inside us until it feels like the walls are closing in, the best thing to do isn't to "communicate," but rather to *pray*. As it turns out, God has a whole arsenal of win-win solutions up His sleeve that far surpass anything we come up with on our own, so we've learned to avail ourselves of Him on a regular basis. And we learned to say to one another, at the slightest hint of hurt or offense or miscommunication, "I'm sorry—will you forgive me?" and to respond in the affirmative, forgiving one another, whether we feel like it in that particular moment or not. In short, we learned the things that give legs to our vows to love, honor, and cherish one another, discovering what it means to live as this new creation, this *one* God promises married couples in the Bible.

There have also been spiritual transitions, as I learned the things that give legs to my vow to follow Jesus. Being part of the family of God is like being part of any other family, I discovered—sometimes you love the people you're with, sometimes they drive you nuts. More than once I resolved, like a child frustrated by some perceived injustice or slight, to pack up my toys and run away. But I never got farther than the corner before the big, wide world seemed like an awfully lonely place, forcing me to admit how much I missed my church family. Jesus described himself as a shepherd, rescuing lost sheep and keeping the flock safe and close together; in my case, at least, he's had his work cut out for him. My friends at the Vineyard—Dave and Grace, Paul and Pascha, Amy, Will, Gwen (the list goes on)—moved heaven and earth to create a place for me to figure out my relationship with Jesus, showing graciousness beyond anything I could have dreamed of. They gave me roots, and that feels good.

I ONCE HEARD a talk by a man named Carl, who described typical Christian evangelism as a bunch of self-righteous people standing in a tight circle around Jesus, with a huge wall around them separating them from the outside world. The goal in such circles, he explained, is to pull as many people as possible over the wall and into the circle by whatever means necessary, thereby rescuing them from the certain destruction (read: hellfire and brimstone) threatening them on the outside. He called this a "bounded sets" approach, where everyone is defined by being either in or out. He wasn't, it seemed, a big fan of this approach.

"What if," he posited, "the important thing isn't whether you are in or out, so much as which way you're facing?" He described an alternative, an "unbounded sets" approach, which keeps Jesus right in the center. Carl drew dots to represent Jesus' followers, still free to edge up as close to him as they want to be. The rest of the world, however—the faraway dots who don't believe in Jesus or don't like him or have given him no thought at all—can, at whatever point they choose, turn to face him to find out what he might be about. There's no wall to climb, no secret password to learn, no "in" or "out" or "us" or "them." Just a standing invitation to turn to face Jesus, and to walk toward him at whatever pace you're called.

This picture stays with me, a perfect description of my slow turn and recalcitrant stroll toward Jesus (then away from Jesus, then off on some wild tangent, then back toward him again). In all my frantic circling, trying to go every direction at once, Jesus was there—I could approach him from wherever I was, however I was; he was always on call. This is, I think, a nice quality in a savior. But I was never pulled over any wall; I never got it "right." All I did was say *yes* when Jesus offered to help me find a way out of my chaos.

Here's a confession: even at the height of my expansive spiritual exploration, it always seemed wrong to me, this idea that *we* define God—that it's up to us to decide who God is and what God likes and dislikes, and he/she/it will be fine with whatever we come up with. I didn't see how it could work this way, as nice as the idea might sound. Honestly, if—as you saw—I couldn't pick a decent man without divine intervention, what on earth made me think I had any business trying to design my own god? The more I struggled to embrace it, the closer I came to the reality that I hated the idea of an amorphous, standardless, undefined deity watching me flounder about and loving me anyway. From this viewpoint, it was all up to me, and God would be fine with however things turned out. The problem was that *I* wouldn't have been fine if my life had continued on its set trajectory for the next thirty, forty, or even fifty years. I needed a God who gave a damn about what I did; a God who was willing and able to help, who would kick my butt back on track whenever I wandered off again following my own broken compass.

So now, when I say *God*, it's a little awkward, because I have to choose: should I be honest, or politically correct? As author Ravi Zacharias aptly puts it, "We are living in a time when sensitivities are at the surface . . . Philosophically, you can believe anything, so long as you do not claim it to be true. Morally, you can practice anything, so long as you do not claim that it is a 'better' way. Religiously, you can hold to anything, so long as you do not bring Jesus Christ into it." Well, I guess I've blown that. Sharing my story would be so much easier if I'd found true love through transcendental meditation, eating kale and mangoes, or even a super-special lip gloss—if my narrative were hipper somehow, or edgier, or at least politically correct. But that's not how it happened.

Here's the honest version: Now, when I say God, it's not a "pick your own definition" kind of thing. I don't mean Buddha, or Allah, or the channeled spirit of Gandhi, or whatever feels right in the moment. I'm not referring to universal energy, or chi running up and down my charkas, or even (especially) some personal capacity for greatness I inherited as a citizen of humanity. I tried all those gods, along with the gods of money, cute outfits, and having the flattest stomach on the beach. Not to mention my ongoing quest to worship Mr. Right, no matter how not-right he might be. But like Baal in the Old Testament, when these gods were put to the test by the fiery trials of my real life, none of them had any power. They either vanished, or

just sort of sat there and burned, staring back at me expression-
less, as if to say, "What did you expect?"

I'm not sorry that I tried all those gods, but that doesn't
change the bottom line: for all my searching for the spiritual
truth that would allow me to *live* the life I dreamed of, none of
these "truths" ever worked. Despite the heart-felt beliefs and
endless good intentions, those paths offered promises but no
answers, hope but no results. But after I'd spent almost a decade
reaching and falling, reaching and falling, Jesus caught me. He
gave me answers, and results. In three years, Jesus exorcized my
demons, healed my wounds, unloaded my baggage, and restored
my hope. He also gave me a new marriage, a new career, a new
self, and a new life. Not a patched-together compilation of the
best I could come up with on my own, but something better
than I could have imagined.

My true fairy tale ending? Seeing the truth of God's promise
in King Solomon's wise words: "A chord of three strands is not
easily broken." I love this picture of how God weaves a man and a
woman together; it's so much better than the other options I explored about formless frames and uncommitted commitments.
Nicole Nordeman, the songwriter who saved my early faith by
admitting that she too had doubts, captured this new feeling of
hope I have in a song she wrote for a friend of hers who thinks
all this Jesus stuff is nuts: "But what if it's *true?*" she asks.

That's the question that changed everything for me. *What if it's
true?* Now, I don't have to pick the petals off of any more flowers,
looking for some sort of hope. The answer, is, *He loves me.*

Acknowledgments

I knew that the hardest part of writing this book would be finding words to tell my family and friends how grateful I am to have them in my life. Still though, it's nice to have a chance to try . . .

Mom and Dad: Thank you for showing me how to love, how to laugh really hard at myself, and how to be part of a family that takes care of each other. And thank you for swooping in to catch me time and time again when most people would have agreed that a good fall might do me some good. If it wasn't for you standing by my side for all these years, I can't imagine where I'd be. Thank God I don't have to.

Meg: Thank you for being my best friend—for challenging me, making me laugh, understanding all the things no one else knows, and showing me options in life I might not have considered. I'm grateful for every vote of confidence.

Chris and Eric: Neither one of you suspects, I'd guess, how your words of encouragement have gotten me over rough patches in the past, or how proud I am of how you live your lives today. Thank you.

The new family I inherited when I became Steve's wife—Mom and Dad Conway, Lisa, James: Thank you for welcoming me with open arms and so much love, not to mention great recipes and political analysis. I'm amazed to be blessed with a second family, and another group of people to call home.

Kristen Fincken Mahan: Thank you for giving me a place to run away to and the space I needed to heal. Thanks for being the one who knows the whole backstory, and loves me anyway.

Everyone at The Vineyard Christian Fellowship of Greater Boston: Thank you for the bagels, the coffee, the music, the prayer, the encouragement, and the love. Thanks for proclaiming, boldly and without embarrassment, that Jesus empowers Impossibly Great Lives, and for sticking by me when it all just felt impossible. Dave and Grace Schmelzer—Steve and I are so grateful for your friendship, leadership, wisdom, and love . . . it's a fun honor to count you as friends and to dream big dreams with you about what might be possible in life. Brian Housman—thank you for your wise counsel, your great sense of humor, and for being there when God knit Steve and I together into one. Chuck and Marianne Snekvik—thanks for showing us what a fun, sexy, Jesus-ey marriage looks like after a few decades. What an inspiration! Christopher Greco, Jordan Seng, Eunice Sim—thanks for writing the songs that drew me toward Jesus. Paul and Pascha Griffiths, Christine Raymond, David Wilmouth, Gwen Bruno, and Chelsea Vessenes—thank you for helping me recalibrate my spiritual compass toward Jesus; I don't think I would have made it to happily ever after without you. Dominic and Kristina Kaiser, Chris and Aimee Radom, Jill Tonelli, Liz Boschee, Bryan and Lisa Graves, Lynette Estes, Emily and Gavin Long, and everyone from SEEK and all the small groups I've been part of—thank you for your friendship, your prayers, the laughs we've shared and hopes we're still holding up, wondering what God will do next.

On the technical side, pulling this book together was a lot like the process Oprah Winfrey described when she talked about posing for the cover of *Vogue*: it took an army of talented people to turn my duckling of a manuscript into a swan.

My wonderful agent, Elisabeth Weed: Thank you for "getting it" right from the start, and being my sounding board and advocate. You're brilliant, and I'm blessed to have you on my team. My editor, Chris Park: Thank you for your amazing heart for this story. You sorted through an awful lot of dross to get to the silver, and I'm so grateful to have had the benefit of your discerning eye, great sense of humor, and tough-love. Thanks for caring enough to tell me when I needed to get back to work! Sarah Sper: Thank you for brainstorming sessions, encouragement, and pitching in your considerable talents to shape my chapters. The other members of the Hachette Team: Rolf Zettersten, Lori Quinn, Harry Helm, Manuel Muñoz, Kathy Antrim, Jana Burson, Preston Cannon, and the amazing sales force—your skills have made my project bigger, better, faster, stronger—you're my heroes! Thank you.

Thank you, Andrea Shea, for making me look so much better than I would if left to my own devices (and keeping me laughing in the process), and Donald Martelli for capturing that on film. Thank you, Meg Raymond, for Web site genius. Special thanks to my patient early readers, Steve Ryan, Paul Griffiths, and Dave Schmelzer—you saw the worst of the early drafts and somehow managed to dig through to the good parts.

While writing this book, I turned again and again to the songs of Nicole Nordeman for inspiration. Thank you, Nicole, for wrenching open the creative side of my brain and bringing order to my questions. I also devoured books by Elizabeth Gilbert, Lauren Winner, Jeannette Walls, Donald Miller, Sarah Dunn, A. J. Jacobs, David Kuo, Madeleine L'Engle, Dave Burchett, Kristin Armstrong, Naomi Wolf, and Peggy Orenstein. Each of you has, in one way or another, raised the bar for me—thank you. I'm also grateful to the following people for their wise words on how to "do" this Jesus thing: Joyce Meyer, Stormie Omartian, Marcus and Joni Lamb, Juanita Bynum, Kevin Lehman, Bill and Lynne Hybels, Brendon Manning, Michelle McKinney-Hammond, and P. B. Wilson.

And finally, to the two men this book is about: the right God, and the right guy.

Jesus: thank you for chasing me so persistently, for offering your hand over and over again, and showing me the difference between a relationship with you and all the stuff I thought it meant to be a Christian. Thank you for making good on all your promises, and for introducing me to a spiritual world that exceeds my expectations every day. Thank you for giving me hope for what is possible for all of us. I love you.

Steve: I'm amazed by how closely my heart for you resembles my thanks to Jesus—thank you for chasing me so persistently, for offering your hand over and over again, and showing me the difference between a relationship with you and all the stuff I thought it meant to be a woman, a girlfriend, a wife. Thank you for making good on all your promises, and for introducing me to a marriage that exceeds my expectations every day. Thank you for loving me like Jesus, and being so very worthy of my respect. I love you.